5/12

Praise for *The Theory Toolbox*:

"The book is an excellent introduction to basic concepts that students in humanities, science, and design need to engage in meaningful discussion of culture and society. Through timely examples from popular culture and working questions that stimulate active discussion in both the classroom and in the online environment, *The Theory Toolbox* is my go-to guide to critical concepts, as it inspires and engenders critical thinking and reasoned dialogue for the beginning theory student."

—Renata Hejduk, Arizona State University

"*The Theory Toolbox* is original and unusual, breaking the standard mold of social theory textbooks. It puts itself in the young theory student's shoes and imagines what s/he needs to know, and how best to convey difficult material. A distinctive feature of this book is its interdisciplinarity, borrowing concepts from humanities disciplines in order to enrich social and sociological theory. My theory students will definitely need this path-breaking book in their toolboxes."

—Ben Agger, University of Texas, Arlington

"As a first introduction for the perplexed and confused to critical and cultural theory, there's no better place to start than *The Theory Toolbox*. The new chapters 'Life' and 'Nature' are engaging and insightful. With its clear, concise, and accurate accounts of often complex theories, instructors will find this an excellent addition to any theory course; with its provocative working questions and up-to-date, funny examples, students will find this book to be illuminating and exhilarating."

—Bruce B. Janz, University of Central Florida

"Students find *The Theory Toolbox* isn't about learning theory through narrow interpretive lenses but thinking critically through theorizing and questioning perspectives."

—Richard Bower, Cayuga Community College

"Students quickly learn to employ theoretical concepts in their own work. The authors support this development by examining theory in relation to material that may at first seem familiar but that the authors then encourage the students to question in complex ways. The new chapters introduce important emerging areas of scholarship that students and instructors should find appealing."

—Tracy Neal Leavelle, Creighton University

"I have used *The Theory Toolbox* several times in my classes, and the response from my students was extremely positive. The theories and concepts in the *Toolbox* are clearly presented and approachable despite the fact that these ideas are often difficult to cover at the undergraduate level. Nealon and Searls Giroux explain complex ideas using everyday poetry, music and pop culture artifacts that are readily accessible to everyone. They really get my students thinking and engaged. The new chapters on 'Life' and 'Nature' promise similar thought-provoking and lively discussions."

—Katy Wiss, Western Connecticut State University

"In our deeply anti-intellectual climate, Nealon and Searls Giroux perform the great act of showing how and why thinking still matters. From their opening engagement with the punk song 'Why Theory?' they give us an impassioned argument for the important uses of theory. As the title suggests, *The Theory Toolbox*, instead of simply reviewing schools of theory and criticism, aims to help students figure out what they can do with theoretical concepts as tools for living. *The Theory Toolbox* engenders pragmatic encounters with theorists from Nietzsche to Deleuze to Agamben and provides productive engagements with key concepts such as agency and ideology. Darwin, Black Sabbath, and Facebook are among a wide variety of examples that Nealon and Searls Giroux deploy to demonstrate why and how theory matters in everyday life. This edition presents compelling new chapters on 'Life' and 'Nature' animated by Foucault and the animal rights movement. For a generation growing up amidst the ruins of capitalism and the endless distractions of social media, this book offers a path for all students desiring to become thinking citizens."

—Kevin DeLuca, University of Georgia

The
Theory
Toolbox

The Theory Toolbox

Critical Concepts for the Humanities, Arts, and Social Sciences

Second Edition

Jeffrey Nealon and
Susan Searls Giroux

ROWMAN & LITTLEFIELD PUBLISHERS, INC.
Lanham Boulder New York Toronto Plymouth, UK

Published by Rowman & Littlefield Publishers, Inc.
A wholly owned subsidary of The Rowman & Littlefield Publishing
Group, Inc.
4501 Forbes Boulevard, Suite 200, Lanham, Maryland 20706
http://www.rowmanlittlefield.com

Estover Road, Plymouth PL6 7PY, United Kingdom

British Library Cataloguing in Publication Information Available

Library of Congress Cataloging-in-Publication Data

Nealon, Jeffrey T. (Jeffrey Thomas)
   The theory toolbox : critical concepts for the humanities, arts, and
social sciences / Jeffrey Nealon and Susan Searls Giroux. — 2nd ed.
      p. cm.
   Includes bibliographical references and index.
   ISBN 978-0-7425-7049-8 (hardback) — ISBN 978-0-7425-7050-4
(paper) — ISBN 978-0-7425-7051-1 (electronic)
   1. Social action. 2. Critical theory. I. Giroux, Susan Searls, 1968-
II. Title.
HM585.N43 2011
301.01—dc22

                                                        2011014879

For

Leisha

Bram

Dashiell

Henry

Jack

Brett

&

Chris

Contents

Acknowledgments

This book has its roots firmly in the classroom—specifically, in the "introduction to theory" course at Penn State. This book owes its largest debt to hundreds of Penn State undergraduates—who helped us to choose, debate, and refine everything in this book.

We've also benefited immensely from discussions with other instructors who've used pilot versions of the text in their classes: Marco Abel, Debbie Hawhee, Jeff Karnicky, Dave Kress, Elizabeth Mazzolini, and John Muckelbauer. Susan Searls Giroux would like to thank her colleague, David L. Clark, for his rich insight regarding all things animal and two graduate students in particular for their unparalleled assistance with the second edition: Jennifer Fisher and Heather Berger. Ben Agger and Michael Greer offered crucial insight in their readings of the manuscript. We'd also like to thank Alison Sullenberger, Alden Perkins, Sallie Greenwood, and the late Alan McClare for their enormous efforts getting this text to publication.

Many thanks to Sarah Tanguy, curator of the Hechinger art collection, as well as to Phil Hetherington, webmaster of Not Great Men, and Andy Gill for their help with Gang of Four's "Why Theory?"

And we've gotten valuable advice, as well as invaluable encouragement, from Henry Giroux and Dean Birkenkamp.

1

Why Theory?

Gang of Four
"Why Theory?"

We've all got opinions
Where do they come from?

Each day seems like a natural fact
And what we think
Changes how we act

We've all got opinions
Where do they come from?

Distant thunder from the East
Won't disturb a morning car wash

Each day seems like a natural fact
And what we think
Changes how we act

So to change ideas,
Changes what we do

Too much thinking makes me ill
I think I'll have another gin
A few more drinks, it'll be alright

Each day seems like a natural fact
And what we think
Changes how we act

Each day seems like a natural fact
Each day seems like a natural fact
Each day seems like a natural fact
Each day seems like a natural fact

—From the album *Solid Gold,* 1981

Y ou can always count on a punk band to ask a good question: "Why Theory?" In our informa-tion-saturated cyberworld, it would seem that the last thing we need is more "theory"—which tends to mean more talk, more abstraction. In fact, there seems to be no scarcity of theories floating around: theories about everything from who "really" bombed the World Trade Center, to the shadowy workings of the International Monetary Fund, to the sinister possibility of the United Nations spon-soring a secret One World Government. Theories abound, and in fact if there's a *shortage* of anything in the contemporary world, it seems to be of theory's opposite: action! Theories are all fine and good, but it's finally what people *do*, rather than what they *think*, that's important. Actions, one might say, speak louder than theories.

And this seems to be the reason why, in almost any teaching and learning situation, theory has a bad name: "Look out, here come the airy, hard-to-understand abstractions, with no concrete examples to back them up or illustrate them." In its very definition, theory seems neatly divorced from commonsense practice, and that's what makes it so frustrating to study: Theory seems separated from what people do.

But if that's the case, we come back again to the conundrum, "Why Theory?" Why bother with it? Well, one might begin to address this question by asking what it costs us to *avoid* theory. If you *gain* an important emphasis on action, what (if anything) do you *lose* when you don't ask the question of theory? Is theory itself the name for a crucial social action? What kind of practice is theory? What does theory do?

Turning back to the Gang of Four song with these questions in mind, we see them immediately translating the question that is the song's title—"Why Theory?"—into another question, the song's first lines: "We've all got opinions/Where do they come from?" "We've all got opinions"; that's easy enough to understand as an emphasis on the everyday, on the active exchange of social discourse. But the song seems immediately to want to shift ground again, away from the simple "fact" that everyone has opinions, to what one might call a question about theory: "Where do they come from?" What, we might ask, is gained or lost in such a change of emphasis—from the social fact that all of us have opinions to the theoretical question of where these opinions come from? And how is this change of terrain related to the song's following stanza: "Each day seems like a natural fact/And what we think/Changes how we act"?

Oddly, it seems that for opinions to be at all productive, we are obliged to ask the question "Where do they come from?" If you've ever been in an argument with someone who simply states and restates his or her opinion about something—with no reasons to back it up, and no reflexivity on other potential points of view—you can quickly see how the pragmatic social fact that "We've all got opinions" isn't very productive. Unless we can ask theoretical questions—larger questions about the origins of knowledges, who holds them, and how such knowledges were formed and might be changed—we're stuck in a go-nowhere exchange of opinions: he said, she said. This is, perhaps, where theory *does* something, where it becomes productive or useful for asking reflexive questions about how things work and how they might work differently. Even people who vehemently deny or disparage theories nevertheless traffic in them all the time. Theory and action are not as neatly opposed as they might appear at first glance.

Take, for example, Jeff's uncle, who lives on the south side of Chicago but drives an hour to a convenience store near the Illinois-Indiana border each week to buy his Lotto tickets. Why does he *act* this way? Well, he has a *theory*: The store near the border sells more tickets than any other store in the state (selling both to local Illinois residents and to Indiana residents coming over the border to take a chance on Illinois's higher jackpots). Because of the store's high-volume sales, Jeff's uncle is convinced that the Lotto officials send more winning numbers to this store. And it's not just that more sales naturally mean more winners; that's too simple. He is convinced that the whole thing is rigged and that the high-volume stores are slated to be winners by the Lotto officials. That's why they *become* high-volume stores, because savvy players know that they sell so many winning tickets.

Jeff, not convinced by this explanation, points out that his uncle doesn't play "quick picks" (where the numbers are supplied by the machine) but rather plays the same numbers every week. In other words, *theoretically* he could buy the damn ticket anywhere: What difference does it make where you buy the ticket if the numbers you play are always going to be the same? But the discussion comes full circle: "No, I have to buy it there, or my numbers will never *be* winners. Don't you see?" In a last-ditch effort, Jeff then points out that his uncle hasn't won after several years of testing out this theory, so that in itself should cause him to question it, but his uncle quickly changes the subject. He's sure that he's right, that his numbers will eventually come to the attention of Lotto officials and somehow be chosen as winners. But he doesn't want to talk about it anymore.

Jeff's uncle has an opinion, sure enough, that comes from somewhere. There is a kind of "theory" at work here, but it's both more and less than that: It's really his uncle's version of an "opinion" translated instantly and unproblematically into a "natural fact." He's not really sure where this belief comes from; he doesn't want to examine his opinion theoretically. But he remains convinced, and it most certainly changes how he acts (although admittedly he acts weird most of the time).

Of course, the point is not that a simple emphasis on "theory" would somehow save Jeff's uncle from this odd behavior, or that he needs to be saved at all; rather, the problem is his firm belief that his "theory" (which would need to be articulated and shown to be useful in action; remember, he's never won) is simply a "natural fact" as far as he's concerned. It doesn't require any further elaboration; it's just true.

If we avoid encountering the reflexive or critical questions of "theory"—if we avoid asking "where do opinions come from?"—then we risk a situation in which "Each day seems like a natural fact": Everything seems self-evident; everything is the way it's always been, the way it's supposed to be. If we really believe that something is "natural" or is simply a "fact," why would we want to challenge it? Think about it. Even the most superficial engagement with the nation's history reveals myriad examples of seemingly natural occurrences, taken-for-granted assumptions, and presumed inevitabilities that have been completely repudiated. Until the early twentieth century, only white men were accorded citizenship and the right to vote; children worked twelve-hour days in factories; the mentally ill were put on circus display; and slavery and segregation were given legal, religious, and scientific justification. It seems pretty obvious that "what we think/Changes how we act," even if what we think isn't always obvious (even to us).

Although theoretical questions may be difficult or seemingly abstract and may even create blockages to simply getting things done, such blockages are often necessary and indeed valuable. The upsetting of the "natural fact" is the beginning of being able to see things differently. If you can't visualize things differently, you're a prisoner of conventional wisdom: "Too much thinking makes me ill/. . . A few more drinks, it'll be alright." Or as the saying goes, "Don't worry too much if you want things to stay the same." But if you want things to change, you have to take a detour through theory; you have to ask what exactly needs to be changed, and how such change might be accomplished.

"Hey," you might respond, "not everything needs to be changed." Sometimes conventional wisdom is *right*—it *is* a good idea to look both ways before you cross the street. This is another situation in which theory often gets a bad name: screwing up something that works well, asking a bunch of critical questions where they're not warranted. From a theoretical point of view, however, the point is never that everything is "bad," that the fascist "Man" is keeping you down with his stifling normality. Rather, the point of theory might be better stated as "everything is suspicious." Everything comes from somewhere and functions in a particular context or set of contexts; there's no such thing as a "natural fact." Call that overly skeptical if you want, but it's theoretical point number 1, and the arrow that gives direction to the rest of this book: Nothing should be accepted at face value; everything is suspect.

This includes our assumptions. In that vein, we offer a word about the book's organization and purpose, about the theory enacted in this book. First, you will note that this book is not an assisted anthology of or introduction to theoretical schools or movements in recent literary and cultural studies; it's not a tour through writings from new criticism, structuralism, feminism, poststructuralism, new historicism, deconstruction, queer theory, cultural studies, postcolonialism, etc.

We assume from the beginning that what attracts people to the humanities or social sciences is *not* the opportunity to become a professional "critic"—a psychoanalytic critic, a structuralist anthropologist, or a deconstructionist. If theory is to be at all interesting or useful, the work that it does really can't be confined or defined in schools and movements. Rather, we're interested in theory as *approach*, as a wider toolbox for intervening in contemporary cultures. The question we'll be consistently discussing is, "What can you *do* with theory?"

This book proceeds under the assumption that students don't "need" theory like they "need" English composition or French 101; you don't need theory because you have to be able to master certain materials or reproduce certain kinds of papers—although those things are important. Rather, you need theory precisely because it does some work for you (and, with any luck at all, it does some work *on* you); it offers angles of intervention that you wouldn't otherwise have. That's the sense of theory that we're interested in introducing here: theory that's less about names or movements or modeling readings of texts than it is about intervening in otherwise inaccessible debates and discourses.

A word about the progression of the text and the concepts covered. The book's larger movement—beginning with "author/ity" and ending with "agency"—mirrors or performs the course we try to chart in each chapter, from examining theoretical concepts to looking at what they can do. We start with authorship not because we feel that literature is necessarily *the* place to begin, but because the "author-function" plays a central role in all humanities, arts, and social sciences. In other words, we start with authorship because it's the most prevalent metaphysical theory of meaning-production (meaning is guaranteed and produced from the interior thoughts and intentions of individuals). From there we increasingly move "outward," toward the production of sense in and through social contexts. The text is then a kind of one-way street, with each new concept taking us ever farther away from merely privatized, hyper-individualist notions of interpretation.

You'll also note that there are no "sample readings" of paintings, films, or texts done in the text: "If you want to deconstruct the *Mona Lisa*, it'd look something like this . . ." We have deliberately avoided including these. Instead, we offer "Working Questions" to provoke discussion, and we assume in addition that any instructor using this text will have myriad other examples for students to think about. We hope this book can be useful for students and instructors across the arts, humanities, and social sciences, and have left the question of interpretive content—whether it be literature, sociology, art history, rhetoric, philosophy, geography, or whatever—wholly up to the disciplinary context in which the book is used. We're relying on the preexisting strengths and interests of individual disciplines, instructors, and students, because the way we look at it, a toolbox shouldn't tell you what to build but offer you opportunities to experiment.

To paraphrase philosopher Gilles Deleuze, we're interested in theory as a *toolbox* of questions and concepts to be built and experimentally deployed rather than as a menu of methods to be chosen and mechanically applied. Of course, this book makes no claims to being an exhaustive introduction; the suggestions for further reading will point you in those directions. Here we're trying to introduce questions and provoke responses, because, as Deleuze says, "Thinking begins in provocation." Thinking begins in response; theory begins as action.

2

Author/ity

So where do our opinions come from? The short answer is, tons of places: from conversation around the dinner table, cereal boxes, YouTube, Facebook, Twitter, reality TV, late-night talk shows, locker room gossip, and a host of other places. But probably the majority of what we know, what we would consider "legitimate" knowledge, comes from more formal sites like schools. School curricula, in fact, are a pretty clear indication of what a society believes constitutes "really useful knowledge," whether or not you happen to agree that classes in advanced math like calculus or four years of English will do any particular work for you. For the most part school knowledge is equated with book knowledge and the traditional canons of "great" thinkers in all the core areas of human thought: science, history, literature, the arts. So maybe locating the folks who penned those great works will suffice in our quest to locate the origin of knowledge. Well, not so fast.

This only begs further inquiry, most obviously the question, "What is an author?" Granted, this seems like a stupid question. Authors are obvious and everywhere. Authors are the bread and butter of various fields across the humanities and social sciences. An English major might observe that they are the people who penned the great English works, from *Beowulf* to Virginia Woolf, as they say, and those American authors who make up the tradition from the Puritans to the postmodernists. But authors don't only write literature. They also produce masterworks of philosophy, history, sociology, and innumerable other disciplines. That's what an author is, plain and simple.

But we need to remember theory rule number 1: Everything is suspect. Even within this seemingly self-evident description of the author, we confront some problems. First, there's the simple fact that there are all sorts of authors outside the narrow confines of an English-speaking humanities or social science major's study. Most obvious are all those authors who write in places other than the United Kingdom, Australia, and North America, in languages other than English. There are thousands of authors in myriad traditions that never show up on a typical course syllabus. And what about those who produce great works outside the culture of print, such as filmmakers and visual artists? Certainly the concept of author needs to accommodate other kinds of cultural producers as well.

Even more broadly speaking, we should also recall that the word "author" can be a *verb* as well as a noun, and that even the noun names a social *action*: Sales managers author quarterly reports, politicians and their aides author legislation, judges and clerks author opinions, we all author grocery lists and personal letters. One might even say that architects and construction workers author buildings, while civil engineers and highway workers author roads. But these are not things we ordinarily study as authored texts in the typical undergraduate course of study. Clearly, then, saying someone is an author is more complex than simply acknowledging that he or she has written or created something, or even that he or she has created something "great" or lasting. Who, after all, gets to determine what "great" is?

Authorship necessarily *begins* as a verb—someone doing something, such as authoring a political treatise, a history, a poem, a play, a film, or a web page. However, before "someone who has written something" becomes "an author," it seems that a number of additional things also have to happen. Maybe your grandmother wrote poetry or your parents made movies of your childhood, but chances are slim indeed that grandma will be studied with the same intensity as Emily Dickinson, or that your home movies will get the recognition of Stanley Kubrick's films. Even writing the most brilliant short story in your fiction-writing class is unlikely to elevate you to the level of being an author.

As we've already suggested, this question of how someone who authors becomes *an* author (or how "author" changes from a verb to a noun) is intimately tied to the question of *canonicity*, which involves the list of accepted "great" works that are deemed worthy of continued scholarly attention. To be an author in the canonical sense is to be invested literally with author/ity, to be taken seriously and even revered for your accomplishments. Canonicity not only establishes "authority" through the designation of "genius" or "greatness," it also establishes a particular relationship to authority, one based on honor and reverence as opposed to critical questioning and challenge. The upshot of this process is that James Joyce, for example, has the status of an author, while Stephen King remains a writer. Of course, even canonicity can be somewhat double-edged. What of the status of recognized authors like W. E. B. DuBois, who wrote across several disciplines: Why, we might ask, is his legacy consigned, for the most part, to English departments, rather than education or sociology, where he made considerable contributions? Among the puzzling questions of authorship are: How do you get from being a writer (a person who writes) to being a canonized author (a person recognized as important)? How does the institutional location of a body of work expand or delimit its impact on culture and society?

And what happens when students learn to substitute reverence for questioning in relation to official knowledge?

Putting those questions aside for the time being, we should note that even if we were able to narrow our focus to "authorship" in the sense of those figures already accepted as worthy of study in the traditional undergraduate curriculum, it would still remain a murky concept. Consider the construction of the canon of English and American literature. Those Puritan writers with whom we often begin American literature surveys (preachers Cotton Mather and Jonathan Edwards, verse writer Anne Bradstreet, historian William Bradford) certainly didn't think of themselves as authors, at least not in the way we think of Willa Cather or Ernest Hemingway as authors, geniuses who produce startling works of the imagination. The Puritans, for the most part, were religious writers who were deeply suspicious of art, artifice, and the imagination; they were much more likely to pen sermons than short stories. Therefore they seem a particularly odd place to begin a history of the great American author. Likewise, it seems immensely unlikely that today we'd refer to TV evangelists as American authors, so why is it that no one blinks an eye when Jonathan Edwards's sermon "Sinners in the Hands of an Angry God" is served up in the first week of an American literature survey course? Why is it seemingly necessary to locate the origins of the American literary tradition here—and necessary to whom, or whose value system?

Maybe this author thing is a little more complicated than it seems. If you think about it, substantial problems and ambiguities remain within even the most seemingly self-evident categories of the canonical English and American authors. Most people would agree that Native American folktales, for example, are an integral part of American literature, and should be studied along with the writings of the Puritans if we are to have anything like an accurate picture of "American" literature's beginnings. But do these Native American tales and religious ceremonies have authors? Clearly they don't have authors in the way that novels do.

Even if you argue that Native American oral traditions *don't* count as American literature because they have no authors (a suspect argument at best), you would still leave open the question of who the first American author is. Where should we begin the canonical listing, if not with Native Americans? Are the first authors the settlers, all of whom were born in England? The first of their American-born children to write? To write *what*? A sermon? A laundry list? A reminder to herself? A poem? Why not nominate Columbus, who kept an extensive diary, as first American author? Clearly we think of Anne Frank's diary as literature, so it seems that would qualify Columbus as the first American author, even though he's neither an American nor an author in any recognizable sense.

It is around issues like this—where authorship is tied intimately to authority—that the question of the canon reemerges and becomes most insistent. Who counts as an author is a much more slippery thing than it may seem at first. For example, the late seventeenth-century British playwright Thomas Otway was hailed as the Shakespeare of his time, but today only a handful of specialists read his work. Likewise, many of the most revered authors in English and American literature (those who now enjoy privileged places in the canon) were virtually unknown, or even scorned, within their own historical context. Herman Melville's *Moby-Dick*, for example, was almost universally panned after its publication in 1851, and it sold precious few copies. In fact, Melville died in almost complete obscurity, broke and bitter. Oddly enough, then, Melville became a canonized author only *after* the fact, while Otway, who clearly attained the status and recognition of authorship among his contemporaries, seems no longer to enjoy that privilege.

The definition of "author" remains complicated even if you look at authors and texts that are clearly canonized. Take a text like *Beowulf,* which has long been accepted and canonized as the beginning text in a survey of British literature. *Beowulf* is considered by most scholars to be an oral poem, passed down through several generations. In other words, like Native American myths and folktales, *Beowulf* doesn't even really *have* an author, yet it is certainly firmly canonized, accepted as a work worthy of study. And as long as we're locating absent authors at the founding of literary traditions, we should note that many scholars argue that Homer, the ancient Greek author of the *Iliad* and the *Odyssey*, is really just a composite figure, the proper name under which a series of oral tales has traditionally been grouped.

Perhaps this problem of canons and authorship is merely a historical problem, and it becomes easier to nail down a definition of *author* as we get closer to our own period. Authors, it seems, are relatively easy to locate in the here and now—at least some of them are. Thomas Pynchon, the paradigmatic postmodern American literary author, hasn't been recognized in public since the early 1960s and gives no interviews or commentary on his work. But he's clearly the exception rather than the rule. In contrast, paradigmatic postmodern philosophers like Slavoj Zizek go on speaking and book-signing tours, teach in universities, and even occasionally show up "live" on the Las Vegas Strip to talk about their work. No elusive oral tradition here in the information age.

But, one wonders, what does this access to the author really get us? Historical parallels might once again prove instructive: We might not have an author for *Beowulf,* but we've got one for *The Canterbury Tales,* Geoffrey Chaucer, and for *Hamlet,* William Shakespeare. For that matter, we know that Pablo Picasso painted *Guernica* and Andy Warhol created *Mao 91.* Of course, the moment of relief—"Whew, we've got an author for these texts!"—doesn't last long. First, it's not at all clear what's been gained by having a dependable author. We really don't know substantially more about Chaucer or Shakespeare than we do about whatever author or authors *Beowulf* had. Historical material remains sketchy on both figures. But—and perhaps more strikingly for our purposes here—even if we knew quite a bit about Chaucer and Shakespeare, if we had some sort of virtual access to their lives, what would that bring us? We know a lot, for example, about Pablo Picasso and Andy Warhol, both of whom have extensively discussed their works and their lives. But does that really tell us what works like *Blue Guitar* or *Campbell's Soup Can* actually *mean*?

◈ Working Question

A close friend—whom you've known since early childhood—writes a poem and shows it to you to get your reaction. You're a little baffled by it but are pretty sure it's about sex—or the lack thereof—in your friend's life. He insists it's about his grandmother's funeral and can't see how you've missed the point so badly. As he explains the imagery to you, you begin to see your friend's point about grandma, but in the end you remain convinced that it's a poem about sex.

In this situation, your friend is the "author," so does his reading supersede yours? If so, why? If not, why not? How do you account for the wildly differing readings? Who finally decides what the poem means?

If you can have a lot of difficulty with the meaning of a friend's poem, it seems unlikely that a ton of information about an author you've never met is somehow going to hand you the meaning of his or her work. It's not that such information is simply irrelevant, either; it seems important—if not essential—to know that George Eliot was an Englishwoman of the nineteenth century and that T. S. Eliot was an American-born man associated with twentieth-century British modernism, or that Toni Morrison is an African-American woman novelist, Van Morrison is a male Irish singer, and Jim Morrison was the lead singer of the Doors.

But although it's helpful to know as much as you can about the circumstances of a text's authorship, it seems clear that the author is far from the final court of appeals when it comes to figuring out the *meanings* of his or her work. Even if the author comes right out and tells you what he or she intended, this doesn't seem to settle very much or tell us very much about how meaning happens. Science fiction author Philip K. Dick, for example, has hundreds of pages of "exegesis" or explanation concerning his novels, but most of Dick's explanations are eccentric to say the least, insane to say the most. And they certainly don't get at what most people like about Dick's work.

In other words, authors may or may not intend for you to perform a certain reading of their work (to "get" a certain "point" out
of it), but there's absolutely no way to guarantee the reception of
that message. Indeed, when you think about it, so-called great
authors are most often people who open up multiple meanings for
their readers; "so, what's the point?" seems like a pretty dumb question to ask about what many see as monumental works like Lévi-
Strauss's *The Raw and the Cooked,* Freud's *Civilization and Its
Discontents,* or James Joyce's *Ulysses.* In fact, we *don't* think of certain texts (like floor plans or interoffice memos) as *authored* because
they seem *not* to be aimed at producing many different readings.

To say something is "authored" in an academic sense seems to
be to say that it offers a maximal amount of interpretative ambiguity or possibility. The question is whether that multiplicity or rich-
ness of meaning comes solely from the author's intention or from
other places as well.

Practically speaking, it seems clear that meaning doesn't exclusively rest in or come from the author's intentions. Any pragmatic
experience of authorship (for example, of essays for classes or poems
shared with friends) should show us this; the author is not simply in
control of meaning. How many times have you written what you
thought was an extraordinarily clear paper for a course and had the
instructor come up with a *very* different reading? How many times
have you sent an e-mail or left a note for friends and had them completely misunderstand the message? As Paul Auster writes in his
novel *Leviathan,* "A book is a mysterious object . . . and once it floats
into the world, anything can happen. All kinds of mischief can be
caused, and there's not a damned thing you can do about it. For better or worse, it's completely out of your control" (5).

Although the author is clearly not in control of meaning, he or she
has nevertheless *functioned* as a guarantee of meaning throughout
much of the history of literary criticism. Even if we don't know a thing
about a text's author, the notion that a piece *has* an author—that someone, somewhere originally had this experience, thought this thing, and

committed it to writing—allows the soothing conclusion that it means something, even if we don't quite know what. Even though we haven't the faintest idea who wrote *Beowulf*, critics cling to the notion that it had an author (often referred to as the "Beowulf poet"). In other words, the author functions as a guarantee of meaning or authenticity behind the text. The line of reasoning here seems to go something like this: If its author were here, he or she could tell us what the text means, and even if we have no access to the author, the very fact that a work has an "author" behind it seems to guarantee meaningfulness.

Curiously, however, this "author-function" is hardly universal; it works differently over time and across disciplines. As philosopher Michel Foucault points out, there was a time when literary texts didn't require an author to validate their truthfulness. In contrast, scientific texts *did*. "Statements on the order of 'Hippocrates said . . .' or 'Pliny tell us that . . . ,'" Foucault writes, "were not really formulas of an argument based on authority; they . . . were statements of demonstrated truth"("What Is an Author?," 150). In other words, the author's name validated the authenticity of texts dealing with mathematics, medicine or illness, the natural sciences or geography. By the eighteenth century, however, scientific texts were increasingly accepted on their own merits and recognized as established truth, without any reference to their authorship. At the same time, literary texts were increasingly deemed worthy or not in accordance with the author's name; henceforth, every poem or piece of fiction had to account for itself: who wrote it, when, why, and under what circumstances. Thus, in scientific texts the author no longer functioned as a guarantee of truthfulness, whereas in literary works the author was granted total sovereignty over meaning (Foucault, "What Is an Author?"). How should we account for such a 180-degree shift in thinking about authorship and authority, as we move from the Middle Ages to the Enlightenment?

And where does this leave us in the present moment, when we know from our own practical experiences of writing that such access to the author guarantees nothing? If the author has functioned historically as a kind of guarantee of meaning behind the words, what happens if we can no longer depend on that guarantee? One might say that theory starts here—with what one French critic called "the death of the author." This death is not a sad one—"There goes the possibility of figuring out what any text is about!"—but is rather an opportunity to free up the multiplicity of meanings in and around a text. Once the author's privilege has been debunked, meaning is then no longer *found* but rather *produced.* The question we ask of the text is no longer "*what* did the author really mean?" but rather "*how* does this text produce meanings?" Certainly one of the ways a text can produce meanings is by reading it through the lens of its autobiographical, historical, and cultural contexts; and obviously authorship and the author's intentions are helpful within such an inquiry. But theory (and its use-value, its necessity) begins in the freeing up of meaning from the iron grasp of the author. Meaning is always more slippery and multiple than any given author's intentions.

Critical reflection about the author-function has also opened up a space for rethinking the question of authority itself. Not only did the author-function serve to guarantee the "truth" of particular discourses, but it also was used to invalidate and exclude other kinds of discourses. In this way institutions performed a gatekeeping function, granting authority to some forms of knowledge and denying it to others, promoting some meanings and disavowing others:

> [T]he author is not an infinite source of significations which can fill a work; the author does not precede the works; he is a certain functional principle by which, in our culture, one limits, excludes, and chooses; in short, by which one impedes the free circulation, the free manipulation, the free composition, decomposition and recomposition of fiction. In fact, if we are accustomed to presenting the author as a genius, as a perpetual surging of invention, it is because, in reality, we make him function in exactly the opposite fashion. One can say that the author is an ideological product, since we represent him as the opposite of his historically real function. . . . The author is therefore the ideological figure

by which one marks the manner in which we fear the proliferation of meaning. (Foucault, "What Is an Author?," 160)

It is precisely the "multiplicity of meanings" that, according to
Foucault, institutions saw as dangerous and sought to reduce.
Conflating "meaning" narrowly with the author was but one mechanism to challenge the proliferation of meanings. We should note further that with the death of the author came the death of the literary
critic, who alone could unlock the mysteries of authorial intention.
The opening up of multiple meanings challenged both the sovereignty of the author as well as that of the professional "expert"—
another mechanism for managing the proliferation of discourse, for
authorizing who can speak to what issues.

Working Questions

1. A physicist recently wrote an article parodying what he took
to be silly and inconsequential work in his field. He sent the article to
a journal specializing in the kind of work he dislikes, and (without
knowing it was a hoax) the journal published it, because the editors
thought that the essay engaged a number of interesting questions.

Is this article then both a parody and a serious piece of scholarly inquiry? How can it be both if the author clearly intended it to
be a parody? Which author/ity do we believe, the author's or the
journal's? How can we know whether the article is any good?

2. A popular theory of constitutional law in the United States
holds that judges should adhere to "the intention of the framers" of
the constitution. This is an author-centered theory to be sure, one
that goes by the name "strict-constructionism" (i.e., making laws
strictly in accordance with what the original authors intended).

Given what you've just read, what—if anything—is suspect
about this "strict-constructionist" view? What *specific* points seem
vulnerable in this legal theory?

3. In *The Archaeology of Knowledge and the Discourse on Language,* written a few years after "What Is an Author?," Foucault further elaborated a theory of language and effects. He postulated that "in every society the production of discourse is at once controlled, selected, organized and distributed according to a certain number of procedures, whose role is to avert its powers and its dangers" (216). So how exactly is discourse "powerful," and how might it possibly be construed as "dangerous"? If ascribing meaning to authorial intention is just one way of controlling the effects of certain discourses, what are other means? For example, how does "expertise" govern who can speak on certain issues and who can't? How do labels like "political" or "unpatriotic" or "emotional," when attached to discourse, serve to contain its effects?

For Further Reading

Auster, Paul. *Leviathan.* New York: Vintage, 1998.

Barthes, Roland. "The Death of the Author." In *Image-Music-Text,* translated by Stephen Heath. New York: Hill & Wang, 1977.

Benjamin, Walter. "The Author As Producer." In *Walter Benjamin: Selected Writings, Volume 2: 1927–1934,* 768–82. Cambridge, MA: Belknap Press of Harvard University, 1999 (1934).

Bledstein, Burton. *The Culture of Professionalism: The Middle Class and the Development of Higher Education in America.* New York: Norton, 1976.

Foucault, Michel. *The Archeology of Knowledge and the Discourse on Language.* New York: Pantheon, 1972.

———. "What Is an Author?" In *Textual Strategies: Perspectives in Post-Structuralist Criticism,* translated and edited by Josue V. Harari. Ithaca, NY: Cornell University Press, 1979 (1969).

Lauter, Paul. *Canons and Contexts.* Oxford: Oxford University Press, 1997.

Said, Edward. *Representations of the Intellectual.* New York: Vintage, 1996.

Sennett, Richard. *Authority.* New York: Vintage, 1980.

Williams, Raymond. "The Romantic Artist." In *Culture and Society: 1780–1950.* New York: Pelican, 1961 (1958).

3

Reading

If the author doesn't hold a patent on meaning, then the next logical question is, who or what (if anything) does? If the producer of a cultural artifact isn't the privileged place to search for meaning, where do we go looking next?

It's tempting here to flip the dialectical coin and say that, after the death of the author, it's the *reader* who is paramount in determining meaning. The death of the author would be the birth of the reader. Active interpretation (the reader *making* meaning) would be substituted for a passive consumption model (the reader *consuming* the author's meaning), and there would be a freeing up of multiple points of view—as many good readings as there are readers. Despite the suspicious theological claim buried in such a formulation ("The author-as-God is dead, long live the revolutionary human reader!"), there is a way in which this displacement of focus from the author's intentions to the reader's production is among the first moves in any "theoretical" discussion.

Reading, in fact, has become a privileged metaphor for perception or experience itself. When we say that we *read* each other's expressions, or golfers *read* greens, or detectives *read* clues, we are speaking more literally than we might think. Like texts, expressions or clues or golf courses don't simply speak for themselves; they don't simply *contain* a meaning. Rather, we must always interpret them. If we really press this line of reasoning, it spreads to literally all phenomena: Everything is in need of interpretation; nothing is merely self-evident. As philosopher Friedrich Nietzsche wrote, "facts . . . do not exist, only *interpretations*" (*The Portable Nietzsche*, 458).

Of course this displacement of meaning from the author to the reader (from "facts" to "interpretations") runs the risk of performing a simple reversal: "It's not what the author thinks that's important; rather, it's what *I* think that's crucial." If we're not careful, the absolute control of the author can give way very quickly to the absolute control of the reader, who then simply usurps the author's privileged role in the game of meaning. If indeed facts don't exist and there are only interpretations, it would seem at first blush that *my* interpretations are then necessarily facts. But this conclusion is a bit hasty. Indeed, the quick response to this line of reasoning might be the old schoolyard chestnut, "Who died and left you boss?" Or it may remind us of the somewhat less kind observation that "Opinions are like assholes: everybody's got one."

If there were *simply* as many compelling readings as there are readers, as many facts as there were interpreters, this would open up a rather pernicious relativism in which all opinions—however uninformed or silly—would be of equal validity or worth. And although citizens of liberal democracies often say that everyone is entitled to his or her opinion, literally no one believes it—or we should say, no one believes it literally.

In other words, no one really believes that any one opinion is just as good or compelling as any other, especially when it comes to matters of importance. No one believes, for example, that a freshman algebra student's opinions about mathematics are on a par with Einstein's theory of relativity. Likewise, no one believes that hate-speech doctrines of racial genocide are simply one set of opinions or interpretations among others, akin to whether or not one likes or dislikes hot weather. And don't expect a judge to go easy on you simply because, in your opinion, robbing liquor stores is a fine, honorable, and harmless pastime. Your interpretations are clearly *not* facts in such an instance.

If meaning is simply shifted from what the author thinks to what the reader thinks, then meaning itself is never examined or questioned, let alone the material relations of power that influence the production of meaning or the human actions that derive from particular perceptions of the world. It is this *examining* or *questioning* of meaning and action that is the cornerstone of social theory. If one conclusion (it means what the author thinks it means) is simply traded for another (it means what I think it means), nothing particularly revolutionary—or even *interesting*—takes place in reading. Absolute authority, in that case, would simply be *moved* from the author to the reader. And if we shouldn't take the author's word for meaning, it seems even less plausible that we should take yours or ours.

Reading or interpretation is not primarily a matter of forming or reinforcing personal opinions but rather a process of negotiation among contexts. What texts mean, in other words, has everything to do with the *contexts* in which they're produced and read. For example, Frederick Douglass's *Narrative of the Life of an American Slave* "means" very different things today than when it was originally written in 1845, in the heat of the abolitionist struggle over American slavery. Or, to put the same point somewhat differently, we read Douglass in vastly different contexts at this point in history: We still read him as an eloquent voice for the abolition of slavery (as he was read in his own time), but today we also read him as a savvy politician, an innovator of the slave narrative genre, a sociologist of the slave system, a rhetorician, a theorist of race, and a canonized author of nineteenth-century American literature. So the "meaning" of Douglass's text is vastly different depending on the context or contexts that it's read within. For example, reading Douglass's book through a rhetorical lens—looking primarily at the ways he persuades his audience—will give you a very different "meaning" of the *Narrative* than if you read it predominantly as a kind of sociological analysis of the Southern slave system. The words are the same, but the meaning changes, depending on the approach taken by any given reader.

Even within these multiple possibilities, it's important to remember that although words don't have simple or singular meanings, it doesn't follow that they mean *anything* you want them to mean. There are many different ways to read Frederick Douglass, but his work *can't* plausibly be read as a dense allegory about space travel. We might wonder, however, why not? If it doesn't have a singular meaning, can't it mean anything? Well, no. Words and events have a *history* of meanings and usages; like the texts in which they are sometimes contained, they only mean something within a specific *context*. Just as the meaning of Douglass's book changes in differing contexts, so the meanings of specific words also change when they're used in differing contexts.

All meaning is contextual because languages are *social* rather than *natural* phenomena.[1] For example, the word "tree" doesn't reference that woody leaf-making machine outside the window in some mystical or natural way, any more than "*arbor*" in Latin or "*Baum*" in German does. There is, in other words, no *essential* connection between a word (in linguistics, a "signifier"), the specific thing that the word refers to (its "referent"), and what the word means in a given symbol system (its "signified").

The relation between a signifier (the word), its referent (the thing), and its signified (the meaning) is *arbitrary*, in linguist Ferdinand de Saussure's famous formulation, and this arbitrariness is consistently shown by the simple fact that different languages have different names and different meanings for the same thing. Many signifiers can be used to designate the same referent; and the same referent has widely divergent meanings in different cultures or contexts. In other words, there is no "correct" or natural name for the thing that English designates as a tree, and trees don't *mean* or signify the same thing in all cultures either: In a Druid culture they signify divinity, in a logging culture they signify profit, in a beach culture they signify shade, and in a bird culture they signify home.

Language is a social system of meaning, and *reading* is essentially the social *production* of a *relation* among a set of signifiers. *Reading*, in other words, is not an exercise in burrowing into the words for their "real" meaning but rather a matter of producing relations among signifiers that have no "natural" or "essential" meaning. Words have meaning only in specific contexts; they don't "mean" something naturally or mystically.

Well, we might counter, what about words that are virtually the same across several languages—say, for example, the English word "difference," for which the French word has exactly the same spelling and the German word is *Differenz*? All these words come from a common root, the Latin *differens*, which would seem to suggest that the relation between signifier and signified (a word and its meaning) is anything *but* arbitrary![2]

"Of course!," Saussure might answer, to say the signifier/signified relation is "arbitrary" is certainly not to say that "tree" or "difference" means just anything you decide it means. Rather, the point is that the relation between the word and its meaning—between a signifier and a signified—is *historical* or *social*. The reason why Latin has such a wide-ranging influence on European languages is a sociohistorical one, not an organic or mystical one: The Roman Empire encompassed much of what we now call "Europe" for many centuries, and during that time the Romans imposed their linguistic and legal codes on their subjects, leaving the lasting legacy of the Latin language with speakers of other European languages. The influence of Latin on other languages, then, shows us the historical and social process of language modification, not some natural connection between a thing, its name, and its meaning. There is no such thing as a "natural" language, with "inherent" meaning or "correct" names. As philosopher Jacques Derrida contends, there is no meaning outside of context, but there is no *final* context, no metacontext that could guarantee the meaning of all the others.

To say that all signifiers are "arbitrary" is merely to say that all meaning is context bound and socially constructed (rather than somehow "naturally found"). "Reading," as we saw above, is one privileged name for that social construction of meaning, for the social negotiation of signifiers in the production of meaning. Like the signification of words, the production of meaning is a social act—which is to say that, like the meaning of a word, the meaning of a sociological study, an advertisement, or a film is neither a predetermined transcendental truth nor a fanciful personal whim. Reading is very much more complicated and very much more open, and the range of possibilities for meanings depends on social *contexts* rather than exclusively on persons (the private thoughts of the reader or the author).

We should also note that Saussurian linguistics has had a profound impact not only in fields of the humanities that deal principally in textual analysis but also in the social sciences and arts. Saussure conceived of "language" and "reading" in the broadest possible terms. A language can be any sign or symbol system that we use to communicate. Semiotics is the study of sign systems. This sounds complicated, but it really isn't. Sign systems abound all around us; what's more, we're pretty capable readers of them, even if we aren't terribly conscious of the ways we negotiate them. Music, dance, and art are all complex, rule driven, nonlinguistic "languages" that we read or interpret every day. Think about all the ways you communicate that require no words; for example, modes of dress, haircuts, body art, and facial expressions. Even what you drive, where you live, what you eat/drink/consume, who you hang out with, where you shop, etc., say something about you.

� Working Questions

1. In your American Lit Survey, a particularly wacky student insists that *Moby-Dick* is not really about whaling at all but is rather about his elderly Aunt Sally, who lives in Passaic, New Jersey. Without reference to the intentions of Melville—who obviously could never have encountered, much less decided to write about, anyone who is alive today—how can you respond to this student without him saying, "Well, that's your opinion, and my opinion is that Aunt Sally's the key."

2. What is your read of the people nearby as you read or discuss this? What elements of their style "speak" to you? What do you suppose is the "intended" effect of their looks? Is there anything, perhaps, unintended?

This insistence on contexts also suggests ways in which "reading" can be an open-ended process of interpretation, without necessarily being an "anything-goes" war of uninformed opinions: "Difference" is historically and contextually tied for its meaning to the Latin root *differens*, but this social fact is of little cultural significance in an argument over the differences between socialism and capitalism. The point is not that either socialism or capitalism is *essentially* better than the other (just as it's not that *difference* has some transhistorical or essential meaning as a word). The argument, rather, is about the social *effects* of certain meanings and policies in specific contexts, about differing *readings* of the historical and social effects of various phenomena. You might favor capitalism or socialism because of the impacts that they've been proven to have or are likely to have. But you're not really arguing over their inherent meaning; no matter which side you favor in such a discussion, it's much too simple to say that one is inherently good while the other is inherently bad. It's the *consequences* that are good or bad, not the *signifiers*.

What something means remains open ended, future oriented, and changeable; the meaning of your education, for example, is yet to be decided. Depending on the contexts in which you find yourself in the future, certain parts of your college training will be crucial, while others may be less so. Some of your training, to be frank, will turn out to have been essentially meaningless. For example, we have yet to find a context in which knowing the International Phonetic Alphabet, which we had to learn as undergraduates, has any meaning at all. But you never know because the future remains open; meaning never stops or rests simply in one interpretation, and this necessarily means that the reader is no more personally in charge of meaning than the author is. We are all parts of a larger social *process* in and through which meaning is produced.

Reading, then, is not an excavation project, trying to strip away inauthentic social meanings to get to the real or metaphysical essence of the word; it is rather a negotiation among signifiers that have socially relevant signifieds. "Reading" is that collision or production of meaning within the context of certain sets of signifiers. Reading, in other words, is about *how* a social system of signifiers works (or how it might work differently). *What* something means is always an effect of *how* something means, and reading is always a *process* in which one must take into account the various *contexts* in which a situation or a piece of writing is produced, read, circulated, and evaluated.

Working Question

In the 1950s "queer" was a particularly derogatory and hateful word to use when referring to homosexuals (and the word "dyke" a specifically pernicious subset of invective referring to lesbians). Half a century later, however, these words seem to have been reappropriated by the homosexual community itself; one often hears of "queer theory" or "queer politics," and many lesbians like to refer to themselves as "dykes." (A popular lesbian comic strip is named "Dykes to Watch Out For.")

How does this happen? Are "queer" and "dyke" hateful words to be avoided or affirmations to be celebrated? Or both? Does the answer somehow depend on a *reading* of the situation to figure out which is the case in a particular context? And do you have to "watch out" when using a word like "queer," if you don't identify yourself as such?

Another way of articulating this point about reading as a process of negotiation would be to look at the distinction between *metaphor* and *metonymy* in literary theory. A metaphor is a figure of speech wherein something sensible is translated into the categories of the intelligible by use of an implicit comparison. When we say that "old age is the evening of life," we take something sensible ("evening") and use it to invoke something that is substantially less tangible ("old age"). The metaphorical relation is, then, similar to the relation of the signifier to the signified; the sensible end of the metaphor ("evening") is akin to the signifier, while the concept that the metaphor alludes to ("old age") is akin to the less concrete signified.

Metonymy, on the other hand, is not so much the substitution of a word for a concept as the substitution of one word for another: "crown" for "king," or "Kleenex" for "facial tissue." Metonymy is different from metaphor insofar as the substitution does not move from material signifier to abstract signified (as it does in the metaphor "evening" = "old age"); rather, in metonymy one material signifier is substituted for another material signifier (as it is in "Ford" = "car").

There's a particularly effective example of the difference between metaphor and metonymy in an episode of MTV's *Beavis and Butthead*. Their ever-gullible neighbor, Mr. Anderson, agrees to give the boys $5.00 to do some yard work. Of course Beavis and Butthead go on to destroy the entire neighborhood in the process of doing this yard work, but at the time of Anderson's offer, little cartoon bubbles appear above their heads, showing us what the $5.00 signifies to each of the boys. Butthead, ever the optimist, conjures up visions of luxury cars, speedboats, and other "cool stuff" that he might be able to obtain with the $5.00 fortune. Beavis's vision of the future, however, is actually of a $5.00 bill. The cartoon-style joke here is fairly obvious: Beavis's seeming lack of imagination is shown in sharp contradistinction to Butthead's wildly unrealistic one.

For our purposes this contradistinction between Beavis and Butthead also shows us the difference between metonymy and metaphor, between a metonymic reading and a metaphoric one. Butthead is the metaphorizer here. He takes the sensible (Anderson's specific promise of $5.00 cash in return for yard work) to be subsumed or understood under the rubric of the intelligible (the potential boat or car); he moves from the material realm of the signifier (the promise of cash for work) to the immaterial realm of the signified (what it might buy in the future). Beavis, on the other hand, is a metonymic reader, moving not from a sensible sign to an abstraction but rather from one sensible sign to another: For Beavis, Anderson's promise of $5.00 is represented by a $5.00 bill; the sensible moves not toward the intelligible but to ever more material signs.

Beavis, in other words, stays in the concrete realm of negotiating signifiers—not, like Butthead, trading signifiers for what they may or may not mean in some abstract sense. Beavis's meaning takes place on a concrete, metonymic plane of signifiers, where one material sign substitutes for another. For Butthead, on the other hand, meaning is a metaphoric action, where the material sign is subordinated to its intangible "meaning."

We tend to understand interpretation or reading as a *metaphoric* process, which is to say, we understand interpretation as allegorical rather than literal. And while it's tempting to think that all good reading is metaphorical, it seems more likely that it is precisely the opposite: Reading is an essentially *metonymic* operation, paying attention to the materiality of the signifiers (the *how* of meaning) rather than hastily translating them into the abstract realm of the signified (the *what* of meaning). We tend to think that reading—or at least good reading—is an exercise in metaphor (trading the words for their abstract meanings), but on further examination, those metaphoric concepts (signifieds) are in reality a species of metonymic substitution (more signifiers). To say that old age is the evening of life is *not*, in the end, to trade a signifier for a signified but rather to trade one set of signifiers for another. A metaphor is always a metonymy *first*; a metaphorical concept doesn't exist without the material or social signifiers that configure the concept. Even abstract ideas are constructed out of concrete signifiers.

Working Question

How do dictionaries work, metaphorically or metonymically? It seems that they should work metaphorically, offering you the abstract "meaning" of a word, the intelligible signified that matches up to the concrete signifier. But in actual practice, when you look up a word (a signifier), does the dictionary give you a concept (signified), or does it give you more signifiers?

Technically speaking, there is no such thing as a "signified," a transcendental or ahistorical meaning for a word. All meaning is socially constructed and decided; all reading is necessarily a socio-historical process of negotiation. Just think, for example, about the practical ways dictionaries (our cultural arbiters of meaning) are put together: Social usage (*context*) is always going to be the final court of appeals for what any given word means. What a word means is nothing other than the product of its usages in a series of social contexts. When we said above that we currently find the International Phonetic Alphabet "meaningless," what we really meant is that we find it "useless" in our present context.

As a concrete example of this point, ask someone from England what the word "football" means. Chances are she'll give you a very different answer than a Green Bay Packers fan would provide, but that doesn't mean either the soccer fan or the American football fan is somehow wrong about the word's meaning. The same word simply means different things—and is used differently—in different contexts, in Britain and the United States.

All supposed signifieds are necessarily then already signifiers, products of social interaction. Signifieds or meanings had to be material before they magically became abstract; and although they are abstract in some sense (meaning isn't something you can touch), that abstraction is itself only accessible through the materiality of the sign. The sign always exists and is used in particular social and historical *contexts*, and it is to those specific contexts—not to supposed transhistorical or metaphysical abstractions—that we turn when we determine meaning.

Working Question

Following is a poem by Wallace Stevens called "Metaphors of a Magnifico" (from *The Collected Poems of Wallace Stevens*. New York: Alfred A. Knopf, 1954).

> Twenty men crossing a bridge,
> Into a village,
> Are twenty men crossing twenty bridges,
> Into twenty villages,
> Or one man
> Crossing a single bridge into a village.
>
> This is old song
> That will not declare itself . . .

Twenty men crossing a bridge,
Into a village,
Are
Twenty men crossing a bridge
Into a village.

That will not declare itself
Yet is certain as meaning . . .

The boots of the men clump
On the boards of the bridge.
The first white wall of the village
Rises through the fruit-trees.

Of what was I thinking?

So the meaning escapes.

The first white wall of the village . . .
The fruit-trees . . .

What, if anything, does this poem have to say about reading? About metaphor and metonymy? Signifieds and signifiers? Context?

Why all the ellipses, which are in the original? Why is it, near the end of the poem, that "the meaning escapes"? What is the effect of the repetition of certain phrases throughout the poem? What are we to make of the fragmentary images that we're left with at the poem's end?

For Further Reading

De Man, Paul. *Allegories of Reading: Figural Language in Rousseau, Nietzsche, Rilke, and Proust.* New Haven, CT: Yale University Press, 1979.

Fish, Stanley. *Is There a Text in This Class?* Cambridge, MA: Harvard University Press, 1980.

————. *The Trouble with Principle*. Cambridge, MA: Harvard University Press, 1999.

Iser, Wolfgang. *The Act of Reading*. Baltimore: Johns Hopkins University Press, 1978.

Mailloux, Steven. *Interpretive Conventions: The Reader in the Study of American Fiction*. Ithaca, NY: Cornell University Press, 1982.

Mitchell, W. J. T., ed. *Against Theory: Literary Studies and the New Pragmatism*. Chicago: University of Chicago Press, 1985.

————, ed. *The Politics of Interpretation*. Chicago: University of Chicago Press, 1983.

Nietzsche, Frederich. "Truth and Lie in the Extramoral Sense." In *The Portable Nietzsche*. New York: Penguin, 1976.

Rabinow, Paul, and William M. Sullivan, eds. *Interpretive Social Science: A Reader*. Berkeley: University of California Press, 1979.

Ricoeur, Paul. *The Conflict of Interpretations*. Evanston, IL: Northwestern University Press, 1974.

————. *Interpretation Theory: Discourse and the Surplus of Meaning*. Fort Worth: Texas Christian University Press, 1976.

Saussure, Ferdinand de. *Course in General Linguistics*, translated by Wade Baskin. New York: McGraw-Hill, 1959.

Suleiman, Susan, and Inge Corsman, eds. *The Reader in the Text: Essays on Audience and Interpretation*. Princeton, NJ: Princeton University Press, 1980.

Tompkins, Jane, ed. *Reader-Response Criticism*. Baltimore: Johns Hopkins University Press, 1980.

Notes

1. There is, by definition, no such thing as a "private" language, because languages are nothing other than translatable symbol systems that, at least in principle, are available to anyone who knows the grammar.

2. Of course it's already more complicated than that in social usage, because in everyday German *Differenz* tends to mean the difference of amounts (e.g., in math problems or monetary exchanges), whereas *Unterschied* tends to be the word used for the abstract category of difference.

4

Subjectivity

I f, as we have seen, the process of *reading* or analysis shifts the production of meaning from the author to the reader (from meaning being *found* to meaning being *made*), it might be a good idea at this point to take a hard look at the reader. Of course, that's going to be difficult, insofar as this entails taking a hard look at ourselves and our social and historical context. Adding to the difficulty here is the fact that, up to this point, we've been trying to *re*define terminology that's already familiar. We assume, however, that the word "subjectivity" is a new one, so perhaps it would be easiest to begin this chapter with a kind of definition.

At first blush this would seem to be relatively simple: "Subjectivity" is the opposite of "objectivity," right? We call something *subjective* when it is relative to a person and his or her opinions, whereas we tend to use *objective* to reference a fact, something not dependent on a specific person's interpretation. Of course this distinction between fact and interpretation has already become suspect and will become even more so as we continue. If, as we have seen, reading is akin to perception itself, then there is at least some level at which seemingly "objective" facts are beholden to "subjective" interpretations. Wherever we see a "fact," an interpretation has been there first.

On one reading, then, "subject" remains just a fancy word for "self." For example, the police will often say that someone is "the subject of our investigation," a queen might refer to her loyal "subjects," a scientist might talk about the "subjects" participating in her experiment, and an English teacher talks about the grammatical "subject" of a sentence. As these examples suggest, when someone says "subject," he or she is just using a more abstract terminology for persons or selves.

So you might wonder, why say "subject" or "subjectivity" if the more familiar "self" or "individual" would do just as well? First of all, the word "subject" carries an importantly different set of associations than the word "self." As you'll note in the above examples (the police, the queen, the scientist, the teacher), the word "subject" carries or conveys the sense of being subject *to* something or someone. The subject in a police investigation or a monarchy is always *secondary*, necessarily defined by his or her position relative to the detective or the queen.

We tend to think of the "self" as that which is *primary*, untouched by cultural influences. We like to believe that our selfhood is the essence of our *unique* individuality: the intrinsic, singular qualities that define us as who we are. We like to think that those intrinsic qualities would preserve our unique individuality, without regard to the circumstances under which we were born and raised. This insistence on selfhood often shows itself in many humanities, arts, and social sciences classes through the "theme" of the individual, often understood *versus* his or her society, as if the individual had to fend off cultural influence or definition to be truly authentic or unique.

In contrast, we understand the "subject" as anything *but* unique or untouched by social factors. By definition, the subject of a scientific experiment or the subjects in a monarchy could be anybody. The subject of a sentence or the subject of a police investigation is nothing other than a kind of position or placeholder, a role that, theoretically at least, anyone could fill. Just as any noun could be made the "subject" of a sentence, literally anyone could become the "subject" of a police investigation, regardless of his or her supposed intrinsic qualities of selfhood. The subject is defined by its place among various social positions: suspect, cop, student, teacher, doctor, patient, electrician.

Unlike the word "self," then, the word "subject" carries a certain anonymous sense, as well as the sense of having one's personhood defined not by intrinsic or internal qualities but by external factors. One is subject to the law, for example, supposedly without regard for the singular or unique qualities that one possesses. Justice, as they say, is blind; it applies equally to all. Likewise, a subject in a scientific experiment is, by definition, replaceable by a number of other subjects, or else the findings of the experiment would be invalid.

We tend to understand the "self" as an inwardly generated phenomenon, a notion of personhood based on the particular (yet strangely abstract) qualities that make us who we are. The self is the strangely intangible core—the soul? the personality? the real me?—that we take for the *cause* of our lives and our actions. On the other hand, the "subject" is an outwardly generated concept, an *effect*, an understanding of personhood based on the social laws or codes to which we are made to answer. We recognize ourselves as subjects most clearly when a demand is made of us: show us your driver's license and insurance card, answer the question, enter your password, check the appropriate box, supply your student ID number.

The "subject," unlike the self, is always understood in reference to preexisting social conditions and categories. We don't get to choose social attributes like our gender, race, class, and ethnicity; nor do we get to vote on what those attributes *mean* in a given social situation. Rather, we are subject to such roles: What these things mean is to a great extent decided before we come along to fit the category. For example, we *learn* what it means to be from a certain social class, just as we learn how to act like a "proper" man or woman. And, of course, we have to *learn* these things precisely because there is no absolute standard for what it means to be rich or poor, just as there is no simple or definitive answer concerning what it "really" means to be a woman or a man.

Kafka wrote a famous text called "Before the Law," and the two senses of "before" alluded to in the title may offer a way to make clearer the distinction between the self and the subject. We tend to think of the self as being *temporally* "before the law": There is a self that's born into the world, and although this self is certainly affected by its surroundings, there always remains at every moment the same core self, the same "natural" body underneath different clothes of "culture." The self comes *before* any laws—social codes or norms of behavior—are "imposed" on it. The subject, in contradistinction, would be formed by that imposition of cultural laws and demands. In this way, the subject suggests another sense of coming "before the law": being called before the judge, made to answer charges, forced to respond by identifying and explaining yourself.

In the end, we tend to understand the "self" as always in the driver's seat, whereas the "subject" is more of a passenger, who may have a say in the destinations and routes but is not wholly or simply in control of them. The self is *causing* things to happen, whereas the subject is necessarily *responding* to things that happen.

Of course, our "driver/passenger" analogy is a loaded example. If we literalize this metaphor for a moment, we are forced to note that the driver is already a kind of passenger; she hasn't produced the car she's driving, nor the signs she's reading, nor the roads she's driving on. Likewise, the driver wasn't born knowing how to drive; she had to subject herself to instruction to gain that skill. Even the fact that she feels like she's in control—independent, free, confident—is a cultural response that's been learned. In the end, the driver, like the passenger, is always *responding* to things that are already there—things that are, for the most part, beyond her control. From the very beginning, it seems that the supposedly free "self" is *already* a responding "subject."

Indeed, as we track an imaginary history of our driver, we're forced to admit that she's been "subject" much more often in her life than she's been "self": subject to her family, her family's economic status and ethnic background, her nationality, her education, her employers, the cultural expectations of her gender and race, and even the language of her native country. All of these things preexist and outlast her, and her life is in large part determined by the ways in which she responds to these social conditions, which she has had little or no voice in determining. Even if she chooses to rebel against the seeming constraints of her life—quit her job, move away, renounce her family, have a sex change operation—she can't merely escape the social processes of subject-formation.

In fact, we'd have to admit that this "rebel-against-authority" narrative is one of the most obvious and pervasive determining narratives of culture, the thing that people as different as rappers and Rush Limbaugh have in common: They're supposedly "selves," unique individuals; and if you buy their books or download their singles, slavishly imitate their actions, and closely follow their lead, you can learn to be a unique self too.

Of course, with our driver/passenger analogy, we've gone a long way on a kind of detour to make a point here: The self, our supposed "driver," is already and always will be a "subject," a passenger. Strictly speaking, there is no such thing as a completely unconstrained "self," somehow free from its social contexts. Even to say "I am completely unique" is to subject yourself to cultural categories of selfhood and uniqueness, referring to some social understanding of subjectivity that you have not and cannot merely create from the ground up. Like the meaning of a literary text, the meaning of a subject/self always exists within a specific cultural *context*; the things that *make* us who we are are found in the context of where we live, where we've come from, and where we're headed. Like other kinds of cultural phenomena, our subjectivity is *socially constructed*, not mystically or naturally *found*. There is no meaning or self that exists *temporally* before the law; meanings and selves are only articulated in terms of certain laws—linguistic, social, economic, cultural, scientific, etc.—and we are born *into* a context where those laws are already at work.

For example, no one asked any of us to vote on what it means to be white, black, Latino/a, or Asian in the place where we live; you know that you are from a particular group—and come to understand what that identity means in America—by the way people recognize you and react to you (or by the ways in which they *don't* recognize you or react to you). Race—what it means to be "white" or "black" or "Asian" or "Latino/a"—is a culturally constructed phenomenon. As another example of this point, recall that under apartheid in South Africa, race was determined by the "one-drop rule": If you had *any* African blood in your past, you were deemed "black." As a number of scientists have pointed out, given such a definition of "black," there was literally no such thing as a "white" South African, but there certainly were plenty of people enjoying the privilege of being "white" under the regime of apartheid. As another example, we might recall that there was a time when people of Irish descent were not considered "white" (the legacy of discrimination against the Irish in British colonial law). This may seem odd to us today, but it does remind us that seemingly neutral or scientific categories like race are not in fact natural but are rather constructed along political and ideological lines. Subjects or selves are constructed by being subject *to* certain social categories or definitions: race, class, gender, ethnicity, etc.

That individuals are socially constructed is easy enough to *say*, but is a bit tough to swallow when *you* are the "cultural phenomenon" that's socially constructed, called before the law. It's tempting to respond, "Well, 'meaning' might be socially constructed, but I'm the one doing the constructing, right? So I'm in control, right?" Well, yes and no. In making meaning, the reader is steering a course, but many potential courses are already mapped when he or she comes upon the text to be read. The reader negotiates meaning by working with, between, and among already existing cultural signs. At some level, that's easy enough to see and understand: The works of Shakespeare or Da Vinci are already there—and have been for centuries—before we come along to read or interpret them. We don't get to choose those cultural signs, just as we don't get to choose where a highway goes or what it means to be Irish in a given society. Rather we must negotiate meaning and destination by *responding* to signs that we come upon.

In other words, the tricky thing that "subjectivity" adds to the vocabulary of the "self" is the fact that the interpreter himself or herself is also one of those cultural signs *within* the process of making meaning; the subject, like the reader, *makes* meanings, but the subject is also *acted upon* by meanings. Although readers interpret texts, they are always subject to—one might say interpreted by—their cultures. If, as we saw, the author is a kind of suspect cultural function that works to guarantee meaning, so also is the reader a suspect category, if we understand readers as "selves," absolutely founding and free grantors of meaning. Such an absolutely "free" interpreter—such a wholly unconstrained self—simply doesn't exist.

As we saw in the relation of the author to meaning, to say that authorship isn't the first and last word in determining the meaning of a text is most certainly *not* to say that authorship is irrelevant. And even more certainly, in any moment of reading (in any sociocultural negotiation among signs with existing meanings), the specific person doing the reading or negotiating is very far from irrelevant. But this is not simply the last word either; the interpreter can no more govern the entire process than the author can. The mystical reader-as-self (rather than the social reader-as-*subject*) is the dream of a reader who could finally control and stop the proliferation of the text's meanings. But this notion of finally *controlling* meaning is impossible (and, it seems, not even desirable). Institutions, laws, social norms, movies, books, and a host of other cultural artifacts influence subjects just as often as subjects influence culture and society, so the subjects that are reading social events or cultural texts—responding to them—can hardly control them at the same time.

Working Questions

1. What the hell does that last sentence mean: "Institutions, laws, social norms, movies, books, and a host of other cultural artifacts influence subjects just as often as subjects influence culture and society"?

Can you think of an example of a film, song, play, sporting event, etc., that's had a wide-ranging influence on what it means to be a self/subject? What, for example, is your favorite band, your favorite sports team, or your favorite actor, and what influence(s) do they have on your worldview? Why do you like band X rather than band Y?

2. Are you "unique"? Assuming that you think you are, how do you *know* that you are? Do other people point to the same reasons for their "uniqueness"? Doesn't everybody think they're unique? And, if that's the case, doesn't this make wanting to be "unique" pretty lame—essentially, wanting to be like everybody else?

So how does this sociocultural "subject" come into being? We tend to experience ourselves as relatively free and autonomous, so how can it be that we are products of culture—a subject rather than a self, a passenger rather than a driver, an effect rather than a cause? Perhaps the first thing to point out is this: To say that the subject is a cultural product is *not* to say that we are somehow simply *controlled* by culture—by parents, corporations, governments, boring textbooks, etc. It is, rather, to say that we are inexorably *dependent* on social and cultural categories for our well-being and satisfaction. To say that the subject/self is *made* or *constructed* is to say that it's dependent on myriad things other than itself.

To put it slightly differently, who you are is dependent on *recognition* of your identity by others. Our various identities—as learner, friend, lover, athlete, partier, etc.—can't come into being divorced from a recognition of those attributes by other people. Like signs, people don't "mean" things inherently; again, all meaning and all identity come into being through a process of social negotiation, and a "successful" negotiation of identity involves recognition by other people. After all, there's no point in being "unique" unless people know it! Perhaps the easiest way to state this point is to say that we are social animals, and one of the things we want from each other is recognition.

Working Questions

1. How many times have you gone out and bought something specifically because of a TV commercial or magazine ad? Assuming that the number you've come up with is relatively small (especially in comparison to the sheer number of ads you confront every day), why then do corporations spend so much money on advertising? It doesn't seem very cost-effective if, given the massive amount of advertising you've seen in your life, it has had relatively little effect on the commodities that you buy.

Exactly how does advertising work, then, if it doesn't merely *determine* each time what you buy? If advertising doesn't control you, then what does it do? Is this an argument for the persistence of the free and independent "self" over the culturally determined "subject": The self refuses to be subject to advertising's ploys? Or does advertising *subject* you by telling you that you're a *self*: "Listen to your gut; not some actor," "Travel your own road," "Obey your thirst," "Just do it!"

2. Consider figure 4.1. Nike ads typically appeal to a strong sense of "self." How does the Adbusters spoof ad challenge that sense of free-wheeling individualism and unencumbered will?

As we noted above, "subject" also comes to mind when we speak of the subject of a sentence, and, as you might imagine, this link is not just one among others. The common link between the subject and language is the common social nature of language and social nature of subjectivity. To put it somewhat bluntly, we speak ourselves into and out of certain categories of identity. To say "I am completely unique and unaffected by culture" is already to posit a subjectivity in terms of existing linguistic and social categories— ones that are far from "unique" and "unaffected by culture." To speak, to say anything at all, is to be "subjected" to language—to culture—in a process that's known as "interpellation."

Interpellation is a word made famous by French political theorist Louis Althusser. For Althusser, the individual is constructed or interpellated as a subject by the institutions of modern life; the so-called unique individual, in other words, is always defining itself and being defined by the generalized social categories of the modern state—worker or boss, husband or wife, son or daughter, student or trainee, etc. For Althusser, the institutions of modern life literally make all of us into subjects. As he writes,

> I shall then suggest that [culture] "acts" or "functions" in such a way that it "recruits" subjects among the individuals (it recruits them all), or "transforms" the individuals into subjects (it transforms them all) by the very precise operation which I have called interpellation or hailing, and which can be imagined along the lines of the most commonplace everyday policeman (or other) hailing, "Hey, you there!"

Figure 4.1 Image courtesy of www.adbusters.org

Assuming that the theoretical scene I have imagined takes place in the street, the hailed individual will turn round. By this mere one-hundred-eighty-degree physical conversion, he becomes a subject. (*Lenin and Philosophy,* 1971: 174)

How, one might wonder, is Althusser's seemingly innocuous scene—being called or hailed by a policeman—of such crucial importance? How can *this* simple act be the key to an interpellation that "recruits" and "transforms" us into subjects? Exactly what happens in the cop's call?

In Althusser's drama, it is the subject's *recognition* that is most important; the "one-hundred-eighty-degree physical conversion" that happens in response to the police officer's call is quite literally the transformation of the "individual" into a "subject." But how? First, of course, there is a kind of cultural coercion featured in this scene: The authority of the police calls upon you to stop and respond, to identify yourself before the law. Clearly this fits all we've been saying about subjects and how they are inextricable from social codes and demands.

However, Althusser adds a slight but very important additional twist to his analysis of interpellation: We *willfully* turn around at being hailed, assuming that the police are calling *to us.* It's here that the line between the supposedly free individual or self and the supposedly constrained subject is most effectively blurred by Althusser: We freely and willfully make ourselves subjects in all of our responses, in all those moments when we recognize *ourselves* as well as others.

We are, so to speak, self-interpellating creatures, which is to say we can only recognize ourselves—much less have others recognize us—in terms of some preexisting social laws or codes. Our identities only take shape in *response* to already given codes, to the "hailing" of the law. So, in the end, every time we recognize ourselves—every time we say "yeah, that's me"—we confront or construct *not* the freedom and uniqueness of our individual selfhood but rather the cultural codes of subjectivity. Wherever we think we see our free and unconstrained self, what we actually see is cultural interpellation.

It's important to recall that this insistence on the subject's interpellation doesn't mean that nothing new ever happens or that any kind of freedom or response to our cultural construction is impossible. But it does mean that any response to cultural construction or interpellation necessarily comes from within the categories of subjection or interpellation itself. You can, for example, quibble with certain labels that may or may not be attached to your subjectivity—slacker, boozer, egghead, suburbanite—but the response itself necessarily comes within culturally supplied and intelligible categories (or else it's not much of an effective response at all). We can always quarrel with specific labels fairly or unfairly imposed in specific contexts, but the very act of labeling—producing signifiers—cannot simply be renounced. When you say, for example, "I hate labels. I'm not part of that GenX group, I'm unique," you're really not abandoning labeling at all. You simply trade one label (GenXer) for another (unique dude). You may like one label better than another, but you can't simply deny the act of labeling, the process of making meaning by using and revising existing cultural categories.

There is no "escape" to some place of perfect freedom where we are untouched by culture, no longer subject to our surroundings. In fact, the dream of such a place is one of the most profound and continuous myths of culture that we have in the West; the dream of an innocent or unconstrained state of nature is a profoundly cultural dream of modernity. However, on further reflection, this dream looks more like a kind of nightmare: What would we be without culture, language, other people, TV, beer? We might not be subjects in that case, but our lives might not be very interesting, either.

Perhaps, folding this chapter into the last two, we might say in conclusion that cultures "author" subjects, but of course those subjects are not merely characters in a book, because those subjects—like *readers*—are able to respond to and remake the signifiers that are placed before them. Interpreting subjects are cultural readers and thereby are not merely passive receptors of preexisting meanings, but, just as important, no meaning or reading can take place outside of a cultural and historical context—and the reading subject is himself or herself subjected *to* the constraints and possibilities of that context.

Working Question

Following is Franz Kafka's "Before the Law" (from *The Complete Stories,* edited by Nahum Glatzer. New York: Schocken Books, 1971).

Before the law sits a gatekeeper. To this gatekeeper comes a man from the country who asks to gain entry into the law. But the gatekeeper says that he cannot grant him entry at the moment. The man thinks about it and then asks if he will be allowed to come in later on. "It is possible," says the gatekeeper, "but not now." At the moment the gate to the law stands open, as always, and the gatekeeper walks to the side, so the man bends over in order to see through the gate into the inside. When the gatekeeper notices that, he laughs and says: "If it tempts you so much, try it in spite of my prohibition. But take note: I am powerful. And I am only the most lowly gatekeeper. But from room to room stand gatekeepers, each more powerful than the other. I can't endure even one glimpse of the third." The man from the country has not expected such difficulties: the law should always be accessible for everyone, he thinks, but as he now looks more closely at the gatekeeper in his fur coat, at his large pointed nose and his long, thin, black Tartar's beard, he decides that it would be better to wait until he gets permission to go inside. The gatekeeper gives him a stool and allows him to sit down at the side in front of the gate. There he sits for days and years. He makes many attempts to be let in, and he wears the gatekeeper out with his requests. The gatekeeper often interrogates him briefly, questioning him about his homeland and many other things, but they are indifferent questions, the kind great men put, and at the end he always tells him once more that he cannot let him inside yet. The man, who has equipped himself with many things for his journey, spends everything, no matter how valuable, to win over the gatekeeper. The latter takes it all but, as he does so, says, "I am taking this only so that you do not think you have failed to do anything." During the many years the man observes the gatekeeper almost continuously. He forgets the other gatekeepers, and this one seems to him the only obstacle for entry into the law. He curses the unlucky circumstance, in the first years thoughtlessly and out loud, later, as he grows old, he still mumbles to himself. He becomes childish and, since in the long years studying the gatekeeper he has come to know the fleas in his fur collar, he even asks the fleas to help him persuade the gatekeeper. Finally his eyesight grows weak, and he does not know whether things are really darker around him or whether his eyes are merely deceiving him. But he recognizes now in the darkness an illumination which breaks inextinguishably out of the gateway to the law. Now he no longer has much time to live. Before his death he gathers in his head all his experiences of the entire time up into one question which he has not yet put to the gatekeeper. He waves to him, since he can no longer lift up his stiffening body. The gatekeeper has to bend way down to him, for the great difference has changed things to the disadvantage of the man. "What do you still want to know, then?" asks the gatekeeper. "You are insatiable." "Everyone strives after the law," says the man, "so how is that in these many years no one except me has requested entry?" The gatekeeper sees that the man is already dying and, in order to reach his diminishing sense of hearing, he shouts at him, "Here no one else can gain entry, since this entrance was assigned only to you. I'm going now to close it."

What (if anything) does this little story have to say about the subject and the self? Is the "countryman" representative of the cultural "subject," always responding to the dictates of the Law? Or is the "countryman" in some paradoxical way the quintessential "self," thinking of himself as unique and untouched by the "Law"? What does it *cost* the countryman to keep safe from the influence of the Law?

Even though he quite deliberately avoids directly encountering the Law, is the countryman nevertheless determined by the Law in some way? How? And what does this have to say about the "unique" and "untouched" self? Does Kafka suggest that such a self is a necessary category, or a dangerous delusion?

For Further Reading

Althusser, Louis. *Lenin and Philosophy and Other Essays,* translated by Ben Brewster. London: Monthly Review Press, 1971. See especially "Ideology and Ideological State Apparatuses."

Foucault, Michel. *Discipline and Punish: The Birth of the Prison.* New York: Vintage, 1995 (1977).

———. *Madness and Civilization: A History of Insanity in the Age of Reason.* New York: Vintage, 1988 (1968).

Freud, Sigmund. *Civilization and Its Discontents.* New York: Dover, 1994 (1930).

———. *Totem and Taboo: Some Points of Agreement between the Mental Lives of Savages and Neurotics.* New York: Norton, 1962 (1946).

Marx, Karl. *Grundrisse.* Harmondsworth, UK: Pelican, 1973 (1858).

Nietzsche, Frederic. *On the Genealogy of Morals.* New York: Vintage, 1967.

Saussure, Ferdinand de. *Course in General Linguistics.* New York: McGraw-Hill, 1966 (1915).

5

Culture

Up to this point we've consistently been on the trail of "meaning," tracking where we might locate it; we've tracked meaning from the author, to the reader, to the cultural considerations of the "subject." Along the way we've been insisting that meaning is brought about by a reading *process* that is *context bound* and *culturally produced*; there is no preexisting metaphysical or transcendental meaning that's somehow found under or above the text. Authors, readers, and subjects always "happen" in a cultural context. As Gertrude Stein so cleverly puts it in her poem "Identity": "I am I because my little dog knows me." Identity, in other words, presupposes a *process* of recognition, and that recognition takes place among a series of differences: straight, gay, white, black, thin, Republican, cute; these are all *cultural* categories of recognition within which our specific identities are located and negotiated.

But, we might ask, what or who makes up this "cultural context"? What is it that makes up a culture? To be sure, there are a host of definitions of culture in circulation in various fields of the humanities and social sciences. For our purposes, we identify two main trajectories of thought: culture as a "whole way of life" and culture as "high culture"—those artifacts representing "the best that has been said or thought." We deal with each in turn, starting with the more anthropological approach to culture coined by Raymond Williams, which entails not only the study of high cultural artifacts but also rituals, institutions, behaviors, and daily practices that constitute the culture as a whole. Yet how does one identify a specific culture? What are its boundaries? Can it be usefully conceived of in such singular terms—or does each culture contain within it several semiautonomous cultures? In this more inclusive definition, there are a series of seemingly self-evident questions that become very murky indeed when you examine them closely. Are cultures or communities defined, for example, by the singularity of race or ethnicity? This seems unlikely; even though ethnic and racial tensions exist everywhere on the earth, the vast majority of cultures in the world today are multiethnic and multiracial. Of course, one could add to the difficulty here by asking exactly what "race" and "ethnicity" mean, or whether they mean something different in different contexts. It seems unlikely, in other words, that race and ethnicity *found* a cultural context, insofar as figuring out what "race" or "ethnicity" means already *presupposes* a context; the very notions of race and ethnicity are already cultural constructs, understood differently at different places or sites. For example, does the identity category "Jewish" name a race, an ethnicity, a nationality, or a religion? Or all four? Or does it depend on whom you ask and where you ask them?

Maybe we could secure a definition for cultural context by looking narrowly at nationality, which seems to be a category configured to give a loose geographical commonality to people from many different races, ethnicities, and religions. Perhaps the nation gives us a way to configure a common cultural context for subjectivity, but at the same time the nation itself seems like a fairly arbitrary construct—especially today, with the contemporary movement of globalization among multinational corporations and the implementation of the European Common Market and the North American Free Trade Agreement (NAFTA). Indeed, a trip to the cinema in Germany will offer you German films as well as a choice of American films dubbed in German; staying home to watch a movie in the United States will likely entail using a TV and Blu-ray player made in Asia; channel-surfing for soap operas in Kenya will turn up *telenovelas* produced in Argentina. Author Salman Rushdie writes novels in English about the Islamic world and lived for many years in hiding (in England? in New York?) under a now-revoked death threat from a now long-dead Iranian leader. Fluctuations on Asian stock markets cause radical economic surges and downfalls in New York and London. All this seems to suggest that the nation as a uniform or common "culture" is quickly becoming an old-fashioned notion in the "new world order."

But even if we stick with the model "nation-as-culture" for a second, it's not clear that it offers very much in the way of common cultural context. It's immensely unlikely, for example, that a sixth-generation American who lives on a family farm in Kansas has the same cultural context as a recent immigrant who has just become a citizen and lives in a tiny apartment in New York City. Indeed, the American rich and poor—as well as the Irish-American and African-American, the gay and the straight American—may share a broad cultural context (something vaguely called "citizenship" in the United States), but they live very differently within it.

As we saw with "subjectivity," cultures influence subjects as much as subjects influence cultures, but even if culture somehow controlled subjects in some simple cause-and-effect way, contemporary culture itself is so diverse and diffuse that those methods of "control" would necessarily produce a very strange being indeed. Insofar as we are cultural subjects, just think for a moment about the complex web of things that we encounter within our "common" cultural context every day: radio, TV, films, newspapers, advertising, family, work, school, the Internet, the telephone, junk mail, friends, enemies, fashion, sex, food, intoxicants, etc.

Even those phenomena that seem most homogenizing and bland in contemporary culture carry an amazing amount of diverse "stuff." Take, for example, TV, which is often criticized for containing too many channels of the same damn thing. At any given moment during the day, your television is spouting news, sports, commercials, videos, talk shows, soap operas, documentaries, shopping channels, sitcoms, *World's Most Dangerous Police Chases*, movies, reruns, cartoons, political roundtable shows, local and national government proceedings, infomercials, non-English programming, C-SPAN book reviews, and the Three Stooges. All of this has effects on us as television viewers and cultural subjects, but those effects could hardly be completely homogenizing. It's not uncommon, for example, for TV viewers to watch "serious" programming like the news or a documentary for an hour, then spend the next hour watching pure trash like *America's Funniest Home Videos*. Certainly both hours of TV will have some effect on the viewer, but the cumulative effect on any particular viewer could hardly be simple or predictable; and the effects of such programs on millions of viewers is even more uncertain. There is no way to simply predict the reception or outcome of a cultural phenomenon.

And, of course, we need to recall that not everybody who's an American watches—or can even *afford*—TV, so even though it seems like the "common" cultural discourse of early-twenty-first-century American culture, TV hardly qualifies across the board.

Indeed, the "stuff" of cultural influence is immensely varied. Wherever we see what looks like a homogenizing influence in culture, we're simultaneously looking at something else as well, a weirdly diffuse force. The things that affect us as subjects are always more than simply singular. Our subjectivity is influenced by our culture, but insofar as our culture is hardly homogeneous, our subjectivity is then necessarily and *already* "multicultural."

Let's face it: We—whoever "we" might be or wherever "we" might live—simply do not live in a monolithic culture. The dream of articulating a common cultural identity remains strong nonetheless—for example, the dream of writing the great American (or Mexican or Scots or . . .) novel remains a powerful pull. But, we might wonder, what would such a book look like? Who could be a "representative" American within the vast array of cultural subjects who fit that description? Who would or could be the protagonist of the great American novel? It seems an impossible question to answer, insofar as American "culture" is already a "multiculture," a "whole" made up of a lot of people who would otherwise have little or nothing in common.

Working Question

Is there such a thing as "American culture"? *Was* there ever such thing? When? Have Americans somehow lost a common sense of identity over the years? Who is the "average American," anyway?

Why do people want to hold on to a *single* identity of Americanness (represented, for example, by English-language-only legislation and stiff immigration restrictions), when in every other sector of their lives (shopping, entertainment, friends) they seem to want increasing choice or diversity?

Multiculturalism

"Multiculturalism" is something of a buzzword these days, taking a lot of criticism and containing a lot of hopes. In certain ways a response to the totalization of "culture as a whole way of life," it poses important—and political—questions: Whose culture? Whose life? What differences among people get covered over in this broad presumption of sameness? Does it presuppose a kind of equality that has yet to be achieved: equal access to material rewards? Equal capacity to influence and shape institutions and political life? Viewed as contentious by some, *multiculturalism* is criticized by those who see it as an attempt at *separating* people rather than bringing them together. Indeed, for some people the contemporary litany of "X-American" identities (African-American, Asian-American, Italian-American, and so forth) signals a decline in the common identity of "American-ness." For others, the proliferation of identities under the common rubric of "American" signals a positive change, the sense of expanding the possibilities to be both a member of the American "melting pot" and yet still affirming some pieces of another (ethnic, racial, religious, etc.) identity at the same time.

From a certain point of view, this "identity politics" debate (is the proliferation of cultural identities a good thing or a bad thing?) is a go-nowhere one. Perhaps more important or at least more productive than this kind of conclusion mongering ("multiculturalism's bad; no, it's good") is returning to the question of what a culture or a community *means*. How does a "common" culture come together; how is it formed and sustained?

The cultural norms by which something becomes meaningful— the definitions of legality, acceptable behavior, womanhood, manhood, etc.—make certain identities and meanings possible and probable, while making other meanings or identities impossible or improbable. For example, the norms of American culture make it easier (across most contexts) to be a white, heterosexual man than to be a gay black man. Whether explicitly acknowledged or not, many of our practices and institutions are set up with this kind of white male "norm" in mind; for example, men are (still) paid more than women for performing the same job, ostensibly because they are to be the head of a household. Of course, they are paid more regardless of whether in actuality they *are* "head of a household" or not—and single mothers are not extended extra pay to close the gap. As another example of this normativity, many corporations and insurance carriers won't recognize gay partnerships as marriages and therefore won't extend basic legal and medical benefits to the partners of their employees.

Although these exclusions are obviously open to debate, question, and change, we must admit at the same time that norms of cultural intelligibility (for example, the use of categories to order our world—being able to differentiate liquids we drink from those we use to run our cars, things we use for lighting as opposed to things we use to sit on) are just as *necessary* as they are inherently *exclusionary*. For there to be a context in which any meaning can happen, an exclusion has to take place; to configure the meaningful context "people in this class" or "eighteen- to twenty-four-year-olds" or "Mexican-Americans" is, by the very nature of the process, to exclude all those who are not "within" the category you're trying to configure.

Exclusion, in other words, is very often a sinister or hateful operation, but it is also, we have to admit, a practical necessity in the postmodern world. If things don't signify in-themselves or universally—if there is only "meaning" within certain contexts—then those contexts need somehow to be narrowed. Think of writing an essay, for example. You have to build a *context* for your argument, and one of the first things you need to do is figure out what to *include* and what to *exclude* so your meaning can be comprehended. You simply can't write a coherent paper on "everything" or "everyone." Likewise, it seems that there is no coherent cultural context that will include "everyone." The world we live in is too complex. And, of course, we'd also want to be careful not to speak for people who may not *want* to be included in our "everyone."

Working Question

At the school where Jeff teaches, Penn State, tens of thousands of people attend football games each Saturday in the fall. One of the rituals of these home games is to consistently shout the chant, "We are Penn State!"

Why, one wonders, do fans shout this at home games, when presumably everyone *knows* that the stands are filled overwhelmingly with

Penn State fans? And why shout it over and over again? Wouldn't once be enough to make the point? What *is* the point of such a practice?

Perhaps the project of multiculturalism is neither an attempt to bring people together under a big homogeneous "we" nor an attempt to separate people along racial, ethnic, class, religious, or sexual-orientation lines; rather, perhaps multiculturalism can call our attention ceaselessly to the fact that the normativity of "our" culture *inexorably* and *necessarily* marginalizes consideration of some people and some groups, and that marginalization has concrete effects on those people. It is undeniable that such an exclusion has serious, concrete consequences, and such an exclusion needs to be highlighted—always kept in mind. Especially in politically charged cases, such as the denial of spousal benefits to gay couples or English-language-only initiatives, the structure of our *norms* must be always pointed out as being both necessary *and* exclusionary. We may not be able to avoid exclusion altogether, but we can keep our attention focused on the exclusionary *effects* of certain kinds of norms.

In the end, it's important to remember that any attempt to configure a "same" (a coherent or narrow group) is always dependent on a *process of exclusion,* and hence on a series of "others." Every "is," to return to Gertrude Stein's wacky but instructive vocabulary, is at the same time a series of "is-nots." To say that one is "white," for example, is to say that one is-not black, Asian, Latina/o, etc. Every "dominant" culture is dependent on its difference from a series of "subcultures," and every majority presupposes a series of minorities. Every culture is inexorably a multiculture.

◈ Working Question

Following is Franz Kafka's (very) short story, "Community" (from *The Complete Stories,* edited by Nahum Glatzer. New York: Schocken Books, 1971).

"We are five friends, one day we came out of a house one after the other, first one came and placed himself beside the gate, then the second came, or rather he glided through the gate like a little ball of quicksilver, and placed himself near the first one, then came the third, then the fourth, then the fifth. Finally we all stood in a row. People began to notice us, they pointed at us and said: Those five just came out of that house. Since then we have been living together; it would be a peaceful life if it weren't for a sixth one continually trying to interfere. He doesn't do us any harm, but he annoys us, and that is harm enough; why does he intrude where he is not wanted? We don't know him and don't want him to join us. There was a time, of course, when the five of us did not know one another, either; and it could be said that we still don't know one another, but what is possible and can be tolerated by the five of us is not possible and cannot be tolerated with this sixth one. In any case, we are five and don't want to be six. And what is the point of this continual being together anyhow? It is also pointless for the five of us, but here we are together and will remain together; a new combination, however, we do not want, just because of our experiences. But how is one to make all this clear to the sixth one? Long explanations would almost amount to accepting him in our circle, so we prefer not to explain and not to accept him. No matter how he pouts his lips we push him away with our elbows, but however much we push him away, back he comes."

What does this story have to say about "community" and how communities are formed?

Popular Culture

Just as the notion of "culture as a whole way of life" begs lots of questions and refinements, so too does the definition of "high culture" advocated by folks like Matthew Arnold, T. S. Eliot, the Leavises, and their contemporary followers, such as William Buckley, Allan Bloom, and E. D. Hirsch. From the start, the phrase "popular culture" can seem like something of a contradiction in terms. If the realm of "culture" is made up of the best that has been thought and written in a society, then anything "popular" is almost by definition not within the realm of "culture," and, vice versa, the things that make up the realm of "high" culture—theater, opera, classical music—tend not to be immensely "popular," at least when measured on the scale of blockbuster movies or mega-popular music stars. If culture is in some sense a repository of "the best," then the successful products of contemporary popular culture—reality TV, soap operas, boy bands, slasher flicks—seem hardly worthy of even sharing the word "culture" with Shakespeare, Mozart, or Jane Austen.

But of course there's something quite suspect about such a definition of "high" versus "popular" culture. First, such a dichotomy tends to presuppose that the person or group making the distinction can somehow tell the difference between high and low, between the best and the worst. But is there, we might ask ourselves, an absolute difference between something that's popular or entertaining and something that aspires to the lofty perch of being serious or high art? Is jazz, for example, a species of high culture or popular culture? Although National Public Radio calls jazz "America's classical music," much of the day-to-day life of playing and listening to jazz continues to go on in small, crowded clubs rather than in ballrooms and symphony houses.

So is jazz a "popular" or "high" culture form? It's difficult to say; jazz isn't stupendously popular when compared to various forms of rock, rap, and country music, but it's certainly more popular than, say, contemporary classical music. To a fan of contemporary classical music, jazz may seem popular or trivial, while to a speed-metal lover it might come across as obscure and pretentious; from another angle altogether, a musicologist might look upon it as a deeply *historical* form of expression growing out of roots in African culture. A jazz musician might look at it as a vocation or an artistic calling, playing it regardless of its popularity or lack thereof.

Indeed, if every culture is a multiculture, and if meaning is not simply inherent in things, we should expect substantial difficulties in any attempt to make a simple high/low culture distinction. One would always be forced to ask, "High culture *to whom*, or to what *group*? By what *criteria* are these distinctions made?" As any trip to an antique store confirms, items that may now count as high-culture treasures (cherry wood tables, Shaker furniture, folk sculpture) were once everyday items within a popular culture of the past.

The distinction between high and low art, like other distinctions we've examined, is a difficult one to make. For example, although the novel seems clearly to be a high-culture form, the fact that Stephen King sells a lot of them continues to cause "true literature" lovers to lose sleep. Perhaps this example gives us a criterion for making a preliminary distinction between high and low; perhaps it is raw popularity (sheer numbers of people participating) that makes something a "low" art form, and a lack of popularity (low numbers of aficionados) that qualifies something as high art. Perhaps the more popular something is, the less likely it is to be truly worthy of serious consideration.

This distinction is tempting, but in the end this doesn't seem likely; for example, while the musical form polka certainly isn't immensely popular, it hardly seems to qualify as a "high" musical form. Appalachian snake-handling religions, although quite rare, certainly don't have the high-cultural feel of midnight mass with the Pope in Rome, but Catholicism is obviously the much more "popular" religious practice. In the end, "high" or "low" culture can't simply correspond to "not popular" and "popular" cultural practices.

So if it's not outward popularity that makes something high or low culture, perhaps it's something inherent in the form itself. On further examination, however, this also seems unlikely. For example, both Orson Welles's *Citizen Kane* and Tim Burton's *Ed Wood* are biographical films, but that fact in itself tells us nothing about where they fit on the "high versus popular" scale of culture. Likewise, are Quentin Tarantino's films best understood as high art or popular blockbusters? Is cinema even a legitimate art form? If it is, then why doesn't all cinema—James Bond movies, pornography, karate movies, instructional videos—qualify as art? Likewise, although painting is certainly a high art *form*, we should note that a painting like the *Mona Lisa* universally qualifies as high art, but paintings of dogs playing cards are just as universally relegated to the low culture bin. Because the same form (painting) can be received in many differing ways, it doesn't seem plausible that there can be inherently "high culture" and inherently "popular culture" art forms.

Working Questions

1. Take a look at Robert Mapplethorpe's photography, such as figure 5.1, *Ken and Tyler*. What is the artist trying to communicate? Is it high art or porn? How do you know? If he had composed nudes in oils, would your judgment be the same or different? Who gets to decide if his images are edifying or titillating?

2. A colleague of ours once said, "It is a grave mistake to assume that a college career spent deconstructing cartoons and song lyrics is tuition money well spent." Clearly this colleague is concerned about too much collegiate focus on "popular" culture to the detriment of "high" culture. Is he right, do you think? If so, why? If not, why not?

No matter how you attack these kinds of questions, it does seem that the more you examine the problem closely, the more you see that there are no clear demarcations between what's called high culture and what's called popular culture. Yet the divide persists. Somehow, everybody on the street knows that a Rembrandt is high art, while a painting of Elvis on velvet isn't; everybody knows that polka is low art, while opera is high art; and no one confuses the

Figure 5.1 *Ken and Tyler*, 1985;
copyright © Robert Mapplethorpe Foundation

merits of porn films with the cultural influence of Oscar-winning dramas. Although the distinction is notoriously difficult to draw, it seems that people do it all the time, and with a great deal of ease.

Perhaps this ease is explained by the fact that the difference between "high" and "popular" culture tends to correspond in many people's minds to a sense of "good" art versus "bad" art: High culture is often seen to be good (good for you—like bran or broccoli), whereas popular culture is often dismissed as irrelevant trash (dangerous to your health—like candy or cigarettes). High art is often understood as bland but edifying (intellectually like a long engagement leading up to an arranged marriage), whereas popular culture is looked upon like a lost weekend of anything-goes debauchery. Consider, for example, Allan Bloom's reading of popular culture's effects in *The Closing of the American Mind*:

> Picture a thirteen-year-old boy sitting in the living room of his family home doing his math assignment while wearing his Walkman headphones or watching MTV. He enjoys the liberties hard won over centuries by the alliance of philosophic genius and political heroism, consecrated by the blood of martyrs; he is provided with comfort and leisure by the most productive economy ever known to mankind; science has penetrated the secrets of nature in order to provide him with the marvelous, lifelike electronic sound and image reproduction he is enjoying. And in what does progress culminate? A pubescent child whose body throbs with orgasmic rhythms; whose feelings are made articulate in hymns to the joys of onanism or the killing of parents; whose ambition is to win fame and wealth in imitating the drag-queen who makes the music. In short, life is made into a nonstop, commercially prepackaged masturbational fantasy. (75)

As far as Bloom is concerned, popular culture is not *merely* vacuous or insipid, devoid of great themes and therefore unworthy of analysis or appreciation (already an argumentative claim). In Bloom's estimation, popular culture certainly *is* all of those things (and less), but the real problem with popular culture is that it's quite literally *dangerous*, a parasite feeding off the "genius" and "heroism" "hard won over centuries" by high culture.

As Bloom suggests in his example of the overstimulated young boy, the category of high-culture art often functions like your parents—it has something valuable (if difficult) to teach you—while popular culture is more like an irresponsible older sibling, offering you cheap gratification, void of any real or substantial meaning. High art in Bloom finds a fairly strict definition: great themes presented in an edifying form. Mozart is taking on the big high-culture themes—death, tradition, love, responsibility—on a grand scale, while silly reality shows play all day on TV.

By its very nature, then, Bloom's conception of popular culture is steeped in a kind of paternalism (*he* knows what's good for *you*), but also buried within it is a very odd notion or definition of "culture." For Bloom, culture isn't those *material* or *contextual* concerns that we've been highlighting throughout this text, the specific and local conditions in which meaning happens. In fact, culture seems in Bloom to be just the opposite, a kind of transcendental "idea," the "soul" or "genius" of a people or nation, "consecrated by the blood of martyrs."

As we've seen throughout this text, there are all sorts of problems with this kind of idea. First of all, any supposedly *transcendental* categories (virtue, wisdom, genius, etc.) are themselves already *social* constructs; lofty goals such as "goodness" and "virtue" grow out of a particular *context* just as surely as *The Simpsons* do. Of course, that doesn't mean that distinctions cannot be made, but we have to insist again that there is nothing *inherent* in a work of art or a person that makes it mean something in particular. Meaning is a *process* of social contextualization; the same signifiers can be read in many, many differing ways.

For Bloom, if you spend your time studying popular culture, all you will discover is some degraded husk of meaning, a "prepackaged masturbational fantasy" determined by the context of a bankrupt culture on the skids. As the antidote to that disease, high culture offers "timeless" or "transcendental" values, meanings that are *not* tied to a specific time, place, or set of (what Bloom might call *merely*) cultural values. So *popular culture* is in this sense another word for a concrete or actual culture, while high culture signifies timeless or transcendent culture, not bound by the times and places in which it is produced, transmitted, and received. For Bloom, "real"—that is, really important—values are "abstract" ones.

It doesn't take a magician to see a bait-and-switch tactic used by Bloom here. What he wants to locate as "timeless" values are themselves "social" values, inextricably tied to a particular time and place. Bloom's book, ironically, was a best-seller largely because of the political context in which it emerged, the conservative backlash of the Reagan 1980s in the United States; in other words (and ironically), Bloom's appeal to "timeless" values found a substantial "popular" audience largely because of the tremendous social and political appeal of the supposedly asocial and apolitical arguments that Bloom put forward. In other words, his argument about high art—the "great" art of the past is good for you, while the products of contemporary culture are dangerous trash—turned out to be quite popular because it tapped into many of the nostalgic social tendencies of the Reagan years.

However querulous Bloom's interventions around popular culture are, his book was nonetheless quite influential in heated curricular debates—the so-called culture wars—that emerged in conjunction with the multicultural turn in higher education in the '80s and '90s. Consider, for example, Dartmouth professor Jeffrey Hart's advice to undergraduates in an essay entitled "How to Get a College Education," published in a September 1996 issue of *The National Review*:

> Select the ordinary courses. I use ordinary here in a paradoxical and challenging way. An ordinary course is one that has always

been taken and obviously should be taken. . . . The student should be discouraged from putting his money on the cutting edge of interdisciplinary cross-textuality.

Thus, do take American and European history, an introduction to philosophy, American and European literature, the Old and New Testaments, and at least one modern language. It would be absurd not to take a course in Shakespeare, the best poet in our language. . . .

I hasten to add that I applaud the student who devotes his life to the history of China or Islam, but that . . . should come later. America is part of the narrative of European history.

If the student should seek out those "ordinary" courses, then it follows that he should avoid the flashy come-ons. Avoid things like Nicaraguan Lesbian Poets. Yes, and anything listed under "Studies," any course whose description uses the words "interdisciplinary," "hegemonic," "phallocratic," or "empowerment," anything that mentions "keeping a diary," any course with a title like "Adventures in Film."

Also, any male professor who comes to class without a jacket and tie should be regarded with extreme prejudice unless he has won a Nobel Prize. (38)

Working Questions

1. What are "timeless" values? Can you think of specific examples? Bravery? Loyalty? Compassion? Family? Can you think of specific or concrete *instances* or *examples* of those values, concrete examples of specific acts that everyone would agree manifest the real meaning of these abstract values? Have the values called "timeless" always been the same?

2. Jeffrey Hart's commentary reflects a common complaint that university education has "become politicized" to the detriment of "disinterested" scholarship. What, if anything, about this claim to scholarly neutrality is suspicious? How do you read Hart's advice to undergraduates, given our discussions of multiculturalism and popular culture? Why the repetition of "ordinary" in his argument? What (or whose) cultural norms and values does Hart advocate? What does he exclude?

So what is to be gained from studying popular culture? What can we learn from popular culture that we can't learn from "the great tradition"? Why even bother to direct our attention to popular culture? First, of course, we should note that popular culture has a lot of influences over our subjectivity; certainly Hollywood holds a lot more sway over contemporary culture than Emily Dickinson's poems do. In fact, one of the most crucial reasons to study popular culture is not so much to *learn* from it but to examine how it *teaches* us certain things: It teaches us how to have fun, how to be sad, how to be in love, what kind of body we should have, what we should be excited by, and what should bore us.

For example, it's fairly clear that Disney movies and Saturday morning cartoons teach children an enormous amount, for better or worse, about gender roles, violence, consumerism, race, competition, manners, and a thousand other things. This kind of pedagogical influence is easy enough to see in children, who slavishly seem to crave and imitate whatever they see on their favorite cartoons, but the power of these influences over children should also draw our attention to the fact that what's called the culture industry—the music industry, television and film, the so-called leisure industry (Disney World, water parks, etc.), advertising—likewise has an enormous influence over our attitudes as adults. What we think of as hip, beautiful, fun, rebellious, authentic, or reprehensible has much to do with the formation of those subject positions within contemporary media culture.

In other words, films, TV, and advertising are never simply about, nor can they be reduced to, "entertainment." Media teach us how to be subjects, or how to be certain types of subjects. *Friends* teaches us what it means to be funny, and soap operas offer us strategies for staging the dramas of our lives; sports stars show us what it means to give 110 percent, while police dramas like *Cops* teach us to be good citizens, or else. So when we study popular culture, we are indeed studying ourselves, but not in the way that people often say. It's not so much that popular culture *reflects* the attitudes of its consumers; rather, the crucial reason to study popular culture is to figure out the ways in which it teaches us how and what to reflect.

Popular culture educates us as it offers us relaxation, excitement, or pleasure; it offers us little pedagogical lessons along with the pleasures that it affords. It is in mapping out those pedagogical effects that much work in popular culture remains to be done. The point, in other words, is not to dismiss popular culture as "dangerous" because it is fun or pleasurable; it is, rather, to study the effects of that industry (and it is very much an *industry*).

Working Question

If something is or becomes "popular," does that necessarily mean that it has diminished "meaning" or "value"?

On the surface, this would seem to be the case all across the cultural board—from grunge and gangsta rap, to pop art and new wave cinema, to *Seinfeld*—the thousands of attempts to try to copy from something new or innovative seem to change the object, transforming it from artistically interesting to pop culture drivel.

But is there something suspect about the "way cool/sold out" dialectic of cultural reception? Is the artist ever in control of the context in which people use or receive art? Would Kurt Cobain really have been better off and happier if no one outside Seattle had ever heard of him?

What, if anything, does the "authenticity" of an artwork have to do with all this? How can you tell an "authentic" original from an "inauthentic" copy? And does this distinction merely repeat the problematic high culture/pop culture distinction? Why or why not?

Media Culture

Let's not be overhasty with that last thought: culture as industry. Given the reach and power of media culture, it would behoove us to take a closer look at it as a specifically *global* industry, and a very powerful one indeed. When we stop to think about it, we're incredibly dependent on media to keep us both informed and entertained. Not only do they tell us stories about our own subjectivities, but they also tell us stories about the world, how it works, and our place within it. Unless you or someone you know has traveled to Pakistan, Sierra Leone, or Argentina, everything you know about those places—their citizens, their culture, their form of government, whether they're allies or foes—derives from the media. But then again, even the firsthand information we've gathered about people we're intimately involved with—family, for example—is deeply influenced by media representations. Would you consider your family rich? Poor? Normal? Insane? How do you know? Based on or compared to what? Years of living with myriad other families, or intense, ongoing exposure to celluloid families ranging from *Leave It to Beaver* to *Keeping Up with the Kardashians*? Thinking about how the media affect our lives, in short, requires thinking about *mediation*.

Mediation refers to ongoing processes by which we negotiate, or translate, flows of signs—words and images—as they circulate or move from place to place. It refers to both the ways in which we make sense of and take on the world and the ways we escape or avoid the world and its responsibilities. Whether in the process of engagement or disengagement, mediation suggests *activity*, as opposed to passivity, on the part of audiences. In contrast to the assumptions that underlie much discussion of what is problematically referred to as "mass culture," media messages don't simply wash over us, nor are their effects in any way homogeneous, uniform, or predictable. We might think reading a novel or attending the opera requires more intellectual effort than watching reruns of *Charlie's Angels* or *The Brady Bunch* on TV Land, but such visual engagement nonetheless requires complex processes of interpretation.

Reading media culture presupposes our ability to account for—more or less unconsciously—the differences among various media forms and their constitutive genres. Making sense of cable and network television programming, for example, requires the capacity to "decode" the structure and rules governing genres particular to that medium. We bring a different set of assumptions and expectations to crime drama as opposed to situation comedy or daytime melodrama. We know, for example, that unless we're watching episodes of the first five seasons of *South Park*, no one dies at the end of sitcoms—particularly the animated ones. With the possible exception of Kenny impaled on the flagpole of his elementary school, we tend not to find death all that amusing, and hence it is well beyond the purview of most comic forms. Our ability to interpret media narratives by contextualizing them in this fashion enables us to make competent decisions about when to read irony, humor, sensation, or candor. Our ability to read *South Park* ironically, in other words, depends on our capacity to situate the program intertextually. For it to work as irony depends on our prior knowledge of similar series organized around packs of eight-year-olds, say *The Little Rascals* or *Peanuts*. Given its departure from the conventions that we've become familiar with, the show potentially raises lots of interesting and pertinent questions: What's it like to grow up in today's very complex world? Are we witnessing the death of childhood innocence or the death of adult illusions that children remain innocent regardless of changing social circumstances? Our capacity to decode media is also evident in the discriminations we make among various sources for news and information. When Marshall McLuhan

famously asserted that the "medium is the message," he was referring, in part, to the distinctions we make all the time between the
news we gather through such venerable institutions as the *New York
Times* and what we learn from tabloids like *People* or *Star* or Jon
Stewart's recap of the day's events on *The Daily Show*.

Currently, however, one could argue that making such discriminations is becoming increasingly difficult as the boundaries between
various media functions—to persuade, to inform, to entertain—and
various media forms are increasingly blurred or subordinated altogether to the imperatives of consumer culture. Cable news channels,
for example, increasingly sound like advertisements pitching new
movies or new CDs in the guise of the "Hollywood Minute" or the
latest computer or cell-phone technology in the "Tech Update." And
conversely, advertisers create infomercials that mimic news copy to
camouflage their efforts to sell products by invoking "scientific
research," often conducted, oddly enough, by the very company
hawking the latest cereal, sneakers, or cosmetics. Further, the contexts of our viewing and the roles we play as audience members are
continually changing as our visual practices shift. Our strategies of
reading change as film moves from the silver screen to the television
screen with video rentals, or the computer screen with the posting
of high-tech interactive trailers. In an information age, representations are constantly in circulation, on the move, and so are their significations. We might see Da Vinci's *Mona Lisa* in the Louvre in
Paris, reproduced in an art history textbook, featured on a coffee
mug in the museum shop at the local mall, or featured on the cover
of *The New Yorker* with someone's head superimposed on the
image—and in each instance the same representation will mean
something different by virtue of its recontextualization. The meanings of mass-mediated images are constantly negotiated by readers,
viewers, and consumers who are themselves situated within constantly shifting social, political, and cultural contexts.

Yet while the capacity for diverse audiences to produce multiple, complex, even paradoxical readings of media should be kept in

mind, it would be a mistake to underestimate the power of an increasingly consolidated media industry to frame meanings, offer pleasures, persuade audiences, and construct communities in very specific ways, more often than not predisposing people to accept established ways of thinking about or acting upon the world. Media culture, like culture in general, tends to favor or encourage the production of certain subjectivities over others—explicitly through the institutions of law and order and implicitly through norms that inform our perceptions of morality and social conduct. This is not to suggest that cultures produce subjectivities like Ford factories produce pickup trucks. Subjects, as we've insisted, also influence culture, and media culture is no exception. While media culture *offers* (as opposed to *determines*) particular identities and meanings, the norms underlying these are resisted all the time. The briefest encounter with the icons of contemporary youth cultures— Eminem, Snoop Dogg, Lady Gaga, and so on—tends to illustrate the capacities of young people to reject outright conventional modes of thought, behavior, style, and interaction. But just as surely, it reveals the capacity of media to appropriate, repackage, and sell such forms of resistance back to youth. In this sense, media culture can be said to exert a regulative influence over—as opposed to crudely determining—our subjectivities. *At the same time, media culture is also subject to particular forms of regulation and control itself.*

But just what kinds of pressure exert a shaping or determining influence on media culture? Where do such forces come from? Where *should* they come from? Such questions demand consideration of what is often referred to as the "political economy" of media culture, a form of analysis that tends to focus on how media texts are produced and distributed rather than on how diverse audiences interpret and engage media. "Political economy" reminds us that the production and distribution of, say, reality TV shows like *Jersey Shore* or *Celebrity Rehab* take place within a specific economic and political system. As the capitalist system, if not the Western version of liberal democracy associated with it, becomes globalized, market imperatives influence much of what gets produced. The drive to maximize profitability, for example, necessitates programming that scores very high ratings while simultaneously incurring low budget costs. In an ever-downsizing economy, the industry loves reality TV in part because it's a lot cheaper for MTV to hire an anonymous teen mom from Des Moines than, say, Charlie Sheen, of millions-per-episode-of–*Two and a Half Men* fame.

Of course, one might point out the obvious: Media have always had a commercial dimension. What's so new and different about media culture today? Advances in telecommunications technologies and three decades of deregulation in the industry have resulted in a global media system dominated, in short, by seven multinational corporations: Disney, AOL–Time Warner, Sony, News Corporation, Viacom, Vivendi, and Bertelsmann. Beginning in the 1980s, the three major television networks were all taken over by major corporate conglomerates: ABC was bought by Capital Cities, NBC merged with General Electric, and CBS was purchased by Tisch Financial Group. And that was only the beginning. Breakneck advances in digital communications and computing have furthered mergers between information and entertainment industries, as older forms of entertainment are increasingly entwined with the Internet and the computer is becoming an indispensable (although not necessarily affordable) household appliance used for entertainment, play, news, information, communication, and connection with virtually all parts of the globe. Dwarfing all previous information and entertainment mergers, the world's largest Internet provider, America Online (AOL), merged with Time Warner in 2000—a merger worth $163.4 billion. The music giant EMI, based in the United Kingdom, quickly followed suit, unveiling plans to merge with Time Warner. The upshot of this massive consolidation of media ownership and control is that among them, these seven conglomerates "own the major U.S. film studios; all but one of the U.S. television networks; the few companies that control 80–85 percent of the global music market; the preponderance of satellite broadcasting worldwide; a significant percentage of book publishing and commercial magazine publishing; all or part of most of the commercial cable TV channels in the U.S. and worldwide; [and] a significant portion of European . . . television" (McChesney, "Global Media, Neoliberalism, and Imperialism," 2). And the process of consolidation is only likely to accelerate in the near future.

Analysis of the concentration of media ownership tells us something about the "economy" side of the contemporary political economy of media, but what about the "political" side? In spite of its obvious power, the "free market" remains something of a misnomer. Although the industry has enjoyed the benefits of "deregulation," it nonetheless remains subject to some form of regulation from the government. Media production responds to both market and democratic imperatives; the latter translate into forms of state regulation and intervention that also affect what media produce and how their products circulate. One such example is the passage of laws requiring not only movies, but also prime-time television programming, to be rated, indicating how much violence, nudity, "adult situations," and obscenity audiences will be subjected to. In addition, music CDs are required to carry warning labels that alert parents to violent lyrics or obscenity. Other forms of state regulation include the prohibition placed on cigarette advertising targeting teens and laws governing the careful placement of "adult magazines" like *Playboy* or *Hustler,* usually under wraps, on store racks—at least back in the day when porn was bought in actual physical spaces as opposed to virtual ones.

Other, less obvious, forms of government regulation of mass media are a bit more suspect. In wartime, U.S. government institutions like the Pentagon can censor if not control the press while claiming to serve and protect national interests and national security. Since the 1991 Gulf War, for example, the U.S. government has prohibited journalists from having any direct contact with soldiers and battlefields through the use of a military pool system, sending one handpicked journalist to the field to report back to all media outlets, thus ensuring only approved images and reporting of the war.

Increasingly, however, it is difficult to distinguish between corporate interests and political interests as they play out on the battlefield of mass media. Currently the wealth generated by any of these first-tier media corporations rivals the GDPs of small nations. And like small nations, they have their own political and economic interests to maintain and protect. Whereas we used to think of media as conduits or appendages of political systems—either in the pocket of specific politicians or parties or a watchdog, the Fourth Estate, ensuring that powerful interests adhere to democratic processes and forms of accountability—we now have to rethink these new media giants as influential political entities *in themselves*. Media corporations produce myriad consumer products—books, music, cable TV, film, news, and Internet services—that we rely on to negotiate an increasingly complex, high-speed, interconnected global society. This provides them with not only billions of dollars of revenue annually but also the capacity to exert political power in both explicit and subtle ways. By virtue of its size, its reach, and its concentration, the media culture industry can influence and change the political process, potentially for democratic ends or very antidemocratic ends. On the one hand, the culture industry can provide people with a wide range of information, opinion, analysis, and debate on the most important public issues of the day; it can do so in a way that gives voice to and reflects the diversity of its citizens; and it can promote transparency and public accountability, curbing the abuse of power in both business and government. On the other hand, the twentieth century is replete with examples of media used for propagandistic and authoritarian ends; Hitler's powerful and persuasive use of the image to forward the interests of National Socialism remains perhaps the most vivid. Of course, one might point out that media, in this instance, were under the control of the national government, whereas now media are transnational and privately owned. But the potential abuses of a contemporary global media system rapidly consolidating into fewer and fewer hands are no less substantial because the interests of particular nation-states have been subordinated to the interests of a global market.

The implications of privately owned media consolidation are problematic in several respects for consumers, small business people, and society at large. For consumers, media conglomerates tend to create less marketplace competition and so less choice. They are averse to risky investment, which translates into less innovation in creative industries like film and music, resulting in the curiously generic, commercially driven rise of the rebellious artist on the music front and more formulaic sex-and-violence blockbusters equipped to serve global markets. Given their broad nationalizing and internationalizing tendencies, media giants offer less access to the concerns and interests of localities and hence declining access to community or regionally based news and information, as well as the marginalization of indigenous art, music, and other cultural forms. For small businesses, the inability to compete with media giants tends to mean either exclusion from the market or being swallowed up by merger or acquisition.

But media consolidation's implications for democracy are perhaps most stark. Most obviously, it poses a serious threat to any notion of a "free" press, given that most news sources are owned by giant multinationals, which puts at risk our access to information that might prove harmful to business interests, impairing our capacity to act as informed, responsible citizens. In their capacity to frame how citizens perceive political issues and the politicians themselves, the media exert a tremendous amount of influence on governments from the local to the national and international levels. Perhaps less obvious is the depoliticizing effect the global media have on their audiences. To maintain profitability, the media industry requires the active participation of consumers, not citizens. To that end, it relentlessly targets audiences as individual consumers while pushing to the margins those long-term social considerations that affect them collectively as citizens. Think of it this way: On average, we are exposed to literally thousands of commercial impressions a day—that's thousands of times every day, seven days a week, that we're appealed to as individual consumers, which doesn't leave a lot of time left over to engage us on issues that affect the commonweal. In short, in their capacity to colonize both space and time through hyper-commercialization, the global media pose a serious challenge to ordinary citizens' relations to the political process.

Media Culture 2.0

Probably at this point many of you Facebook and Twitter fans, citizen journalists, bloggers, gamers, and video artists are wondering what the hell we're talking about when we speak to the potential threats to democracy that ongoing media consolidation harbingers. What about the impact of new interactive technologies and forms of digital participation they enable, which would seem to inspire a new, participatory culture that promises precisely to democratize global media production? To be sure, much of the excitement and the hype (if not hyperbole) around new digital technologies rests on a felicitous set of assumptions that they do indeed produce alternative forms of knowledge, create community, empower users, and revolutionize communications—in some cases even foment actual revolution, given the role that social networking has been said to play in the Tunisian and Egyptian uprisings in 2011 as well as Iran's violently preempted Green Revolution some eighteen months prior. As early as December 2006, in fact, *Time* magazine anointed "you" its person of the year "for seizing the reins of the global media, for founding and framing the new digital democracy, for working for nothing and beating the pros at their own game" (Grossman, "*Time*'s Person of the Year"). But even this heady praise is a bit suspicious—"seizing the reins . . . [to work] for nothing"? Sounds like "you" been punk'd. Although Grossman's comment is meant to underscore the meteoric rise of collaborative sites and technologies such as YouTube, Flickr, podcasting, wikis, and the general intensification of user-generated content, it should also raise some pointed questions. As Craig Calhoun reminds us, the new information technologies and modes of interactivity they enable "are powerful, but not all powerful" in that they "are introduced into a world of existing social relations, culture, capitalism and inequalities" ("Information Technology," 240). Rather than giving in to a kind of technological determinism in which digital participation is uncritically celebrated as the outcome of technological innovation and youthful genius, these advances should be taken up as sites of struggle within the realm of capital, new forms of immaterial labor, potential solidarities, subject formation, social relations, desires, and "life" itself—as we discuss a few chapters down the road. And that means questioning just how digital participation will be framed and configured, maintained and contained, enabled and surveilled— and for whose benefit.

Digital participation offers a staggering diversity of opportunities for personal enrichment and social assertion, from online educational opportunities for learners who live in remote areas or who negotiate physical challenges that make attendance at brick-and-mortar institutions difficult if not impossible, to the direct confrontation with governmental power and authority used to legitimate invasion and war, as seen in the 2010 release by Wikileaks of more than 92,000 classified military documents relating to the war in Afghanistan. But the possibilities that new interactive technologies offer are as contradictory and uncontrollable as they are increasingly ubiquitous, as intention and action can be at once achieved and appropriated, turned to socially just or socially repressive ends. The 2008 presidential election, on one hand, has offered a powerful glimpse of how new media can be harnessed for progressive ends, as the Obama campaign successfully used the Web to mobilize notoriously hard-to-reach youth voters among other constituencies in the interests of generating a grassroots movement that sought to redefine the nation's political culture. But the fact that such massive political mobilization efforts quickly dissipated after the election also says something about the contexts in which digital technologies are used. Digital participants, on the other hand, seem no less immune to the relentless privatization of public discourse, no less obsessed with the consumption and production of personal narratives of attained or desired "wealth, sexual conquest, and fame" that has come to dominate celebrity-infused media culture (Hedges, *Empire of Illusion*, 2009). In many ways the arrival of new digital technologies has accelerated what the sociologist Richard Sennett identified several decades ago as the ascendancy of an "intimate vision of society," a form of "tyranny" that erodes robust forms of public life animated by intense political debate and impersonal exchange among strangers, as it simultaneously and ironically renders implosive much-vaunted private, intimate relations that increasingly seize people's wholehearted interest and imagination. Just as every successful campaign has done in the last half century, team Obama spent millions in campaign funds to appeal to and manipulate this kind of political illiteracy and illogic as the electorate was invited to focus increasingly on the person of this potential leader. Obama's youthful promise, his intellectual gravity, his soaring rhetoric, his unfailing cool, and most of all his compelling personal narrative that simultaneously invoked the triumphalism of America's beloved immigration mythology and offered a redemptive conclusion to its most egregious racial sins—all these personal attributes took consistent priority over the specificities of his political platform.

The highly influential MIT scholar who once expressed tremendous optimism about the wealth of opportunities available to an increasingly wired world, Sherry Turkle has radically revised her position about the psychological and sociopolitical effects of new digital technologies. In *Alone Together* she alerts readers to what she sees as a fateful collapse between our online life and life itself:

> Only a decade ago I would have been mystified that fifteen-year-olds in my urban neighborhood, a neighborhood full of parks and shopping malls, of front stoops and coffee shops, would feel the need to send and receive close to six thousand

> messages a month via portable digital devices or that best
> friends would assume that when they visited, it would usually
> be on the virtual real estate of Facebook. (16)

Has technology lead to increased social contact or radically circumscribed it? Has it created more effective communication or
facilitated the exchange of mountains of gossip and trivia? Has it
enriched our emotional lives or depleted them, saved us valuable
time or emptied it of meaning? Echoing Sennett's concerns, Turkle
openly worries about the normalization of a wired world, to the
detriment of our ability to connect outside of it. She writes, "Life in
a media bubble has come to seem natural. So has the end of a certain public etiquette: on the street we speak into the invisible micro-
phones in our mobile phones and appear to be talking to ourselves.
We share intimacies with the air as though unconcerned about who
can hear us or the details of our physical surroundings" (*Alone
Together*, 16). To be sure, these technologies have revolutionized
family life, medicine, education, and business as parents experience
greater ease of access to their children, patients to doctors, students
to teachers, salespersons to customers—to say nothing of the vast
wealth of information all have at their fingertips. But at what costs?
For Turkle, the "connected life encourages us to treat those we meet
online in something like the way we treat objects—with dispatch.
It happens naturally: when you are besieged by thousands of
e-mails, texts and messages—more than you can respond to—
demands become depersonalized" (*Alone Together*, 168).

Even the hype around the use of social media in the context of
Egypt's Tahrir Square—what one reporter from CNN called the
"most fascinating aspect of this whole revolution"—had to take a
backseat to social reality. The Egyptian government successfully dis-
rupted access to the nation's four main Internet providers, and the
protests only got stronger. An exacerbated Richard Engel, a foreign
correspondent on the scene and reporting on MSNBC, eventually
set the record straight: "This didn't have anything to do with Twitter

and Facebook," he said. "This had to do with people's dignity, people's pride. People are not able to feed their families" (cited in Rich, "Wallflowers at the Revolution," WK8). From this perspective, the tools that protesters used to communicate with one another may well be the least interesting fact of all. Indeed, even among the young and semi-wired populace of Egypt, only some 20 percent have access to the Internet. Such are the concerns of scholarly participants in evolving debates over what social media mean for governmental regimes that run the gamut from democratic to totalitarian. Evgeny Morozov's recent book, *The Net Delusion: The Dark Side of Internet Freedom*, challenges what he calls the now conventional wisdom of "cyber-utopianism." Taking on what many American pundits hailed as the "Twitter Revolution" in Iran, he notes that there were only 19,235 registered Twitter accounts in the country at the time, or about 0.027 percent of the population. More disturbingly, Morozov documents the ways in which "digital tools so useful to citizens in a free society can be co-opted by tech-savvy dictators, police states and garden-variety autocrats to spread propaganda and to track (and arrest) conveniently networked dissidents, from Iran to Venezuela" (cited in Rich, "Wallflowers at the Revolution," WK8). Hugo Chavez, for example, "first vilified Twitter as a 'conspiracy,' but now has 1.2 million followers imbibing his self-sanctifying Tweets" (Rich, "Wallflowers at the Revolution," WK8).

To be sure, digitally assisted circulation of images and videos on the Internet has challenged the abilities of nation-states to "control the message" to the degree that these once sovereign entities no longer exert an exclusive or overly determined influence on media and its economies of spectacle. No longer the exclusive tools of state power, digital technologies have been used, as we have recently seen, to challenge corrupt governmental power and authority for democratic ends through the exposure of illegality and brutality in leaked documents or documentary footage. But such cyber-imagery and testimony has also been used to advance violent and extremist ends. Henry A. Giroux has documented the ways in which video technology has become a primary tool used by terrorists to distribute images, including speeches by terrorist leaders, gruesome beheadings, jihadist hip-hop music videos, and suicide bombers using cell phones to document their own deaths, and also to bear witness to the victims of state terrorism as in the images of Muslims being killed by American and British soldiers . . . or experiencing indignities at the hands of American soldiers, especially [in] the images of torture and abuse of detainees at Abu Ghraib prison. (*Beyond the Spectacle*, 50–51)

Indeed, the ongoing "war on terror" is fought not only on the rocky terrain of places like Afghanistan, but also on the fluid terrain of cyberspace; in fact Gary Bunt (*Islam in the Digital Age*) uses the term "cyber jihad" to describe how adept various insurgent groups have become in utilizing the Web to communicate their demands to domestic and international audiences. Of course, the usage of violent imagery and insurgent rhetoric is hardly confined to Islamic extremism; it finds commensurate expression in far-right organizations and extremist militias globally. Lest we forget a certain American ex-governor criticized for her placement of rifle crosshairs over the congressional districts of rival politicians and aggressive "don't retreat, reload" rhetoric in the days following the Tuscon, Arizona, massacre of 2011.

Ongoing popular struggles against governments and corporations, whether for progressive or reactionary ends, remain decidedly one-sided and uneven, given the extreme differential in power and resources. Governments and corporations, as Giroux argues, "work incessantly in both limiting Internet freedom through censorship and surveillance and allowing advertising to permeate every corner of cyberspace" ("Crisis," 13). The educator and media theorist Catherine Burwell ("Rewriting the Script") has rightly argued that understanding the social and political implications of expanding digital participation as it shapes everyday life and communicative exchange particularly in the overdeveloped West means paying careful attention to at least four interrelated issues. First, there is the challenge of the increasing commodification of said participation, which influences and transforms not only how but why, or for what purposes, users negotiate various Internet sites. The global media giants who own newspapers, magazines, cable channels, and other media also seek ownership of new social networking sites. Within the last few years, Google has taken over YouTube; NewsCorp purchased MySpace; and NBC gobbled up Television without Pity (Burwell, "Rewriting the Script," 386). As important as the issue of ownership is the issue of how these commercial enterprises transform the way users behave on these sites—the shift that invariably occurs, in other words, from "vibrant online communities to shopping destinations and 'light virtual communities'" (Burwell, "Rewriting the Script," 386). And make no mistake, the bottom line for multinational corporations is not about enhancing communication or community but rather building an attractive base of viewers for their ads. The competition for your attention here is fierce. Consider the refreshingly blunt response of venture capitalist Todd Dagres to the pressure confronting Google, given that over two-thirds of all Internet users in the United States have now joined rival Facebook: "There is nothing more threatening to Google than a company that has 500 million subscribers and knows a lot about them and places targeted advertisements in front of them" (Helft, "Facebook Makes Headway"). Dagres, a partner at a firm that has invested in Twitter and other such companies, adds, "For every second that people are on Facebook and for every ad that Facebook puts in front of their face, it is one less second they are on Google and one less ad that Google puts in front of their face" (Helft, "Facebook Makes Headway").

Second, digital interaction, as these examples suggest, inevitably take shape within structural relations of power, surveillance, consumption, cultural privatization, and the curiously "cold intimacies" that mark what Eva Illouz calls "emotional capitalism." Thus there is the question of user agency, or how users are positioned by digital media producers and texts and how they position themselves in these forces, including the degree to which users take an active role in shaping interactivity as against being steered in particular directions by a site's interface (Burwell, "Rewriting the Script," 386).

Third, the aforementioned forms of free labor associated with collaborative technologies and user-generated content constitute another set of pressing issues. To what extent is said labor structured and shaped by late capitalism versus the ability of users to labor outside of and subvert capitalist acceleration? Is there really even a space "outside" of capital from which to resist it, as we discuss in chapter 11? Finally, and directly related to this issue of labor, there are issues around intellectual property and digital rights, among other issues. Consider the vast amounts of user-generated content garnered by wildly popular websites like Colbert Nation. As Burwell argues, "fans' labor provides free content for both the Web site and the broadcast, not only now but in the future, as all content is uploaded to the Colbert Nation Web site becomes the property of Viacom 'perpetually and indefinitely' (Terms of Use)" ("Rewriting the Script," 394). In fact, Burwell adds, television producers frequently mine user-generated content to create new storylines and ideas, just as corporations mine users' personal data to be bought and sold. In the end, to theorize the impact of the new digital communication systems on individual and social life is to take note of the way these novel forms of interactivity blur the lines between a whole slew of once stable distinctions: between work and play, production and consumption, coercion and choice, submission and subversion, publicity and privacy.

The unprecedented power of the new global telecommunications industry, then, provides us with yet another reason for studying popular culture, and media culture in particular. Not only do media teach us how to be subjects by fostering particular kinds of identifications, channeling desires in certain directions, and framing how we understand ourselves and the world, but they also play an increasingly influential role in the political and economic life of nations in a rapidly globalizing world. Highlighting the pedagogical and political impact of commercial media on our daily lives, however, doesn't mean that we're controlled, like so many mindless zombies, by the industry. But neither can we simply "turn off" its influence by pressing a button on a remote, abstaining from Facebook, or refusing to buy the latest issue of *Vogue* or *Rolling Stone*. Commercial images are now ubiquitous—on the Internet, television, cable, and radio; in magazines, movie theaters, stores, schools, and ballparks; on billboards, buses, T-shirts, coffee mugs, even produce at the local grocery. Brand names and logos are carefully insinuated into the storylines of TV and movie scripts and popular songs. They're even plugged on the evening news. As we've already suggested, there's no way for us to remove ourselves from the influences of culture, to step outside of culture so to speak, and now more than ever that includes media culture as well.

In spite of its insidious commercialism, it isn't clear that we'd want to abandon media culture and new forms of digital communication anyway, even if we could. Media afford us a great deal of pleasure, fantasy, and spectacle, in addition to being a primary source of vital information and exchange. A key issue then is not to renounce or dismiss media culture but to become more savvy readers and producers of media as we work to make them a more genuinely shared and democratic entity.

Working Questions

1. We often hear that the news media have a "liberal bias," that the people producing the news are far more liberal than the public at large, and hence the media favor a left-wing viewpoint. Many people have contested this notion, but let's assume for the moment that it's absolutely true. Why, then, do the people who run the entertainment and news empires—who we can safely assume are as conservative as the day is long—allow this to happen? What's in it for a hyper-conservative CEO to hire a left-wing anchor, and an army of unreconstructed hippie writers, for the company's news program? Is it that these CEOs have no control over the organizations they're running? That they're not paying attention? Is this finally the paradox that puts to rest the myth of the liberal media? Why would the media be any more liberal than the people who own and run them?

2. In what ways have the rise of citizen journalism and blogging been a response to the existing highly concentrated and corporate-owned media landscape? In what ways has it influenced said landscape, for better and worse? Where do *you* go for news and information? Why?

3. How would you assess the consequences of new forms of digital media participation for democracy? Does it strengthen democratic subjectivities and social relations or weaken them or a little bit of both? What kinds of information do citizens need access to? What new kinds of literacy should mediate it? How much of a concern is the corporate influence on social networking and other sites rich in user-generated content in terms of the tensions that inevitably swirl around questions of access, control, creativity, ownership, and profit?

4. In the film industry, which now has global reach, the bottom line tends to dictate the production of violent, high-octane action films, which are cheaper to produce than comedies, although comedies are actually more popular. Humor is culturally specific and often difficult to translate for audiences in such diverse places as Hong Kong, Copenhagen, Buenos Aires, and San Francisco, thereby limiting from the start its global reach. In contrast, a twenty-minute car chase—heavy on crashes, explosions, and death-defying stunts and very light on dialogue—requires very little if any translation. In addition to influencing the kinds of films that get made, market imperatives also shape the content of film, as producers discovered that film delivers as a vehicle for selling all sorts of products. Not

only are films peppered with various product placements, but they also generate an incredible amount of spinoff merchandise in the form of action figures, T-shirts, coffee mugs, posters, games, CDs, and new rides at theme parks.

So, do the media simply reflect popular tastes, "giving the people what they want," or are massive box office sales for, say, tons of violence and hyper-commercialization a result, more or less, of what is made available to global audiences rather than what those audiences actually want?

For Further Reading

Multiculture

Anzaldua, Gloria. *Borderlands/La Frontera.* 2d ed. New York: Consortium, 1999.

Bennett, David. *Multicultural States: Rethinking Difference and Identity.* New York: Routledge, 1998.

Bloom, Allan. *The Closing of the American Mind.* New York: Simon & Schuster, 1987.

Castells, Manuel. *The Power of Identity.* Cambridge: Blackwell, 1997.

Giroux, Henry. *Border Crossings.* New York: Routledge, 1992.

Goldberg, David Theo. *Multiculturalism: A Critical Reader.* Oxford: Blackwell, 1994.

Gomez-Pena, Guillermo. *The New World Border: Prophecies, Poems, and Loqueras for the End of the Century.* San Francisco: City Lights Books, 1996.

Hall, Stuart, and Paul du Gay. *Questions of Cultural Identity.* London: Sage, 1996.

Lorde, Audre. *Sister Outsider: Essays and Speeches.* Trumansburg, NY: Crossing Press, 1984.

Parekh, Bhikhu. *Rethinking Multiculturalism: Cultural Diversity and Political Theory.* Cambridge, MA: Harvard University Press, 2000.

Rajchman, John, ed. *The Identity in Question.* New York: Routledge, 1995.

Reed, Ishmael, ed. *MultiAmerica: Essays on Cultural Wars and Cultural Peace.* New York: Viking, 1997.

Rutherford, Jonathan, ed. *Identity: Community, Culture and Difference.* London: Lawrence Wishart, 1990.

Taylor, Charles. *Multiculturalism: Examining the Politics of Recognition.* Princeton, NJ: Princeton University Press, 1994.

West, Cornel. *Beyond Eurocentrism and Multiculturalism.* Monroe, ME: Common Courage, 1993.

Popular Culture

Adorno, Theodor, and Max Horkheimer. "The Culture Industry." In *Dialectic of the Enlightenment,* translated by John Cumming, 120–67. New York: Herder and Herder, 1972 (1944).

Benjamin, Walter. "The Work of Art in an Age of Mechanical Reproduction." In *Illuminations: Essays and Reflections,* edited by Hannah Arendt, 217–52. New York: Schocken Books, 1968.

Bourdieu, Pierre. *Distinction: A Social Critique of the Judgement of Taste.* Cambridge, MA: Harvard University Press, 1986.

Gans, Herbert J. *Popular Culture and High Culture: An Analysis and Evaluation of Taste.* New York: Basic, 1974.

Giroux, Henry A. *Breaking into the Movies.* Malden, MA: Blackwell, 2002.

———. *Disturbing Pleasures: Learning Popular Culture.* New York: Routledge, 1994.

Grossberg, Lawrence. *Dancing in Spite of Myself: Essays on Popular Culture.* Durham, NC: Duke University Press, 1997.

Grossberg, Lawrence, Cary Nelson, and Paula Treichler. *Cultural Studies.* New York: Routledge, 1994.

Hebdige, Dick. *Subculture: The Politics of Style.* London: Routledge, 1988 (1979).

Huyssen, Andreas. *After the Great Divide: Modernism, Mass Culture and Postmodernism.* Basingstoke, NH: Macmillan, 1988.

McRobbie, Angela. *Postmodernism and Popular Culture.* London: Routledge, 1994.

Storey, John, ed. *Cultural Theory and Popular Culture: A Reader.* New York: Harvester, 1994.

Media Culture and Media Culture 2.0

Bourdieu, Pierre. *On Television*. New York: New Press, 1998.

Bunt, Gary R. *Islam in the Digital Age: E-Jihad, Online Fatwas, and Cyber Islamic Environments*. London: Pluto Press, 2003.

Burwell, Catherine. "Rewriting the Script: Toward a Politics of Young People's Digital Media Participation." *The Review of Education, Pedagogy, and Cultural Studies* 32 (2010): 382–402.

Calhoun, Craig. "Information Technology and the International Public Sphere." In *Shaping the Network Society: The New Role of Society in Cyberspace*, edited by D. Schuler and P. Day, 229–52. Cambridge: MIT Press, 2004.

Castells, Manuel. *The Rise of the Network Society*. Vol. 1. Cambridge: Blackwell, 1996.

Chomsky, Noam, and Ed Herman. *Manufacturing Consent: The Political Economy of Mass Media*. New York: Pantheon, 2002 (1988).

Debord, Guy. *The Society of the Spectacle*. New York: Zone, 1995 (1983).

Giroux, Henry A. *Beyond the Spectacle of Terrorism: Global Uncertainty and the Challenge of the New Media*. Boulder, CO: Paradigm, 2006.

———. *Channel Surfing: Racism, the Media and the Destruction of Today's Youth*. New York: St. Martin's Press, 1998.

———. "The Crisis of Public Values in the Age of the New Media." *Critical Studies in Media Communication* 28, no. 1 (2011): 8–29.

Grossman, Lev. "*Time*'s Person of the Year: You." *Time*, December 13, 2006. Available at http://www.time.com/time/magazine/article/0,9171,1569514,00.html. Accessed February 10, 2011.

Habermas, Jurgen. *The Structural Transformation of the Public Sphere: An Inquiry into a Category of Bourgeois Society*. Cambridge, MA: MIT Press, 1991 (1989).

Hedges, Chris. *Empire of Illusion*. Toronto: Knopf Canada, 2009.

Helft, Miguel. "Facebook Makes Headway around the World." *New York Times*, July 7, 2010: B1. Available at http://www.nytimes.com/2010/07/08/technology/companies/08facebook.html. Accessed July 7, 2010.

Illouz, Eva. *Cold Intimacies: The Making of Emotional Capitalism*. Cambridge: Polity, 2007.

Kellner, Douglas. *Media Culture: Cultural Studies, Identity and Politics between the Modern and the Postmodern.* New York: Routledge, 1998.

McChesney, Robert. "Global Media, Neoliberalism, and Imperialism." *Monthly Review* 52, no. 10 (March 2001): 1–19.

———. *Rich Media, Poor Democracy: Communication Politics in Dubious Times.* Urbana: University of Illinois Press, 1999.

McLuhan, Marshal. *The Global Village.* Oxford: Oxford University Press, 1992.

Morozov, Evgeny. *The Net Delusion: The Dark Side of Internet Freedom.* New York: Public Affairs, 2011.

Rich, Frank. "Wallflowers at the Revolution." *New York Times*, February 6, 2011: WK8. Available at http://www.nytimes.com/2011/02/06/opinion/06rich.html. Accessed March 15, 2011.

Schiller, Herbert. *Culture, Inc.: The Corporate Takeover of Public Expression.* Oxford: Oxford University Press, 1990.

Silverstone, Richard. *Why Study the Media?* London; Thousand Oaks, CA: Sage, 1999.

Turkle, Sherry. *Alone Together: Why We Expect More from Technology and Less from Each Other.* New York: Basic, 2011.

Williams, Raymond. *Communications.* 3d ed. Harmondsworth, UK: Penguin, 1976.

———. *Raymond Williams on Television: Selected Writings,* edited by Alan O'Conner. London: Routledge, 1989.

6

Ideology

deology is a tough thing to get at, and not *just* because the concept itself is difficult to understand. In its most basic semantic meaning, "ideology" is the "study of ideas" in the same way that "psychology" can be defined as the "study of the *psyche*" or "biology" suggests the study of "*bios*," life. That being the case, however, we note that ideology is born out of a contradiction: It is the *material* study of *immaterial* things, ideas. The word's earliest uses (by, for example, Napoleon) were derogatory or pejorative; to be an "ideologist" was to be someone with his or her head in the clouds, trying to delude or persuade people with mere *ideas* rather than hard *realities*.

It is in this sense that ideology, defined as "false consciousness" (an inability to see real conditions because they are masked by false ideas), is taken up in Marxist discourse of the nineteenth century. This constitutes the first definition of ideology: something that's *false* or *misleading* because it's *mystifying*. Ideology in this sense is a discourse that always misrepresents concrete conditions and specific causes, trading concrete realities for murky, vague, metaphysical explanations.

Such understandings of ideology-as-falsity tend, of course, also to contain a notion of how things *ought* to be: If you say that people are now in the grip of false consciousness (deluded by ideologies), you necessarily commit yourself to a state in which people aren't deluded, in which the real truth behind the false ideology could be known. Ideology in this first sense is *prescriptive*, offering a kind of new course that might somehow be free from the mystifications of false ideas.

As an example, we might note that politicians tend to be purveyors of ideology par excellence, always looking for some murky generalization to cover over a social or political problem. For example, we're used to hearing that teen crime is caused by neglectful parenting, bad genes, insufficiently disciplined teachers, society's turn away from religion, rap music, movies and television, etc. An ideology critique would suggest that these are all mystifying explanations for a social phenomenon that seems to have more easily identifiable causes. Simply put, a shortage of legitimate opportunities for many poor young people leads them to choose crime. As any number of economists have pointed out, crime can look like a perfectly rational career choice—big money, quick promotion, excitement—especially when your alternatives are crippling poverty, underfunded and crumbling schools, and a lifetime of jobs where the most exciting component is enticing the customer to "super size" his or her order of french fries.

Why should that simple truth about crime be so difficult to understand, the prescriptive critic of ideology might ask? Could it be because the murky generalizations shift the blame onto victims, thereby obscuring the real causes of social problems and failing to address the real work that would have to be done to deal with such problems? An ideology critique would point out the material truth under the mystical explanation: Teen crime is finally about *money—*

about who's got it and who wants it—and such crime cannot be accounted for by merely "ideological" explanations like bad parenting or faulty genes or violent films. Such interpretations of teen crime are "ideological" to the extent that they are not only misleading but finally false. In its most basic sense, then, ideology critique is an attempt to show the rational kernel—the concrete explanation—that's hidden inside the ideological or mystical shell.

◈ Working Question

There's much discourse in the press these days about "binge drinking" as an epidemic on college campuses. When asked for explanations, the experts round up the usual suspects: poor parenting, kids without moral standards, lax administrators and faculty, TV commercials that glamorize beer, etc.

Is there a way in which these explanations strike you as "ideological" in the sense outlined above? Are these explanations, in other words, misleading at best and simply false at worst? Conversely, and as an exercise in ideology critique, are there more concrete explanations for heavy drinking on college campuses? Simple boredom, perhaps?

There is, however, another sense of ideology, and this one is perhaps even more slippery than the one noted above. If ideology is a kind of study of ideas, the unmasking of a misleading metaphysical abstraction behind the concrete realities, it necessarily remains a part of any culture. In fact, ideology seems inseparable in this way from the definition of *knowledge* itself, which is necessarily both abstract and concrete. For a culture to produce ideas (or new ideas), for example, there has to be some consensus on what the present material conditions *mean*, a kind of common agreement about the way things are. If you're going to do scientific research, you'd better know a thing or two about scientific method in the community of scientists you wish to address. Other scientists can disagree with your results (calling your hypotheses ideological or false), but for any scientists to see your work as at all relevant, the work has to have been produced within a recognizable framework of accepted ideas.

For there to be any knowledge at all, there has to be ideology in this sense; there has to be some preexisting agreement concerning what will *count* as knowledge, or what criteria will be used to judge new or developing knowledges. In this second sense, ideology is a *descriptive* (rather than prescriptive) word, attempting to show the way things are, a whole way of life in a social group.

But at the same time, these larger social ideological criteria—a descriptive understanding of what it means to "do" science in a particular context, for example—are also the *stakes* of ideas produced within a culture. Science, philosophy, politics, and religion are all involved with trying to articulate what specific material conditions mean in a more abstract or general way; they are involved in the production of knowledge. Science produces knowledge about the physical world, philosophy about the metaphysical world, and politics about the social world. But the very meanings of such inquiries or knowledges—which in turn make further additions possible or understandable—are sometimes changed in the course of performing the research that is supposedly based on them.

This happens all the time in science: Someone sets out to do research in a given field, and her research changes our whole understanding of the field. The research that discovered DNA, for example, both *used* the preexisting methodologies of the life sciences and inexorably *challenged* these understandings as well. The discovery of DNA certainly took place within a tradition of research in the life sciences (natural law, evolution, cell biology, etc.); but it also changed the meaning and methods of that tradition through its discoveries.

So ideology, as a network or consensus of interconnected ideas, is in some sense *both* the *source* of cultural discourses *and* their *out-*

come. For example, you'd need to know how photosynthesis works to research green plants, but if your work is successful, it may change the way we understand what photosynthesis *means.* Dominant theories about the way things work—knowledges and ideologies—obviously change over time.

If this second sense of the word is even more difficult, this is because such a notion of ideology names a kind of slippery consensus or "common sense" that a culture, people, or group shares among its members. Plant biologists, for example, know how photosynthesis works; they share an accepted set of ideas, a common sense or knowledge concerning photosynthesis. By definition, however, this sharing happens without conscious acknowledgment of ideology's or common sense's content: No vote was taken among plant biologists to choose or affirm their common understanding of photosynthesis.

In fact, this is where the two senses of ideology come together: Ideology is that group of intertwining beliefs that makes possible certain kinds of cultural consensus or knowledge, but precisely because it is everywhere and nowhere, ideology tends to disappear—so to speak—"into" the things that it makes possible. Paradoxically, ideology is the metaphysical "airy abstraction" that is simultaneously a kind of concrete "common sense." As we saw in Kafka's parable about community, for example, there certainly is a commonsense version of what it means to be part of a group or clique, but often one is unsure exactly *why* one belongs or wants to belong to that group. When you get right down to it, common sense—or the seeming ability for lots of people to share a notion of common sense—is actually very complicated.

Ideology, understood as a kind of cultural common sense, doesn't need to be articulated, discussed, or justified. Anything that's *ideological* in this sense seems like it just *is*—it's the way things are, case closed. "Progress," "freedom," and "citizenship" are "ideological" notions—strong beliefs to be sure, but ones that are, strangely enough, held more or less unconsciously. For example, in an argument you seldom have to defend "freedom" or "progress" or your participation in a representative democracy. It may be immensely unclear what these things *mean* in any specific *context*, but the terms are thrown around all the time as if they were unproblematically "good" notions. Ideology is the making natural of cultural phenomena.

Recently there have been lots of ads on TV suggesting that drug traffickers support terrorism against the United States, and that if you buy or sell drugs you're a terrorist, too. Told in the cadences adults use to narrate fairy tales to young children, the argument avails itself of the voice of common sense, relating a simple, unassailable morality tale. And common sense is itself seen as an unproblematically good thing. Yet this is the voice of ideology, the voice of supposedly flawless "reason," frustratingly difficult to spot because it sounds so sensible and just.

At another level, however, the ideologist is *extremely* easy to spot: He's the one most vehemently denying that he's employing "ideology," the one who insists that he's simply speaking the voice of informed and impartial "reason," telling you the truth rather than some misty soup of delusionary "ideas." Politicians, of course, are best at this, accusing their rivals of engaging in "politics" (meaning mere wars of words or ideas) at the expense of the real work of governing. Criticizing a policy for "political" reasons tends to mean criticizing it not for its merits but for how well it conforms to a pet ideological agenda. For example, critics of the antidrug/antiterrorism campaign aired an ad of their own (although it was given very limited play). Mimicking the childlike simplicity of the antidrug message, this campaign argued that drivers of SUVs support terrorism, underscoring the role of oil (and the U.S. government's indifference to environmental protections) in fomenting conflict in the Middle East.

This, however, brings out the paradoxical nature of ideology yet again: Any appeal to "common sense" or "real work" is itself thoroughly ideological. It is completely mystifying insofar as common sense, again *by definition*, can't be examined or challenged or rearranged. You have to agree with ideology, or there's something wrong with you. You can't question common sense or the rightness of something like "reason" or "knowledge"; it just *is*. As cultural critic Stuart Hall writes,

> It is precisely its "spontaneous" quality, its transparency, its "naturalness," its refusal to be made to examine the premises on which it is founded, its resistance to change and to correction, its effect of instant recognition, and the closed circle in which it moves which makes common sense, at one and the same time, "spontaneous," ideological and *unconscious*. You cannot learn, through common sense, how *things are*: you can only discover *where they fit* into the existing scheme of things. In this way, its very taken-for-grantedness is what establishes it as a medium in which its own premises and presuppositions are being rendered *invisible* by its apparent transparency. ("Culture, Media and the 'Ideological Effect,'" 325–26)

As an example of Hall's "spontaneous" ideology, we note that the American belief in the "free" and unencumbered "self" is deeply ideological in both senses of the word. It is first of all a *mystification* that ignores the cultural constraints of subjectivity; it is simply not true that people are free to do whatever they want. But at the same time this free "self" is also the baseline *common sense* understanding of what it means to be a person for most Americans. Most people experience themselves as "naturally" or "spontaneously" free, but of course that experience is at some level patently false, or at least misleading.

Ideology, in the end, is what you think *before* you think or act—what thinking and action silently take for granted. As such, ideology is another way that our attention is diverted from the *how* of meaning to the *what*; in other words, ideology is one of the devices by which cultural meanings—which are by definition "arbitrary," not necessary in any mystical or transcendental way—are seen as "natural," "inevitable," and "good." Ideology is that which allows us to say that our values are "better," without any reflection on who "we" might be, and without the slightest shred of evidence to back up the claim about "our" superiority. Ideology is the thing that entices you to forget that meaning always happens in a context. Ideology leads you to accept each day as a natural fact: Things are the way they are; case closed.

Working Questions

1. One thing that's sure about college: It's about learning to get along with people. Is there anything that your roommates or new friends do that just drives you nuts, but that they think is perfectly "natural"—and they can't understand why it bothers you? Are these "ideologies" differing versions of common sense? And if you identify them as such, how is this helpful to you in getting along with others?

2. On the topic of "mystical explanations," Friedrich Nietzsche wrote, "Mystical explanations are considered deep. The truth is that they are not even superficial." First of all, what might this mean? Is Nietzsche asking us to be "superficial"? Why would we want that? Also, what might this quotation have to say about "ideology" as a "mystical explanation"? Is ideology critique then a way to recover the "superficial"?

Given this kind of definition, it should become clear that there's a particularly odd problem when discussing ideology in terms of social and cultural theory: Both high and popular culture art forms are, it seems, purveyors of ideology *par excellence*. If ideology can be described as the tendency to misrecognize the literal (exchanging it for the metaphorical), then it seems to be very much in tune with literary and cultural production on the whole. For example, in the movement from the material act of stealing bread, to that act's novelization in Victor Hugo's *Les Misérables*, to the ultimate spectacle-ization of that event in the Broadway megamusical *Les Miz*, we see the increasingly metaphorical and mystifying (ideological) rendering of a specific cultural act.

The more misty the explanation, one might say, the more ideological it is; the more an explanation appeals to an unexamined "common sense" that can't be interrogated, the more it is dependent on "ideology." Of course, at the same time we could note some important discriminations in our example: Hugo's novel seems an attempt to render a *critical* account of the ideologies surrounding crime and punishment, whereas Alain Boublil and Claude-Michel Schonberg's musical seems to be a pandering piece that actually *promotes* ideological mystification: happy poor people crooning on cue. Of course, our reading of this example is *itself* ideological; it appeals to a number of unarticulated premises—to various common senses concerning critique, reading, the flatulence of Broadway musicals, etc.—that are by no means incontestable.

In fact, all cultural acts take place in some relation to ideology: critical, complicit, a little of both. There is no simple escape from ideology, just as there is no premise-free (that is to say no merely "objective") knowledge: All meaning is contextual; all contexts are social; and all societies have ideologies, recognitions of common sense. The task of literary and cultural theory, then, is *not* to *escape* ideology but to account for its workings in the seemingly disinterested and neutral presentations of culture, as well as in our interpretations of those cultural artifacts. There is no escape from ideology, but there is a kind of constant vigilance that ideology *critique* calls for: What unarticulated premises stand behind our "knowledge"? This is the first and last question of ideology critique, and it is necessarily an *ongoing* question.

And this in some sense explains the path we've been traveling throughout this book. We haven't been interested in offering ideological answers to difficult questions, but in fact have tried to confront the difficulties and challenges that abound in notions that already seem familiar to us: authorship, reading, media, popular culture. The task of ideology critique is to make the familiar seem a bit more strange and thereby to make us consistently examine the things that we all too often take for granted. This, as we intimated in chapter 1, might be called the productive *work* of theory.

Figure 6.1 *This Modern World* by Tom Tomorrow

Figure 6.2 *This Modern World* by Tom Tomorrow

❖ Working Questions

1. French theorist Louis Althusser wrote that ideology is made concrete in *structures,* in the ways that space is arranged in modern societies.

What "ideologies" (or "natural" presuppositions) do you see around you in classrooms and in the architecture of the campus (or the dorm)? What "commonsense" decisions have been made to arrange the physical space of this classroom, this campus, this building, the time allotted for this class, and the ways that it proceeds?

To use Hall's terminology, these "commonsense" decisions are nearly "invisible" in the architectural spaces we inhabit, so what, if anything, do we learn by teasing out the ideological presuppositions that ground our everyday lives? How does the "common sense" of space naturalize certain assumptions about the ways the world should work?

2. Watch the film *Dirty Harry.* Certainly Dirty Harry (played by Clint Eastwood) is one of the icons of recent film history, starring in a number of films after this one. What are the "ideologies" at work in this film? In other words, what "commonsense" premises do you have to accept to enter the film's portrait of crime and punishment?

Think about the following "superficial" or "commonsense" questions: Why is Dirty Harry such a popular character? Why is the film (made in 1970) set in San Francisco, rather than, say, Milwaukee or Denver? Does San Francisco in 1970 signify anything in particular that's important to the film?

What does the film (however silently) ask us to think about crime and society? What causes crime, in the world of the film? What combats it effectively? What gets in the way? What drives the criminal "Scorpio"? Does he fit any recognizable profile? He seems, for example, to be a kind of free-love hippy but also a greedy capitalist (extorting money from the city), an expert with a rifle, a racist, and a child molester. What drives the cops in the film? Is Harry's motivation the same as the mayor's? What "common sense" does the film create about crime? Is that common sense accurate?

3. How do popular comic strips like *This Modern World* (figures 6.1 and 6.2) function as a form of ideology critique? How do they disrupt the consensus of common sense? What kinds of contradictions do they expose? Whose interests?

For Further Reading

Eagleton, Terry. *Ideology: An Introduction.* London: Verso, 1991.

Gouldner, Alvin. *The Dialectic of Ideology and Technology: The Origins, Grammar, and Future of Ideology.* New York: Oxford University Press, 1982 (1976).

Gramsci, Antonio. *The Prison Notebooks,* edited by Joseph A. Buttigieg, translated by Joseph A. Buttigieg and Antonio Callari. New York: Columbia University Press, 1992.

Hall, Stuart. "Culture, Media and the 'Ideological Effect.'" In *Mass Communication and Society,* edited by J. Curran et al. Beverly Hills, CA: Sage, 1979.

Hall, Stuart, and James Donald, eds. *Politics and Ideology.* Milton Keynes, UK: Open University Press, 1986.

Jameson, Fredric. *The Political Unconscious: Narrative As a Socially Symbolic Act.* Ithaca, NY: Cornell University Press, 1981.

Mannheim, Karl. *Ideology and Utopia: An Introduction to the Sociology of Knowledge,* translated by Louis Wirth and Edward Shils. San Diego: Harcourt Brace Jovanovich, 1985 (1936).

Marx, Karl, and Friedrich Engels. *The German Ideology.* London: Lawrence and Wishart, 1965 (1846).

Thompson, John. *Ideology and Modern Culture.* Stanford, CA: Stanford University Press, 1990.

———. *Studies in the Theory of Ideology.* Berkeley: University of California Press, 1984.

Williams, Raymond. *Marxism and Literature.* Oxford: Oxford University Press, 1977.

Zizek, Slavoj. *The Sublime Object of Ideology.* London: Verso, 1989.

tion of the wheel is no more inherently meaningful than the invention of WiFi; it is only in a particular context—the history of mobility or the history of fishing—that such events *become* meaningful (or not). In short, historical meaning, like literary meaning, is actively *produced* rather than dispassionately uncovered or rendered visible.

Having disabused history of any neutral or objective claims it might make, it might be tempting at this point to reject the category of history altogether, not as "fiction" but as simply propaganda, by virtue of its ideological nature. But that move would be hasty indeed. As discussed in the last chapter, dismissing history as merely ideological is to partake in a theory of ideology that separates "false consciousness" from "true consciousness," the presupposition being that out there somewhere is a pristine vision of "the past" that history is insufficient to represent in objective terms. Rather, what we're arguing, after Benjamin, is that our only access to "the past" is through mediation—whether in images, symbols, artworks, architecture, or written or spoken language. Our only way to make sense of the past, to learn from the past, is through an engagement with multiple, often conflicting, historical narratives.

History, as an inherently meaningful development of events ("manifest destiny"), is indeed bunk. But this opens history to the multiplicity that we find in the present; the *meaning* of these events for future history remains to be decided—or is never *finally* decided—because history is constantly under construction. To say that history is open to interpretation is not, however, to say that historical events mean anything at all; it is rather to say that history itself needs to be historicized—or that historical events need to be subjected to the same scrutiny as other ideological truth claims. Nor does it take away our ability to assert that, for example, the Holocaust happened and was a horrible, reprehensible episode in Western history. Of course genocide is terrible. But this characterization hardly tells us everything we need to know about what the Holocaust *means* or will mean in history.

As a sort of thought experiment, think of genocide or a deadly disease like AIDS or cancer; these too are terrible things, and must be named as such. But if what you want to do is *stop* the effects of AIDS, cancer, or genocide (i.e., if you want to learn from events so that deaths *don't* happen in the same way again), denunciation is certainly a place to start—it must be remembered that people have died cruelly and unjustly, and this is something that we must fight against and hold in contempt. But more important than the commemoration is the *action* that one might undertake to prevent its happening again. The historical event of the Holocaust is irreducible, and one must bear witness to it, always remember it. But the event itself—or our condemnation of it—doesn't tell us how to keep it from happening again. In other words, the event itself doesn't tell us what it means or how it functions in an ongoing narrative of history. Events in history, like words in a narrative, don't *contain* meaning.

We can of course still make judgments about these things; even if we accept a "narrative" conception of history, we can still confidently say that murder, poverty, or the bombing of innocent civilians are very bad things indeed. But to say that something is bad is not at all to say how it came about, how it might best be understood, and ultimately how one might prevent it from happening again. Historical meaning is not inherent in the events that make up history, just as narrative meaning is not inherent in the words that make up a novel. Meaning is made in responses to the event, and there's a considerable distance between *interpreting* events and responding to them. History is not simply about *interpreting* various dead artifacts, looking at past events as safely in the past. It's about inventing strategies for the present.

Working Question

The following sections are from one of the earliest histories written in (Old) English, *The Anglo-Saxon Chronicle*:

7

History

istory, like many of the critical terms we've encountered thus far, seems like a fairly self-evident concept. History is a record of things that have happened, an archive of the past's most important and pivotal events. Accordingly, we tend to think of history as a *reconstruction* of actual events as they unfolded in time, as distinct from a poet's or novelist's *construction* of a historical past, which may refer to real events and lives but is free to ignore or transgress available historiographic evidence in its pursuit of "higher truths." Apparently purged of any subjective elements, history appears as factual, objective, and neutral as any discipline in the sciences. In fact, historians often compare themselves to archeologists or anthropologists, excavating or uncovering various artifacts—documents, memorials, traditions, cultural practices, institutions—that contain vital information about the past.

In the terminology we've been using, then, history would seem to give us a stable, neutral "context" for interpretation. Perhaps the dictum of theorist Fredric Jameson, "Always historicize!," might solve all our problems when confronted by the difficulty or ambiguity of meaning. If no meaning can be determined outside of context, then history would seem to be that "meta-context" to which we could always refer when we hit a slippery patch on the superhighway of meaning. "History" could be that "context" that would finally determine meaning.

Unfortunately, it's not quite that easy. History is indeed a context in which interpretation takes place, but history itself must always *be interpreted*. The critical theorist Walter Benjamin once noted that "the past can be seized only as an image which flashes up at the instant when it can be recognized and is never seen again" ("Theses on the Philosophy of History," 255). The past, in other words, is not accessible to us as stories with their meanings already intact but as fleeting "images" to be deciphered. Benjamin reminds us that meaning doesn't simply emanate from random events; rather, it is the historian who not only assigns order and coherence to events but also renders them significant, or not. Because the meaning of these images from the past is not transparent or self-evident, reading history, then, requires something extra-historical: a politics or an ethics. But Benjamin's insight suggests something else at least as important: We have no access to the past that is *unmediated*. Not necessarily in the sense that we addressed in chapter 5, that various mass media such as television and film offer us specific images of the past, which is certainly true. Rather, we refer to mediation in the broader sense. The past is available to us only through representations—words, images, symbols—whether these derive from film, advertising, legal records, oral history, or personal recollections. We often assume that we can determine the "truth" of particular representations of the past by measuring them against "reality," but Benjamin is suggesting that we have no access to a past "reality" that is not already a representation. And try as we might to find one, there is no singular "true" or objective description of any historical context or any aspect of it. Rather, what we invariably discover upon closer investigation are many different representations of past events and people. These may be "true" at the level of facts, but they offer at times radically different interpretations of the historiographic evidence they assemble to tell particular stories. Of course, historians aren't free to make up events and personalities as they go along, but they do make choices about the different meanings they assign to factual data. Thus it is possible to read historical accounts of the U.S. bombing of Hiroshima and Nagasaki in World War II that describe the event as a necessary and strategic retaliatory strike in a cosmic battle between good and evil, or as a massacre of hundreds of thousands of innocent lives that was as senseless as it was horrific. Is the (real) use of atomic weaponry on Japan more appropriately narrated as triumph or tragedy? Such a decision not only will take into account past facts but also will reflect contemporary beliefs about the use of vastly more devastating nuclear warheads.

All of which is to say that histories are *narrated* from a point of view; "important" events are *chosen* according to certain criteria; and those events are *explained* in terms of certain paradigms that promote particular visions of the past, present, and future. Because factual accounts of the past involve this process of selection and emphasis, they turn out to be interpretations, or *constructions*, of history rather than objective *reconstructions* of past realities.

In fact, history might be compared more fruitfully with the study of literature, at least in one very important respect. Divergent in their *content*, both literature and history share a narrative *form*. If past events are available only as images, not as stories, then they must be constructed as such. We might even say, for example, that history itself is made comprehensible to us through the use of a widely recognizable narrative genre, the *Bildungsroman*, in which history unfolds as a kind of a coming-of-age story that has a people or a nation as its central character. Writing a history is very much akin to writing a story with a plot—focusing on the development of an idea, the causes and effects that have led up to the present. Events within such a story must be ranked according to their significance and evaluated in terms of the larger developing plot. As historiographer Hayden White writes, historical "events must be not only registered within the chronological framework of their original occurrence but narrated as well, that is to say, revealed as possessing a structure, an order of meaning, that they do not possess as a mere sequence" (*The Content of the Form*, 5). The simple flow of events, in other words, is not history, just as random jottings of words is not necessarily a poem, or a mass of people is not necessarily a nation. It's the overarching plot, the "master narrative," the bigger *context*, that gives meaning to the otherwise random events of history or the otherwise random words that can make up a poem, or the ways in which people are gathered together into nations.

If history is indeed written in narrative form, it follows that it necessarily contains many of the other qualities of a narrative as well. It is written from a point of view, out of a certain cultural position, and its author, like the author of a literary narrative, does not simply control its meanings. History itself not only requires interpretation, but it also opens up many other interpretations. Rather than being a disinterested archeological uncovering of the past, historical narrative is inescapably political in that it contains or reflects certain *deeply ideological* presuppositions, a point to which we will return.

It bears repeating, however, that to say that history shares many qualities with literature is not to suggest that it is simply "fiction"—mythical or fanciful—but to underscore that historical facts, like literary meanings, are not *inherently* meaningful. Rather, they are always beholden to something "other" for their meaning; historical facts themselves require a context (a larger narrative in which they can be rendered recognizable, useful, and/or meaningful), and that context is consistently *made* rather than *found*. By itself, the inven-

733   In this year AEthelbald occupied Somerton, and there
       was an eclipse of the sun.
734   In this year the moon looked as if it were suffused with
       blood, and Tatwine and Bede died.
735
736   In this year archbishop Nothhelm received the *pallium*
       from the bishop of the Romans.

Is this "history"? Why or why not? It's certainly not history as
we understand it, but what *exactly* is different about it? For example, did nothing happen in 735, which is blank in the *Chronicle*?
Why is 734's "bloody moon" important, in fact seemingly more
important than the death of the venerable Saint Bede? What needs
to be added or subtracted to make it more in line with our notion
of history? And what, if anything, does that tell us about our notion
of history and the Anglo-Saxon's notion of it?

Although it won't offer us an objective, "true" context or transcendent meaning, history at its best does teach us about larger patterns of events—the *why* in addition to the *what*—so that we may
avoid certain pitfalls of our predecessors. Recall the famous warning, those who do not learn from history are doomed to repeat it.
But this truism begs a rather complicated question: How do we
move from learning *about* history to learning *from* history? The radical historian Howard Zinn has argued that history has meaning in
a double sense. One is concerned with the *narration and interpretation* of actual events in the past that have shaped, or determined,
our present circumstances, and the other is concerned with the *present action* that specific understandings of the past might give rise
to. The former involves textual analyses of isolated words on a page,
fueling various debates over what a writer like de Toqueville or
Michelet or Hegel "really meant" to communicate about a specific
historical event or era and its relative significance. The latter is a bit

more tricky, as it not only engages specific statements about the past (what happened?) but also asks what effects such statements have on the real world (what are the consequences of different interpretations of, for example, FDR's New Deal, the Vietnam War, or the Reagan administration, for contemporary society?). Further, we might add, a commitment to avoid "repeating the past" requires both thinking about how to use the past to alter present conditions (which in turn means being able to conceive of an alternative to the present, without the burden of seeing certain changes as inevitable) and thinking about the future society we'd like to live in. Historians, then, not only construct a coherent past, they also *construct a particular understanding of the present* for which the past has significance. Any appeal to history—far from being an objective "meta-context" in pinning down decisive meanings—involves a staggering amount of textual interpretation as well as ethical judgments about the past, the present, and the future. Thus, to paraphrase Zinn, there is no question of a "disinterested" or neutral history, only a question about what kinds of interests history can serve in a divided world.

Needless to say, when one looks to history to engage certain present questions, many elements of the past are excluded. But a history that lacks focus (in an effort to "tell everything") also leaves things out, while producing a much more abstract understanding of the past. A history of the United States, for example, or even a history of your hometown, isn't going to include everything that ever happened within its boundaries, just as a map of either site isn't going to include every landmark. Historians, like cartographers, are necessarily selective; they focus on significant events and places. And it's a good thing, too—who wants to wade through fifty (or one hundred? or two hundred?) volumes of everything that happened in Allentown, Pennsylvania, in 1986? Although we might marvel at the inclusivity of such a project, one might well wonder if the historian's real purpose is to assert the equal importance of every shred of detail, without discrimination. What would one learn from such a history, assuming one ever got through it? And a map of Allentown that included literally everything would pretty much have to be as big as Allentown, wouldn't it? While we might note that it's left nothing out, we'd simultaneously have to recognize that it won't help us get anywhere, either.

So while the issue of whether this or that history is selective or partial in its retelling of the past is moot, we can—and must—raise other kinds of questions, such as: What are those criteria that determine "significance"? Who determines them? If interpretations of past events are "true" at the factual level, are they all equal? If not, how do we evaluate them? What are the consequences of different selections of past facts? In other words, how do different historical narratives of the same event color our understanding of it, and how do these in turn shape our actions, or the collective action of communities, militaries, governments, and nations? Using the terminology we've been working on, what kind of subject do certain histories put into place? Do they reinforce passivity or motivate us to act in some way? Do they induce cynical acceptance of the way things are or inspire us to change things with visions of the way things might/should be?

High school textbook history, for example, is full of kings, queens, generals, and battles, but it seldom gives us any indication of what everyday life was like for an ordinary man or woman, or what a particular battle might have looked like to a soldier rather than to a general. In other words, rather than being an impartial archive of the past, much history seems to be an archive of certain, narrowly chosen "great" events of the past. History in this sense tends to focus on certain kinds of events and the meaning of those events to the people who were seemingly in charge of them. For example, in American history classes, students can learn quite a bit about the planning of the battle of Gettysburg and what that battle meant for President Lincoln, General Lee, and General Mead, but we don't hear very much about what it was like for an average soldier to *fight* at Gettysburg. What did they eat? How'd they go to the bathroom? Did they know it was a decisive battle? Did African-Americans participate in the battle? What role(s) did women play? Is Gettysburg only important after the fact, because Lincoln made an address there?

History teaches us about the outcomes of events like Gettysburg, but we hear little about the participants who performed the grunt work. Nor do we hear about other potential outcomes: alternative battle plans; dissenting voices; those citizens protesting the war in both the North and South; or the stories of the families who lost fathers, brothers, and sons at Gettysburg. Indeed, to an average family of farmers in rural Maine or Vermont, losing two sons in a battle is of far greater historical significance than who won the battle, or maybe even who won the war. But we tend not to study these events.

Well, you might think, of course we don't. History is concerned with the recording of significant, public events that affect larger collectivities—communities, regions, nations—as opposed to the private concerns of individuals and their families. The nineteenth-century German philosopher, G. W. F. Hegel, asserted that "Family memorials, patriarchal traditions, have an interest confined to the family and the clan . . . which is no subject of serious remembrance. . . . It is the state that first presents a subject matter that not only is *adapted* to the prose of history, but involves the production of such history in the progress of its own being" (in White, *The Content of the Form*, 26–27). Distinguishing between public and private acts of remembrance, Hegel locates history in the public sphere, associated with the activity of men (who are recognized as citizens) and excludes the domestic sphere, associated with the activity of women (who are not citizens). He also suggests that history is primarily political history, concerned with (and implicated in) the politics of "the state." It is both these crucial observations that inform much contemporary debate and criticism of traditional historiography in terms of its complicity with power.

To be sure, the dominant tendency is to see history from the top, as it is often based on the accounts of the most privileged, most educated members of society. And as we have already noted, it is not only the concerns of "the family and the clan" that are excluded from high school textbooks. Traditional versions of history—what Hegel would call "State histories"—are generally unconcerned with the activities of everyday life; nor, strangely enough, are they concerned with ordinary people, common practices, or popular culture. Accounting for and legitimating the rise of a particular nation-state, such history is written solely from the vantage point of the most powerful. It serves the interests of those in power because it reinforces the mythology that only they—as opposed to ordinary people—make history; it deadens people's awareness of the abuses of power, as evident in inequalities all around them; and it covers over the failure of those in power to alter unjust social conditions. It distorts our understanding of how people actually live by underemphasizing poverty and social suffering, while rendering certain populations such as women and people of color all but invisible.

History, as they say, is written by the victors, and chance events are often taken as some kind of historical mandate or necessary development. But this isn't always the case. Returning to our history/literature analogy, it has sometimes been said that history narrates the lives of the victorious and powerful from their perspective, whereas literature tends to side with the vanquished and powerless, recounting their version. Although a tempting formulation at first glance, this nonetheless does an injustice to those histories that have emerged particularly since the 1960s—postcolonial and feminist, for example—that have challenged the conventions of traditional historiography while bringing critical attention to questions of power, politics, and public consciousness. The postcolonial theorist, Edward Said, for example, has summed up postcolonial historiographical efforts in the phrase "history as critique." In doing so, Said underscores not only the efforts of Third World intellectuals to write their own histories from their perspectives—and the implicit challenges such scholarship poses to "imperialist" histories—but also possible transformation of the concept of history itself.

In sum, we argue that history is neither objective or neutral. Nor is it inevitably useful. In the words of Howard Zinn,

History ... can bind us or free us. It can destroy compassion by showing us the world through the eyes of the comfortable.... It can oppress any resolve to act by mountains of trivia, by diverting us into intellectual games, by pretentious "interpretations" which spur contemplation rather than action, by limiting our vision to an endless story of disaster and thus promoting cynical withdrawal, by befogging us with the encyclopedic eclecticism of the standard textbook. (*The Politics of History*, 54)

The challenge we confront as engaged readers of history is not one of cynicism or resignation because we know that historical reference can be abused or that we can never finally get at "the truth." Rather, our task is both critical—to complicate our understanding of history by virtue of its complicity, at least potentially, with power—and creative—to consciously construct meanings that inspire action in and for the present. History

can suggest to us alternatives that we would never otherwise consider. It can both warn and inspire. It can warn us that it is possible for a whole nation to be brainwashed, for "enlightened" and "educated" people to commit genocide, for a "democratic" country to maintain slavery, for oppressed to turn into oppressors, for "socialism" to be tyrannical and "liberalism" to be imperialist, for whole peoples to be led to war like sheep. It can also show us that apparently powerless underlings can defeat their rulers. (*The Politics of History*, 281)

Working Questions

1. When we were in grade school and high school, we remember Western Civ classes spending an inordinate amount of time talking about the differences between Athens and Sparta in ancient Greece. The Athenians were always represented as peaceful, knowledge-loving

democrats, while the Spartans were warlike conquerors with no time for higher pursuits (watching *Star Trek* [the original one] after school, the Klingons reminded us a lot of the Spartans).

In any case, why do you think our history teachers spent so much time on this topic? What's so important about Athens and Sparta? Does the mere information offered in the comparison have another historical purpose or use? Can you think of contemporary conflicts that have been similarly taken up as a "clash of civilizations"? What does this tell us about how traditional history is written? What histories, ironically enough, does history leave out?

2. As we've attempted to demonstrate in this chapter, history remains to be written and rewritten; the past is never simply over, done, decided once and for all. Such an understanding of history is what allowed music critic Griel Marcus to write in 1989, "listening now to the Sex Pistols' records, it doesn't seem like a mistake to confuse their moment with a major event in history" (*Lipstick Traces,* 5). One could of course agree or disagree with this statement, but what possibilities does such a historical claim—one might call it a history of the present—open up? In what ways does it make history more complex, conflicted, and open ended?

3. In Ishmael Reed's *Flight to Canada* (a kind of postmodern slave narrative, written in 1976), he writes about the American Civil War: "When will we realize that Poe was the principal historian of that strange war?" (10). This seems like an odd statement, on several counts: First of all, Poe died a decade before the Civil War started; and secondly, Poe wrote gothic horror tales, not histories. What sense can we make of Poe as a "historian" of the Civil War?

For Further Reading

The Anglo-Saxon Chronicle, translated by Dorothy Whitelock. New Brunswick, NJ: Rutgers University Press, 1961.

Benjamin, Walter. "Theses on the Philosophy of History." In *Illuminations: Essays and Reflections,* edited by Hannah Arendt, translated by Harry Zohn. New York: Schocken Books, 1968 (1955).

Dirlik, Arif. *Postmodernity's Histories: The Past as Legacy and Project.* Lanham, MD: Rowman & Littlefield, 2000.

Foucault, Michel. "Nietzsche, Genealogy, History." In *The Foucault Reader,* edited by Paul Rabinow. New York: Random House, 1984 (1972).

Friedlander, Saul. *A Conflict of Memories? The New German Debates about the "Final Solution."* New York: Leo Baeck Institute, 1987.

———. *History and Psychoanalysis: An Inquiry into the Possibilities and Limits of Psychohistory,* translated by Susan Suleiman. New York: Holmes and Meier, 1980.

Genovese, Elizabeth Fox, ed. *Reconstructing History: The Emergence of a New Historical Society.* New York: Routledge, 1999.

Himmelfarb, Gertrude. *The Old History and the New.* Cambridge, MA: Belknap Press, 1987.

Jenkins, Keith. *Why History? Ethics and Postmodernity.* London: Routledge, 1999.

Marcus, Griel. *Lipstick Traces.* Cambridge, MA: Harvard University Press, 1989.

Nietzsche, Friedrich. *The Use and Abuse of History,* translated by Adrian Collins. New York: Liberty Arts Press, 1957 (1874).

Scott, Joan Wallach. *Gender and the Politics of History.* Rev. ed. New York: Columbia University Press, 1999.

White, Hayden. *The Content of the Form.* Baltimore: Johns Hopkins University Press, 1987.

———. *Metahistory: The Historical Imagination in Nineteenth-Century Europe.* Baltimore: Johns Hopkins University Press, 1973.

Young, Robert. *White Mythologies: Writing History and the West.* London: Routledge, 1990.

Zinn, Howard. *The Future of History: Interviews with David Barsamian.* Monroe, ME: Common Courage Press, 1999.

———. *The Politics of History.* Boston: Beacon Press, 1973.

8

Space/Time

I t seems rather banal to point out that our daily practices—routines of going to school or to work, leisure activities, our encounters with other people, our very biographies—unfold in time and space. No doubt this is why we rarely think of how these categories shape our daily lives or the various meanings we assign to places, spaces, time, and history, and why it would never occur to most of us to debate what those categories mean. Like many of the concepts we've encountered so far—author, reader, culture—space and time seem given and self-evident. Yet, on closer inspection, space and time are deeply social as opposed to natural phenomena.

Take the question of time. True, we register the passage of time in seconds, minutes, hours, days, weeks, months, years, decades, centuries, and so on using a single, objective scale. Yet our experiences of time hardly conform to this rigid model. In fact, our perception of time seems to have a lot more to do with how we're spending it. Sitting through Economics 101 on a Friday afternoon while the professor drones on over various charts and graphs can feel like weeks, whereas spring break spent frolicking in the sun on Miami Beach seems over before you've finished your first margarita. To carry the point even further, our experience of time is also heavily mediated by our access to material resources. For some people, time is a luxury—like the Stones' song, "time is on [their] side"—while for others, time is a burden. How well you do in that Econ class will be contingent on your particular relationship to time, among other factors (like your capacity to stay awake). Some students have to work at a menial job twenty or forty hours a week during an average semester; some don't. Some have cars to travel between work and school or to run various errands; some have to wait for public transportation or walk. Should their cars break down (presuming ownership), some students can whip out a cell phone and call for maintenance or towing, whereas those without the cell or extra cash are out of luck. Some students have their own laptop computer to use when and where they need, others have to shlep to the nearest campus computer lab and wait for a vacancy to open up at a work station. Even the lure of spring break in Miami differs for those who can hop a two-hour flight with cash on hand and a credit card subsidized by mom and dad, in contrast to those who can look forward to a two-day bus ride twice with a week's worth of ramen noodles in tow to compensate for the price of the ticket.

Without question, we experience time in individual, often idiosyncratic ways, but these experiences are also shaped by larger social processes. As the preceding examples make clear, how we experience time is not necessarily a function of our choosing, a simple assertion of will ("Carpe diem!" as the saying goes). In other words, our capacity to "seize the day" differs according to material resources as well as our abilities to negotiate how we use our time versus how our time is used by others, the amount of "free" time we have at our disposal versus the amount of time we spend punching in on someone else's clock. Although we tend to focus on the accumulation of wealth or political pull as barometers of social power in advanced capitalist societies like ours, it is also crucial to recognize that implicit in such power is the capacity to control one's own as well as other peoples' time or location in space.

An obvious example of this is the centuries-long, ongoing battle between labor and management—organized primarily around time. (Yes, of course, money was also a key factor—but it's difficult to conceptualize the "objective value" of either labor or consumer goods outside of questions of time.) Marx traced the struggle over the length of the working day back to Elizabethan England. With the passage of the Enclosure laws, which violently expelled peasants from their ancestral homes and forced millions to move from the countryside to new urban industrial centers, the government legislated an increase in the working day for laborers recently arrived in the city. The idea was that the state imposition of time-discipline would keep the newly dispossessed and unruly masses in check and out of trouble. It was clever, when you think about it—nothing like twelve- to fifteen-hour days of intense physical labor for slave wages in crowded, unventilated factories to take the edge off thousands of angry, frustrated people who might otherwise take to the streets. Of course, workers eventually organized and learned to fight the dehumanizing and alienating conditions of their labor, championing, among other human rights, the eight-hour work day as a necessary means for fulfilling the obligations of citizenship, community and family, and the life of the mind. But such battles, we should note, were fought on the terms—the timetables—established by their employers. The historian E. P. Thompson explains:

> The first generation of factory workers were taught by their masters the importance of time; the second generation formed their short-time work committees in the ten-hour movement; the third generation struck for overtime and time-and-a-half. They had accepted the categories of their employers and learned to fight back with them. They had learned their lesson,

that time is money, only too well. ("Time, Work Discipline, and Industrial Capitalism," 90)

Some four hundred years later, in the now rapidly deindustrial-izing cities of the West, the battle between workers and management is still waged in terms of minutes and seconds, days and weeks, years and life spans—in campaigns for lunch hours and half hours, fif-teen-minute breaks, the pace of a day's work, paid vacations, family leave, "free time," and compensation in retirement. Ironically, how-ever, in the new "postindustrial" era, workers are less concerned with too many hours than too few, as full-time, salaried careers (with medical and retirement benefits) disappear and part-time, minimum wage McJobs (with zero benefits) endlessly proliferate. Those older battles for a short working day have shifted to the so-called indus-trializing Third World, where nonunion laborers are pushed to work twenty-four- and even thirty-six-hour shifts for less than a dollar an hour in sweatshops owned by multinational corporations. The demand for decent living wages is on the rise everywhere.

During the aforementioned industrializing era, not all laborers were able to organize and fight back in a similar fashion to Britain's working class. Slaves similarly expropriated from their lands in Africa and brought to the United States, for example, had no recourse for making demands on their masters—they could neither make claims to rights nor draw any meaningful line of separation between work and life. Both were owned by the master, whose chief concern was the eradication of "free time," which could lead to (lit-erally) free time. Political scientist Michael Hanchard makes this crucial distinction in his analysis of "racial time," a social construct that serves to mark out "the inequalities of temporality" between various social groups when linked to relations of domination.

Following this line of thought, Hanchard notes three concep-tual facets to racial time: waiting, time appropriation, and the ethical relationship between temporality and progress. Waiting pertains to the experience of time lags or disjunctures that result from the imposition of racial rule. For example, members of subordinated racial groups are literally made to wait for goods and services that are delivered first to members of the dominant group ("Afro-Modernity," 256). To be black in the United States under Jim Crow meant waiting for pretty much everything: health care, police protection, transportation, education, and a host of other provisions citizens are entitled to receive *as* citizens. Martin Luther King Jr. captured the frustration with structurally imposed time inequality in his 1968 collection of essays, *Why We Can't Wait*, forcefully rejecting white liberal appeals to "be patient" and "go slow." "We can, of course, try to *temporize*," King wrote, "negotiate small, inadequate changes and prolong the timetable of freedom in the hope that the narcotics of delay will dull the pain of progress. We can try, but we shall certainly fail" (cited in Hanchard, "Afro-Modernity," 265). Thus King recast waiting as procrastination and patience as immorality. Time appropriation, conversely, involves challenging the temporal dimensions of inequality associated with segregation—"seizing another's time and making it one's own"—as captured in Black Panther Bobby Seale's exhortation to "seize the time" ("Afro-Modernity," 266). Time appropriation in this instance is revolutionary time, when members of a subordinated group reconstitute themselves as a social movement and intervene in the public sphere of politics in the interests of equality and social justice. The third conceptualization of time refers to belief in the future as improvement on the present, often with religious references to a second coming or encounter with and the arrival of an angry God. In his "Notes on the State of Virginia," Thomas Jefferson invoked this sense of millennial time in his ruminations on the consequences of slavery: "Indeed I tremble for my country when I reflect that God is just: that his justice cannot sleep for ever" ("Notes on the State of Virginia," 215). Similarly, revolutionaries like John Brown and Nat Turner invoke a vengeful God who will wreak havoc on sinful whites, as does the more contemporary writer-activist James Baldwin in *The Fire Next Time*, an allusion to impending confrontation and conflict.

❖ Working Question

How does your daily experience of time differ from that of your roommate or friends? What are the implications of these differences for how well you perform in school? Your economic situation? Your social life? Your health? Suppose you win the lottery or become heir to a long-lost uncle's millions—how do you imagine your relationship to time would change?

Like time, space is a taken-for-granted conceptual category, a given. In fact, we tend to think of space as a mere stage, setting, or backdrop for the unfolding of a film or novel's plot—or the dramas of our own lives. But space is neither so empty nor so neutral. Our experience of space is no less social and no less complicated than our relationship to time. Some might even argue that it is more complex than our relation to time, although the two are increasingly difficult to separate; we experience space temporally and time is registered spacially. With the possible exception of cyberspace, moving through space takes time, but again, the more resources you have to alleviate the burden of distance, the less time it requires. Conversely we map time spatially, using, for example, wristwatches, wall clocks, and calendars (Harvey, *The Condition of Postmodernity*).

Like time, the spaces we occupy—geographic regions, nations, cities, hospitals, prisons, home, our bodies, not to mention those mental spaces and maps we sometimes inhabit—provide a framework for our experiences, as we learn who and what we are in society, our "proper place." Far from a neutral category, space is often perceived in racial and gendered terms. The categories of West and East, suburban and urban, for example, carry with them, however silently, certain racial designations. But such significations don't simply mark spaces racially, they also order them hierarchically. Thus, the West comes to stand for technological and industrial innovation, democracy, and progress, whereas the East signifies its opposite: orientalist despotism, religious mysticism, backwardness. True, the suburbs are often decried as sterile, hygienic, irredeemably boring spaces, but they also generate images of safety, security, order, wealth, and whiteness. And similarly, every city seems to offer a tale of two cities: exciting, culturally enriching spaces marked by the seats of government, the marketplace, institutions of learning, art, music, and dance on one hand, and nightmare spaces of danger, decline, disorder, and blackness on the other—and there is nothing natural or given about these categories. Similarly, the designations of "public" and "private" are often conceived of in masculine and feminine terms, respectively. Marking space in this way is hardly innocent; as feminist historians have pointed out, it served to legitimate male political power through the legal disenfranchisement of women (a woman's place, after all, is "in the home") until the early twentieth century. Even today, such boundaries remain in place, as when working mothers are blamed for the transgressions committed by their children. The presumption is that a more "natural" arrangement—the mother in the home—would putatively end children's misbehavior. The possibility of "stay-at-home dads" is rarely proffered as a solution to family dysfunction or "breakdown." As these examples make clear, social spaces are also constructed in ways that promote particular kinds of social relationships, creating the conditions for contact or isolation, integration and exclusion. In addition, social spaces also facilitate the capacity of governments, the state, to impose law and order (as in the ways schools, factories, and prisons organize space—in oddly similar ways, we might add).

Many contemporary theorists such as Michel Foucault have written about the space of the body as the irreducible element in the socially symbolic orderings of time and space, as it is in this space that the operations of socialization, repression, confinement, discipline, and punishment are performed. Foucault's preoccupation with the rise of modern institutions—the clinic, the prison, the asylum, the school—have been profoundly influential in this regard, reflecting his interest in post-Enlightenment modes of social control.

According to Foucault, the simultaneous transition from monarchical to parliamentary rule and from feudalism to industrialism posed new challenges for the imposition of social order over large populations. If earlier epochs relied on visual spectacles of public torture to keep royal subjects in line, the modern era devised new methods of large-scale city planning, information collection, and bureaucratic organization in the interests of surveillance and control over rapidly expanding populations in Europe's urban centers. To better visualize this transition, recall, for example, the British crown's response to the leader of Scottish anti-imperialist rebellion in the concluding scenes of the public torture and execution of Mel Gibson's renegade character in the blockbuster film *Braveheart.* This would be the medieval, pre-Enlightenment solution to the possibility of social disorder and rebellion: the spectacle of power literally inscribed on the body in full public display. To grasp the newer, micro-operations of a much more decentralized form of power at work in the modern period, think of the institutionally sanctioned response (in the form of lobotomy) to Jack Nicholson's defiant character in the final scenes of *One Flew Over the Cuckoo's Nest,* or the myriad rules of conduct for disciplining soldiers in Kubrick's *Full Metal Jacket.* Among the many differences between the *ancien régime,* which relies on the spectacle of violence to keep people "in their places," and the modern regime, which operates modern bureaucratic techniques of information collection distributed across institutions and careful urban planning, Foucault underscored the power of "panoptic" organization of institutional spaces—the capacity for surveillance that he located in schools, shop floors, prisons, and military barracks—to instill in individual subjects a sense of being watched. The upshot of this asymmetrical and omniscient gaze is the creation of a self-disciplining subject—an individual who will behave in socially prescribed ways without the threat of immediate physical harm or even the presence of a figure of authority. Clearly space, thought of in these terms, is not a mere setting for the unfolding events of our lives but a force actively involved in shaping our experiences.

At the dawn of an entirely new era of global capitalism—sometimes referred to as "postindustrialism" or "post-Fordism" to mark the deindustrialization of cities in the West—the organization of time and space (and the means for maintaining social order) have once again undergone a rather profound transformation. To sum up in the words of postmodern theorist Paul Virilio: "Time and space are shrinking." In contrast to the modern era of industrialism, moving through space took time, communications took time, as we've already observed, and progress seemed to be measured in terms of the speed with which distance could be overcome. David Harvey illustrates this point by providing four variously sized maps of the world in descending order, with the following notations:

- 1500–1840 (best average speed of horse-drawn coaches and sailing ships was ten mph)
- 1850–1930 (steam locomotives averaged sixty-five mph and steam ships averaged thirty-six mph)
- 1950s (propeller aircraft averaged 300–400 mph)
- 1960s (jet passenger aircraft averaged 500–700 mph) (*The Condition of Postmodernity,* 241)

Harvey's point, of course, was to draw attention to how changes in travel time inaugurated new perceptions of global space. Now, given the revolutionary advances in technology, movement through space is greatly accelerated and communication is instantaneous. Given the new possibilities of being able to communicate instantaneously with various parts of the globe, distinctions between "close" and "far away" have become less important, if not altogether irrelevant. Similarly, notions of community bounded by "locality" have seemingly given way to the concept of the "global village." Such time-space compression has enabled the transition from advanced capitalism to global capitalism, both in terms of production and consumption. And these changes, in turn, have implications once again for how time and space are organized and experienced.

With the rise of finance capital, the end of the Cold War, the advent of new technologies, and the increasing mobility of industry, it seems that the nation-states of the West have little use for massive reserve armies of laborers that once filled their factories. The panoptic institutions designed to organize and discipline such large populations have become largely outmoded. With the flight of industrial work in search of cheap labor and deregulated environments, societies in the West have become bifurcated. About one-third of the new workforce is geared toward research and development of the new information society, while two-thirds of the workforce is organized around a service economy, cleaning up around the new technologies. What appears to unite such a divided society is the spectacle of consumption. The decline of the panopticon marks the rise of synoptic institutions. Rather than the few (prison guards, factory managers, doctors, teachers) watching the many, the many now watch the few (the pageantry of celebrity—Hollywood starlets, famous athletes, political leaders, rock legends, and other global elites). Similarly, the primacy of panoptic institutions such as schools and prisons (themselves transformed into privatized or for-profit ventures) gives way to media spaces devoted to the cult of celebrity and the aesthetic of wealth (from MTV's *Cribs* to *Martha Stewart Living*) and to spaces of consumption: the megamall, the Home Shopping Network, the Internet. Comparing the impact of this world of global celebrity on the watching populations bounded by locality to the impact of Christianity, Zygmunt Bauman, in *Globalization: The Human Consequences*, observes:

> In the Synopticon, the locals watch the globals. The authority of the latter is secured by their very remoteness; the globals are literally "out of this world," but their hovering above the worlds of the local is much more, daily and obtrusively, visible than that of the angels who once hovered over the Christian world; simultaneously inaccessible and within sight, lofty and mundane, infinitely superior yet setting a shining example for all the infe-

riors to follow or to dream of following; admired and coveted at the same time—a royalty that guides instead of ruling. (54)

Submission to the demands of the working day is no longer garnered through surveillance and disciplining but through voyeuristic seduction and desire, the promise of wealth and fame just around the corner. As "sociologist" Jennifer Lopez reminds us: "Don't be fooled by the rocks that I got, I'm just, I'm just Jenny from the block." With a little ingenuity and a lot of luck, anybody can supposedly make it.

◆ Working Question

Take a look at figures 8.1 and 8.2. How do these spaces—a correctional facility on one hand and a movie theater on the other—shape normative behavior and social relations? What or who in each case is watching or being watched, and with what subjective and social effects? How might the prison and the theater be said to represent synecdochally panoptic and synoptic societies respectively?

To preclude ending on such a cynical note, this might be a good time to recall Michel de Certeau's important corrective to Foucault. Social spaces cannot be reduced to their most repressive functions; they are also open to human agency, creativity, and action. The key question for us is how our concepts of space and time evolve, change, and give meaning to various cultural forms and practices. Take, for example, the set of material practices we associate with the culture of hip hop, ranging from breakdancing and go-go to the brief vogue of graffiti art to rap music, which began in the late 1970s and remains today a dominant force in popular culture. The rise of hip hop, we would argue, is impossible to understand without reference to the shifting conditions of time and space that transformed and continue to transform U.S. cities from the 1970s to the present.

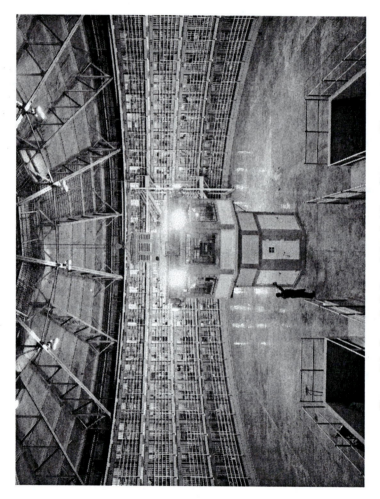

Figure 8.1 Doug DuBois and Jim Goldberg/Magnum Photos

Figure 8.2 J. R. Eyerman/Getty Images

How is this so? The historian Robin D. G. Kelley, in *Yo' Mama's Disfunktional!*, has persuasively argued that the culture of hip hop is a creative response to urban postindustrial decline and the new social conditions with which it is associated: the rise of permanent unemployment, the transformation of public space, and the shifting meanings of "play" for African-American urban youth. Critiquing the ad campaigns run by multinational corporations such as Nike, LA Gear, and Reebok, which romanticize deteriorating urban spaces in which black and Latino youth must play, Kelley ironically notes that such corporations have made huge profits from the postindustrial decline they inaugurated. Not only have they moved factories from urban centers in the United States to "developing" countries in search of cheap, nonunion labor, they have also created a vast market for overpriced sneakers (some going for $200 a pair) among young black males who have nothing to do *but* play. Kelley notes:

> The most striking element in this postindustrial urban spectacle are the people who occupy these urban spaces. Parks and schoolyards are full of brown bodies of various hues whose lack of employment has left them with plenty of time to "play." In other words, while obscuring poverty, unemployment, racism and rising police repression, commercial representations of the contemporary "concrete jungles" powerfully underscore the link between urban decline, joblessness, and the erosion of recreational spaces in the inner city. At the same time, they highlight the historic development of "leisure" time for the urban working class and, therefore, offer commodities to help fill that time. The difference between the creation and commodification of urban leisure at the turn of the century and now, however, is that opportunities for wage labor have virtually disappeared and the bodies of the displaced workers are overwhelmingly black and brown. (*Yo' Mama's Disfunktional!*, 44–45)

In other words, the economic restructuring we associate with globalization has meant permanent unemployment for some populations and hence the declining infrastructures of urban spaces; shrinking social services; the flight of middle-class residents to the suburbs; and the deterioration of public schools, play areas, and parks. As a result of the movement of transnational corporations, unemployment was 50 to 70 percent among young black males in Midwestern cities by 1985. The departure of all remnants of a formal economy created the conditions for underground economies—criminality and drugs—to take hold and flourish, furthering the deterioration of inner city space. The rise in crime and the ascendance of the crack economy in turn lead to greater police repression and the militarization of city space, as ghetto spaces become renovated along the lines of minimum security prisons and subject to surveillance by helicopters, tanks, and various electronic means. The cordoning off of school property, the privatization of parks, and the increasing surveillance of what remained of urban youth centers meant that black and brown urban youth, the throwaways of global capitalism, had only the streets in which "to play." And the logic of survival meant trying to turn that play into a means to get paid. Given that the chances of attaining professional status in sports are 2 in 100,000 for black men and 3 in 1,000,000 for Latinos, there are real limitations in imagining a future in basketball or other sports as an answer to the disappearance of wage labor and a means of escape from poverty, although it remains the dream of many. Other youth look to alternative means for getting paid from play-labor: graffiti art, breakdancing, emceeing, rapping, and various forms of public performance requiring no or inexpensive equipment, thus providing the necessary options. Kelley's point is not to celebrate hip hop for generated spaces of resistance to the forces of global capital (especially given the way that hip hop has been appropriated by multinationals to hock consumer goods from Burberry to Prada, as in the work of J Lo, Nelly, and Snoop Dogg) or to offer "success stories" to prove that kids can make it if they work hard enough. Rather, he is offering a crucial set of contexts for understanding the cultural productions of urban youth formed in the intersections of time and space as these have been reordered by transnational capital.

To conclude, the social meanings we assign to spaces and times and the ways they are organized or produced in the material world tend to reproduce the existing social order. The commonsense assumption that "everything has a place and time" naturalizes how spatial and temporal meanings get mapped onto the fault lines of social conflict. The degree to which you will feel safe or endangered, at home or out of place, legal or illegal, in private or under surveillance, capable of movement or confined, free or policed has everything to do with the spaces you occupy. It seems unlikely, then, that any single, homogeneous, and objective sense of time and space can adequately measure the incredible diversity of human experiences.

Working Questions

1. Of the many truisms of late capitalist society, one reigns supreme: Time is money. We've all heard it, but what does it really mean? How does this logic inform a "just in time" economy? The politics of the shop floor—speed ups and slowdowns? Worker compensation? The demands of organized labor? The value of consumer goods?

2. Marshall McLuhan coined the phrase "global village" in the 1960s to signal the ways in which advances in media and communication would overcome vast distances to connect disparate parts of the world, collapsing in a sense time and space with the immediate contact that telephones and televisions seem to provide. "Global village" not only invokes the shrinkage of time and space, it also carries positive connotations of community, contact, closeness, and the ethical obligations these imply. But has the capacity to "reach out and touch someone" lent itself to greater human interaction or less? Greater ethical awareness of "the other" or less?

For Further Reading

Bachelard, Gaston. *The Poetics of Space*, translated by Maria Jolas. Boston: Beacon Press, 1972 (1964).

Bauman, Zygmunt. *Globalization: The Human Consequences.* New York: Columbia University Press, 1998.

Davis, Mike. *City of Quartz: Excavating the Future of Los Angeles.* London: Verso, 1990.

Foucault, Michel. "Space, Knowledge, and Power." In *The Foucault Reader*, edited by Paul Rabinow, 239–56. New York: Pantheon, 1984.

Gregory, Derek, and John Urry. *Social Relations and Spatial Structures.* New York: St. Martin's Press, 1985.

Hanchard, Michael. "Afro-Modernity: Temporality, Politics, and the African Diaspora." *Public Culture* 11, no. 1 (1999): 245–68.

Harvey, David. *The Condition of Postmodernity.* London: Blackwell, 1989.

———. *Justice, Nature, and the Geography of Difference.* Cambridge, MA: Blackwell, 1996.

———. *Spaces of Capital.* New York: Routledge, 2001.

———. *Spaces of Hope.* Berkeley: University of California Press, 2000.

Jefferson, Thomas. "Notes on the State of Virginia." In *The Portable Thomas Jefferson*, edited by Merrill D. Peterson. New York: Penguin, 1977.

Kelley, Robin D. G. *Yo' Mama's Disfunktional!: Fighting the Culture Wars in Urban America.* Boston: Beacon Press, 1997.

Lefebvre, Henri. *The Production of Space*, translated by Donald Nicholon-Smith. Oxford: Blackwell, 1991.

Massey, Doreen. *Space, Place, and Gender.* Minneapolis: University of Minnesota Press, 1994.

———. *Spatial Divisions of Labor: Social Structures and the Geography of Production.* 2d ed. New York: Routledge, 1995 (1984).

Soja, Edward. *Postmodern Geographies: The Reassertion of Space in Critical Social Theory.* London: Verso, 1989.

———. *Thirdspace: Journeys to Los Angeles and Other Real-and-Imagined Spaces.* Cambridge, MA: Blackwell, 1996.

Thompson, E. P. "Time, Work Discipline, and Industrial Capitalism." *Past and Present* 38 (1967): 90.

Virilio, Paul. *Speed and Politics: An Essay on Dromology*, translated by Mark Polizzotti. New York: Columbia University, 1986.

Posts

It seems that we live in a world of "posts": We're postmodern, postindustrial, postfeminist, postcolonial, and, given the advent of e-mail, perhaps we're becoming post–post office. This chapter takes a look at some of those "posts," taking the advice offered in the first part of the book—always contextualize—and applying it to our contemporary moment.

Postmodernism

"Postmodern" is one of those words that's getting thrown around a lot these days. We're perhaps used to "postmodern" as an adjective used to describe fiction like Thomas Pynchon's or Ishmael Reed's, but it's also noteworthy that Clint Eastwood's *Unforgiven* was hailed as a "postmodern Western"; *Seinfeld* has been called postmodern television; Stanley Tigerman, who designed several Hard Rock Cafes, is routinely called a "postmodern" architect; and visual artists Barbara Kruger (who splashes provocative words across her photographs) and Andy Warhol are called "postmodern" in the same breath. Performance artist and former porn star Annie Sprinkle calls one of her performances "Post-Porn-Modern." The possible references go on and on: from rap to acid jazz to the films of the Coen brothers, the list of things labeled "postmodern" grows by the day.

What, one might wonder, could all these disparate things have in common? How could "postmodern" (or any category, for that matter) possibly encompass an impeccably diverse grouping like Snoop Dogg, Clint Eastwood, Jerry Seinfeld, Annie Sprinkle, and Andy Warhol? It seems impossible, but on further reflection, some general connections might be made. There seems to be a certain sense of *style* shared by many of the things labeled "postmodern," a sense of disjunction or deliberate confusion, irony, playfulness, reflexivity, a kind of cool detachment, a deliberate foregrounding of constructedness, a suspicion concerning neat or easy conclusions.

Following up this preliminary sense of postmodern, we might note that Eastwood's *Unforgiven* is postmodern insofar as it plays with the good/evil dichotomy running through so many Westerns; it coolly and ironically exposes the constructedness of the Western myth, and in the process challenges this myth's seemingly natural validity: The gunslinger is not a hero or a God; he's just a hired killer. Similarly, *Seinfeld* is postmodern insofar as it is *par excellence* the sitcom that foregrounds and plays with the fact that nothing ever happens on sitcoms; the show doesn't even pretend to have a plot most of the time, and when it does, the plot is so contrived and full of planned "coincidences" as to be obviously and deliberately ridiculous. And the rap practice of sampling—using cuts from other recordings—always emphasizes the fact that the music and the sound is *constructed*, put together in a certain way in the hope of producing a certain set of effects in the listener. As rap producer Hank Shocklee says, "Music is nothing but organized noise. You can take anything—street sounds, us talking, whatever you want—and make it music by organizing it" (Rose, *Black Noise*, 82).

Maybe all this suggests a postmodern insistence on *process* rather than *product*: A "postmodern" cultural artifact is one that consistently questions itself and the context that it seems to fit within. Perhaps, preliminarily, we could say that postmodern cultural artifacts are constantly calling attention to the ways in which both the work and the viewer are constructing, deconstructing, and reconstructing meaning.

In the end, then, one might say that *Seinfeld* is "postmodern" insofar as it's a sitcom about sitcoms, and *Unforgiven* is a postmodern Western about Westerns. Similarly, Warhol's art is primarily about producing art, and postmodern architects might be said to produce buildings that are about buildings: The hallways that go nowhere, the exposed beams, and the see-through elevators that characterize postmodern buildings all point to the fact that space is constructed rather than merely found. And these deliberately difficult architectural constructions challenge the user of the building to think about the ways in which his or her movements are unconsciously channeled (one might even say controlled) by architects.

Although this kind of description gives us a beginning handle on "postmodern," it also raises a host of questions. Most pressing among them, perhaps, is not so much figuring out what the "post-" means but rather understanding what the "modern" means. If postmodern signifies, at least in part, "after the modern," then what is or was "modern"? Is modern over? Modern what? Modern art? Modern history? Modern painting? Modern love? So-called modern rock? When did the modern period begin, much less end? Why weren't we informed?

In literary history, "modernism" tends to mean an international aesthetic movement that began to take hold in the late nineteenth and early twentieth centuries and ended around the time of the second World War. As a reaction to the Romanticism of the early and middle nineteenth century, modernism as a literary and artistic movement tended to stress form over Romantic feeling; so the poetry of Ezra Pound or T. S. Eliot is *modern* insofar as it is impersonal, complex, and allusive, especially when compared with the Romantic verse of Wordsworth. Likewise, Hemingway's short and clipped modernist prose style stands in stark contrast to the voluminous Victorian novel. It's not so much that modernism abandons the subjective feeling of Romanticism, but the subject or self in a modern work is troubled, psychologically and physically. The kind of fragmented subjective vision that one sees in Picasso's modernist work, for example, stands in marked contrast to the gentle color schemes of Monet's neo-Romanticism.

On the other hand, if you go to the philosophy department and sign up for "Modern Philosophy," you're not going to get philosophy beginning with Nietzsche at the end of the nineteenth century. In fact, in philosophical parlance, the "modern" period begins with Descartes (born in Shakespeare's time) and ends in the early nineteenth century. Modern philosophy tends to mean the philosophy of subjectivity from Descartes to Kant or Hegel. If you go to the history department and sign up for "Early Modern Europe," you'll be looking at the beginning of the sixteenth or seventeenth centuries, not the beginning of the twentieth. In historical parlance, "modern" tends to mean the history of industrialization and the rise of towns and commerce, beginning after the medieval or feudal period.

And, just to make things really confusing, in literary and visual arts, as we saw above, "modern" tends to mean a historical period following the Romantics, beginning around the turn of the twentieth century and ending in 1945. So if you take the "Modern American Novel" course at our university, you're taking "American Novel 1890–1945"; after 1945, the course is called "Contemporary American Novel," or perhaps one might call it the "postmodern" novel course. But, all that considered, we seem to find ourselves farther from—rather than closer to—a concrete definition of either modernism or postmodernism. Is "postmodern" a style, or is it a historical period? Or is it both?

In his essay "Toward a Concept of Postmodernism" in *The Postmodern Turn*, critic Ihab Hassan lays out a list of "schematic differences" between modernism and postmodernism in literature and the arts. Perhaps highlighting certain of Hassan's differences will bring the question more clearly into focus (see table 9.1).

Hassan's list tends to emphasize very concisely the *stylistic* differences between modernism and postmodernism. As we saw above, the unexpected, questioning, or process-oriented form of *Seinfeld* or *Unforgiven* is the thing that makes people call it "postmodern," in contradistinction to the highly designed, totalized, "finished" quality of traditional TV shows or Westerns. It is some deliberate sense of *indeterminacy* or *uncertainty* that would seem to make an artifact "postmodern."

However, this list—as convenient as it is—introduces a truckload of problems. For example, T. S. Eliot's 1922 poem "The Waste Land" is a landmark of modernism, but it seems to have all the

Table 9.1

Modernism	*Postmodernism*
Form (closed)	Anti-form (open)
Purpose	Play
Design	Chance
Hierarchy	Anarchy
Finished Art Object	Process/Performance
Distance	Participation
Totalization	Deconstruction
Centering	Dispersal
Metaphor	Metonymy
Signified	Signifier
Depth	Surface
Determinacy	Indeterminacy

Source: Ihab Hassan, "Toward a Concept of Postmodernism," in *The Postmodern Turn*. (Columbus: Ohio State University Press, 1987).

artistic *markers* of postmodernism: The poem seems to have an incredibly "open" form that relies much more heavily on "dispersal" than on "centering." One could say the same for famous modernists Gertrude Stein and William Faulkner, whose works seem to have all the markers of "postmodernism." This gets even trickier if we consider the incredibly open and dispersed character of an eighteenth-century novel like *Tristram Shandy*, or even of Chaucer's *Canterbury Tales*.

Perhaps one could solve this problem, though, by insisting on the more literal, *historical* meaning of postmodern: after the modern period, after the end of World War II, roughly after 1945. Of course, the problem there is that not everything produced in this period is "postmodern" in the sense outlined by Hassan's list; for example, the fiction of John Updike or Joyce Carol Oates don't easily fit the "postmodern" suit. So maybe the most cogent definition of "postmodern" is disjunctive, ironic, and/or reflexive artistic work produced after 1945.

Working Question

Given this definition, why would the date 1945 be crucial? What happened after 1945 that seems to have altered the world, our lives, and our consciousness in such revolutionary ways?

Once you can nail down a kind of definition for "postmodern," the next logical question haunts you almost immediately: Is "postmodern" art any good, or is it interesting? In much current critical discourse in newspapers and journals, postmodern artistic markers—disjunction, irony, reflexivity, deliberate confusion, a kind of cool apathy—are routinely celebrated or denounced by critics in familiar ways: Postmodernism, they say, celebrates the freedom of possibility, but it also seems to make agency or concrete decision impossible.

Postmodernism demystifies logo-phallo-Euro-Theo-centrism and in the process preserves the status quo because it leaves us without direction. The postmodern artwork foregrounds the complexity of our epoch, thereby remaining an elitist diversion for a leisure class of overeducated white folks who "get the joke."

◈ Working Question

Perhaps the questions surrounding "postmodern" boil down to this: Does postmodern art pose interesting questions that demand your response, or does it just ask you to smirk knowingly if you're part of the crowd that is "in" on the joke? Is postmodernism, in other words, a reactionary or progressive phenomenon? This question is the hot one surrounding "postmodernism," and one that you could take up in class, using your examples and/or some of the ones we've mentioned here: *Seinfeld, Unforgiven,* Hard Rock Cafes, Warhol, Pynchon.

We provide a place to start with two paintings, which critic Fredric Jameson has pointed to as representative of their epochs: Vincent Van Gogh's *A Pair of Boots* (modernism) and Andy Warhol's *Diamond Dust Shoes* (postmodernism) (figures 9.1 and 9.2, respectively). Consider the differences between these two paintings for a class discussion.

Poststructuralism

As a term, "poststructuralism" presents much the same problem as "postmodern": Before you can get a handle on the "post-" part, you need to know something about structuralism, which logically came *before* poststructuralism. Structuralism is or was a cross-disciplinary movement in the humanities and social sciences, having the greatest impact on linguistics, ethnography, anthropology, and literary criticism. Essentially, structuralism is interested in the study of sig-

Figure 9.1 Vincent van Gogh, *A Pair of Boots.*
The Baltimore Museum of Art

nifying or symbol systems, and its basic premise gives structuralism its name: For any given signifying phenomenon, there must be
an underlying *structure* that makes the signifying act possible and
governs it in some way.

For any given speech act to be intelligible, for example, there
must be a common grammar that helps to explain the specific word
order, sentence pattern, and position of subjects, verbs, objects, etc.
Any signifying or meaningful phenomenon presupposes a kind of
structure, a system of rules and values by which it is produced and
in which it is at least minimally intelligible to someone else who knows
the system. In this way, the sense of "structure" in "structuralism"

Figure 9.2 Andy Warhol, *Diamond Dust Shoes.*
© 2003 Andy Warhol Foundation for the Visual Arts

has some overlap with "ideology," in its second definition as the baseline "common sense"—the shared but largely unconscious consensus—of a social body.[1]

As an example of a kind of structuralist analysis, we note that for a person to understand the simple English command, "Shut the door!," both the speaker and the listener must already possess a staggering amount of "structural" information, both about the language they're speaking and the situation they're in. The command form is a particularly slippery one in English, relying on tone of voice and other contextual issues (relative social positions of the speaker and listener, some mutual understanding of the "problem" created by a door being left open, etc.) as much as the "content" of the message; in addition, the subject of the command is implied rather than stated directly, so to know that it really is *you* who is being addressed is, strictly speaking, impossible to pick up from the sentence itself. To pick up the meaning of this simple command, you need to possess an underlying understanding of both the grammar of English and the situation in which this sentence is uttered.

In other words, a number of complicated "structures" must be learned before a simple symbolic act can be rendered meaningful, and structuralism is interested in uncovering these underlying phenomena. As Robert Scholes writes in *Structuralism in Literature,* "in order to exist, any human science must move from the phenomena it recognizes to the system that governs them" (14). In fact, one might say that this movement from *things* to the *structures* that govern them is the central movement of all structuralisms.

Of course, each one of us performs such "structuralist" movements—from the particular symbolic act to the structure that renders it intelligible—all the time, more or less unconsciously sorting signs and symbols according to the structures of intelligibility that we learned long ago. For example, raising your middle finger toward someone is, in itself, a meaningless act, but when you understand this gesture in terms of the structuring grammar of American society, it takes on a very specific meaning. In fact, this process of reference is often so automatic that we tend to notice it only when it breaks down in some way, when, for example, words or images become difficult because they are "overcoded" with multiple meanings (as in literary or poetic language), or when we try to get by in an unfamiliar or foreign language, where we don't know the underlying social and linguistic structures.[2] In other words, it is when you *don't know* or can't figure out the underlying structures of meaning that the existence of these structures becomes most apparent.

✦ Working Question

Think about and describe the last time you were in a situation where you didn't know the underlying structures of meaning that govern a conversation. A visit to another country, for example? A neighborhood, store, or bar in your own city, perhaps? Attending an office party at a place you don't work? A cricket match on TV? Or a night out with people who all perform the same job—dentists or computer experts or Deadheads or truck drivers or plumbers or musicians—and who talk endlessly about their jobs or hobbies in a technical language you don't get?

What specifically didn't you understand when you were last in such a situation? What effects did it have on you? Is it really the case that you need to know a lot of complex structures to enter into simple conversations?

Perhaps the paradigmatic discourse for structuralism is the linguistics of Ferdinand de Saussure, which we looked at briefly in chapter 3. Recall that Saussure distinguishes between the material *sign* or *speech act* and the underlying structures—respectively, the *signified* and the *grammar*—that render such symbolic acts intelligible. Saussure remains crucial for poststructuralism as well, but poststructuralism picks up and questions structuralism at its most central point, the movement from the particular (the signifier) to the structure that governs it (the signified).

Certainly, poststructuralists will agree, it is in a situation where you *don't* understand something that the underlying structures of meaning become most apparent: When the plumber is describing to you in excruciating detail the inner workings of a toilet, you realize that she is referring to structures that you don't understand; likewise, when you order breakfast in Germany and get what looks a lot like lunch, you realize—like Dorothy—that you're not in Kansas anymore. You haven't made a mistake in ordering, but what breakfast means in Germany (what one might call the signified of breakfast) is different than it is in the United States.

However, to these little dramas, the *post*structuralist will add another observation: With the realization that you don't understand the plumber or can't order a proper breakfast in German also comes the realization that the structures of intelligibility are *not* universal or abstract. When *your* system breaks down, you see that the underlying structures of meaning (the *contexts* that render meaning) vary from place to place. The structures of meaning, like meaning itself, are *not* abstract or transcendental: The signified (the concept of breakfast, for example) is just as material (dependent on context for its meaning) as the signifier ("breakfast" in English or *Frühstück* in German); the seemingly abstract and universal grammar (*what* you're ordering) is just as concrete and changeable as the *sentence* or *word* that refers to it.

For a poststructuralist, both the signifier *and* the signified are "arbitrary" in this way. There is no essential (or structural) connection between a word and what that word means. This, perhaps, is poststructuralism's most crucial addition to structuralism: Even the deep or underlying *structures* of meaning are themselves *arbitrary*; what we take to be the *cause* of meaning or intelligibility is itself already an *effect*; wherever you think you see *nature, culture* has already been there.

To say something is "arbitrary" generally means that it's based on individual preference and therefore easy to change. In this sense, what you had for lunch yesterday is "arbitrary"—it's a fairly inconsequential personal preference that changes from day to day. Of course, this is certainly *not* the sense in which the Saussurean signifier is "arbitrary." In English, that midday meal was referred to as "lunch" yesterday and for many years before that, and it's a pretty good bet that it'll be called "lunch" tomorrow and well beyond. You may exhibit an individual preference to call it "flanjor," but don't expect anyone to know what you're talking about if you say, "Hey, let's have flanjor sometime." The signifier, although it is "arbitrary," is *not* an individual preference.

In fact, as Saussure writes, the "arbitrary nature of the sign is really what protects language from any attempt to modify it" (*Course in General Linguistics,* 73). This seems pretty strange: If "arbitrary" means that there is no "natural" connection between sign and signified (that the relation is "culturally constructed" as opposed to "essential"), wouldn't that also suggest that the relation is easier to change or modify? If the relation between word and meaning is "arbitrary" rather than "essential," then isn't every word subject to easy "modification" in this way?

Working Question

What sense does it make to say something is "arbitrary" but is therefore *resistant* to change? To change something, don't you have to show how it is not "natural" and thereby able to be changed? If the signifier is "arbitrary" or merely "culturally constructed," why don't a lot of people refer to lunch as "flanjor"?

In the wake of structuralism, to say that something is "culturally constructed" rather than "essential" or "natural" has somehow come to suggest that it's easy to change: If it's not essential or natural, then it should be really easy to modify, right? Well, no. For example, most people would agree that the pressing problems of our day are wholly socially constructed: poverty, crime, discrimination, high taxes, wars. Everyone *knows* that these things are socially constructed; discrimination is not a "natural" phenomenon, any more than high taxes or wars are; people *become* bigots, they are not born that way. This fact, however, doesn't seem to have much effect on the discourse of racism or gender discrimination. Most people seem to agree that women's roles are not simply to be wife and mother, but that doesn't change the social fact of gender discrimination. As feminist theorist Eve Kosofsky Sedgwick writes,

"I remember the buoyant enthusiasm with which feminist scholars used to greet the finding that one or another brutal form of oppression was not biological but 'only' cultural! I have often wondered what the basis was for our optimism about the malleability of culture by any one group or program" (*Epistemology,* 41).

In fact, if discrimination *were* a "natural" thing, and it could be somehow scientifically invalidated, it would in fact be much easier to "change" it than if one agrees that discrimination is and has been a socially constructed phenomenon from the start. Social habits are in fact notoriously difficult to change, and not because they're "essential" but precisely because we're so used to them. There's no necessary reason to play most American football games on Sunday (just as there's no essential connection between the word "football" and the American version of the sport), but the fact that there's no necessary reason why it's done this way certainly does not mean that it would be really easy just to decide to do it another way.

Since "arbitrary" means "socially constructed" to Saussure, it then necessarily also means "resistant to change." Social customs are deeply ingrained, and the conventions of social systems are therefore impossible to change simply through any given individual's action. Language, Saussure points out, is perhaps the greatest example of this point: *Because* language is an arbitrary social system of meaning based on long-held conventions, it's highly resistant to change. What would be the point of changing the word "lunch" to "flanjor," when "lunch" continues to work like a charm in everyday usage? To point out that something is constructed or structured is *not* the same thing as finally understanding it or being able somehow to change it wholesale.

In many of its variants, however, structuralism dreams of finding a kind of universal structure for symbol systems and a kind of ultimate grounding of *nature* that comes *before* any culture. Structuralist anthropology, for example, argues that the incest taboo is the founding or underlying structure of all symbol systems in all societies. As Jacques Derrida writes about structuralism's claims concerning the founding principle of the incest taboo:

> Society, language, history, articulation . . . are born at the same time as the incest prohibition [which] is the hinge between nature and culture. . . . [The incest prohibition] is moreover not simply one element of culture among others, since it is a sacred and universal interdict. It is the element of culture itself, the undeclared origin of passions, of society, of languages. (*Of Grammatology*, 265–66)

For Derrida, a poststructuralist, what is suspicious here is the "sacred and universal" quality of structuralism's claim for the incest taboo. In other words, what is suspicious for a *post*structuralist is structuralism's trace of a certain theological or transcendental claim for "structure." However, the structures that seem to *govern* cultural practices are themselves *products* of cultural practices. This is the lesson of poststructuralism, and the point where it most easily hooks back up to postmodernism: Both the postmodernist and the poststructuralist will insist on and foreground the provisional nature of any claim to truth. Truths come about in specific contexts, which is not to say that anything we think is true (as we have seen throughout the course of this text), but rather that truths are beholden to specific contexts.

Working Question

The big bang theory seems to be the accepted scientific version of the birth of the universe: It all started in one huge mass that broke apart in a huge explosion. The universe will expand as far as it can go and then begin again to contract, bringing everything crashing back into one undifferentiated mass. (This theory also helps to explain gravity, entropy, thermodynamics, and a series of other scientific concepts.)

Is there anything suspicious about the big bang theory from a "poststructuralist" point of view?

Postcolonialism

As with "postmodernism" and "poststructuralism," the first question begged by "postcolonialism" is the status or meaning of the root word, "colonialism." As we remember from world history, the "discovery" of the Americas in the fifteenth century was actually a subplot in the history of colonialism: The United States's original thirteen states were first colonies of England, much of what is now Canada and the central United States was claimed by France, and large parts of what is now Mexico and South America were colonized by the Spanish. And the legacy of such colonialism remains to this day, most obviously in the languages spoken by modern nations: Brazilians still speak Portuguese; Mexicans speak Spanish, along with many native languages; French is spoken throughout much of colonial Africa; and there remains an intense cultural battle between French- and English-speaking Canadians. Such a battle is in fact looming in the postcolonial United States, where native Spanish speakers will soon constitute a significant percentage of the population. These linguistic heritages and conflicts are the most obvious legacies of colonialism in the new world(s).

Throughout the history of colonialism, colonies provided raw materials and new products for European markets; the colonization of the United States, for example, pioneered the European marketing of tobacco, and the colonization of the Aztecs and Incas provided much gold for Spain and Portugal. European colonialism, then, was a race for territory and wealth that began in the sixteenth and seventeenth centuries; it spread from the Americas to Asia and Africa throughout the eighteenth and nineteenth centuries, and in fact such empire-building colonialism officially ended only relatively recently (and only, one might argue, when there was no "new" territory left to colonize). Due to increasing unrest among colonial peoples (unrest akin to the revolution that manifested itself in the American colonies in 1776), throughout the twentieth century there has been an increasing and inexorable decolonization that has returned sovereignty to many former European colonies. In the 1950s and 1960s, for example, in the face of uprisings by the colonized peoples, the French gave up control of Algeria and Vietnam; in 1962, the English renounced their claim to Jamaica; and more recently, under intense worldwide pressure, the white Afrikaner minority in South Africa held free and open elections, sweeping the formerly imprisoned Nelson Mandela into power. Perhaps *the* most high-profile case of decolonization was Britain's handover of Hong Kong to the Chinese in 1999. It is this movement of decolonization that has given rise to "postcolonialism," the period after the heyday of colonization.

We should note here that for important reasons the "post" in postcolonialism remains subject to much contestation. Many theorists see "*neo*colonial" as a more apt term for describing the status of so-called developing countries in the New World Order. Since for many recently established independent nations, formal political sovereignty did not translate into economic self-sufficiency, many newly created African and Latin American states and eventually India gravitated toward one or another of the then two great superpowers—the United States or the Soviet Union—to prevent economic collapse or civil war, in spite of a proclaimed policy of "nonalignment." The upshot is that after the fall of communism and the subsequent end of the Cold War, Western European powers and the United States established a new institutional framework for engaging in projects of global economic and political restructuring: the U.S.-dominated World Bank and International Monetary Fund. These lending institutions provide aid to developing countries in exchange for neoliberal free-trade policies. A former British colony, the United States ironically has emerged at the dawn of the twenty-first century as the most recent reigning empire.

Colonialism, thus, would seem to be a crucial historical and economic consideration, helping us to understand the history of colonial powers and the legacy of those powers in present-day post-colonial countries. In other words, the history of colonialism seems to provide a necessary context for situating past and present economic and political conditions in a number of formerly "colonial" countries, from the United States to South Africa. Such considerations are also essential for explaining the politics of race in the former colonial powers: the status of North Africans in France, for example, or the attitudes of the English toward Caribbean immigrants from former British colonies.

It seems fairly evident why an analysis of postcolonial relations is necessary to disciplines in the social sciences, such as sociology, political science, anthropology, and economics. But what, one might profitably ask, does all this have to do with the study of literature, art, history, philosophy, or other disciplines in the humanities? On the surface, these postcolonial concerns seem primarily economic and political and so rather marginal to a discussion of, say, film or art theory. However, the realms of politics and culture are not so easily separated from each other. One might even say that politics and culture work in collusion. On the one level you might think, why is this news? As we've already learned, representations—historical, artistic, popular—are always mediated by the artist's or the producer's subjectivity and they are always ideological in that they participate in the production of forms of common sense. But these assumptions frustrate much more deeply held, centuries-old assumptions about "high culture": that it springs forth from pure, imaginative genius, and it is therefore unsullied by the messy world of politics. Culture in this sense represents a kind of autonomous site from whence to critique this social and political world: that it is truth, it represents a world that ought to be. But in fact we discover that, far from being autonomous, culture—art, literature, history, philosophy, etc.—as we've been insisting all along, reproduces certain interests and in doing so reproduces stereotypes about men and women, the sane and the mentally ill, the whites and the dark, the foreign "other," the rich and the poor.

To understand this relationship further, the Italian theorist Antonio Gramsci made a useful distinction between civil and political society. The former is made up of voluntary (or at least rational and noncoercive) affiliations like schools, churches, and trade unions. The latter is made up of state institutions like the army, the police, and the central bureaucracy, whose role in the polity is, among other things, the maintenance of law and order. In the name of protecting citizens from enemies either within or outside its borders, it can employ the use of force, or direct domination. Culture is to be found operating in civil society, where the influence of ideas, imbibed pedagogically, works not through domination but by what Gramsci calls consent. In any society that isn't totalitarian, rule by consent is always preferred to rule by coercion and force, which is notoriously unstable. Thus, certain cultural forms predominate over others; certain ideas have more influence than others. The form of this cultural leadership is what Gramsci called *hegemony*.

Cultural representations of the Middle East, Africa, and other colonies at the high point of empire—of colonial rule by British, French, Belgian, and other European powers in the nineteenth century—fostered particular understandings of "the idea of Europe," a collective notion identifying a "we" against all "those" non-Europeans. Here it might be useful to think back not only to such literary classics as Conrad's *Heart of Darkness*, but also to all those Tarzan movies, Looney Tunes cartoons, or issues of *National Geographic* you grew up with that portrayed "darkest" Africa in ways generally accompanied by corresponding, opposing images of Western European "civilization." The major component in European culture is precisely what made that culture hegemonic both in and outside of Europe: the idea of European identity as a superior one in comparison with all the non-European peoples and cultures.

"Okay," you might still be thinking, "so the United States used to be an English colony, or the Congo used to be a colony of Belgium.

But what could that possibly have to do with the study of any of the art produced in any of these places, either now or in the past?"

A student of American literature might respond that colonization seems to have had quite a bit of influence on both its past and present configuration. For example, an overwhelming amount of "classic" American literature—for example, that of Poe, Emerson, Hawthorne, and Whitman—is overtly obsessed with the problem of writing a postcolonial literature, an American literature that is not merely a copy of British models. Consider Emerson's insistence, in his 1837 address "The American Scholar," that American artists and thinkers leave behind the models of colonial Europe: "Our day of dependence, our long apprenticeship to the learning of other lands, draws to a close" (*Selected Essays*, 83). Or Poe's thoughts in his 1842 review of Hawthorne's *Twice Told Tales*: "As Americans we feel proud of the book," he wrote, because "we have very few American tales of real merit" (*Great Short Works of Edgar Allan Poe*, 523).

Of course, that student might also point out that the entire enterprise of literary education itself emerges out of a colonial context. Ever wonder where English departments come from? Curiously enough, the first courses in English literature were not taught in Britain but rather in nineteenth-century India. With the passing of the Charter Act of 1813, Britain assumed a new responsibility for the education of its colonial subjects. The motive? "Civilizing the natives"? Not exactly; colonial administrators recognized that the most effective means of quashing rebellion against foreign rule was to assimilate young minds into the prevailing order, to confer upon them the urgent necessity of identifying with British social and cultural authority. As one high-ranking British official in the Bombay administration put it: "The Natives must either be kept down by a sense of our power, or they must willingly submit from a conviction that we are more wise, more just, more humane, and more anxious to improve their condition than any other rulers they could possibly have" (Viswanathan, "Currying Favor," 86). English literature, a suitably nationalist course of study, proved an effective means of introducing the native population to the image of the "ideal" Englishman in the ongoing effort to secure popular consent for imperial rule. The colonial origin of literary study offers an unusually clear and distinct instance of the Gramscian notion of hegemony.

So if these images of cultural inferiority and superiority are associated with colonialism and the age of empire, and these images are entirely the product of a European imagery, it seems only fitting that in an era of postcolonialism, formerly colonized peoples will want to assert their own identities. In other words, they will produce their own histories, literatures, and philosophies in part to challenge the inferior identities that have been imposed upon them. The project here is not simply one of rewriting the often violent misrepresentations and exclusions that have informed colonial versions of the history and culture of oppressed groups, but also one that levels, in good poststructuralist fashion, the entire system of reference. Not only is the mythology of "darkest Africa" or the "mystical Orient" subject to implosion, but so too is its equally mythical flip side: the "civilized West," the identity of which now is understood to be entirely dependent on the image of colonial savagery and superstition. In addition to struggling for political and economic autonomy, then, the cultural moment in the postcolonial project reflects the slow, often painful process of articulating an identity separate from the one imposed by the former colonial power. And throughout the long history of colonization and decolonization, literature has been one of the most important and privileged media for articulating this distinct identity. In that spirit, one recent collection of postcolonial writing is called *The Empire Writes Back*.

Of course, part of the paradox and difficulty is the fact that colonial power remains active in such a project: The postcolonial author, whether she likes it or not, often works in the language of the colonizer, with forms of the colonizer, and, in some cases, in the tradition of the colonizer, having gone to colonial schools and learned the imperial power's customs. So the breaks and rearticulations of postcolonial identity are never simple or unproblematic.

Working Question

In *Decolonising the Mind,* the Kenyan writer and activist Ngũgĩ Wa Thiong'o describes the difficulty formerly colonized peoples face in their struggle to establish independence in the following terms:

> The oppressed and the exploited of the earth maintain their defiance: liberty from theft. But the biggest weapon wielded and actually daily unleashed by imperialism against that collective defiance is the cultural bomb. The effect of a cultural bomb is to annihilate a people's belief in their names, in their languages, in their environment, in their heritage of struggle, in their unity, in their capacities and ultimately in themselves. It makes them see their past as one wasteland of nonachievement and it makes them want to distance themselves from that wasteland. It makes them want to identify with that which is furthest removed from themselves; for instance, with other people's languages rather than their own. It makes them identify with that which is decadent and reactionary, all those forces which would stop their own springs of life. It even plants serious doubts about the moral rightness of struggle. Possibilities of triumph or victory are seen as remote, ridiculous dreams. The intended results are despair, despondency, and a collective death-wish. Amidst this wasteland which it has created, imperialism presents itself as the cure and demands that the dependent sing hymns of praise with the constant refrain: "Theft is holy". Indeed, this sums up the new creed of the neo-colonial bourgeoisie in many in "independent" African states. (3)

What is the "cultural bomb" to which the author refers? How does it work?

Many critics locate Shakespeare's *The Tempest* as the first literary work to deal seriously with European colonization, both from the perspective of the colonizer and, perhaps more important, from that of the colonized. Recall that in Shakespeare's historical moment, European colonization was just getting into full swing, with many strange and exciting discoveries making their way from far-off colonies back to Shakespeare's England. *The Tempest* (first performed in 1611) is very much an attempt to capture the *wonder* of those encounters with new people and new lands; but, at the same time, Shakespeare also calls our attention to the power relations that necessarily accompany such a colonialist movement.

One of the characters in the drama, Caliban, already lived on the island when Prospero (a sorcerer of sorts and the play's main character) arrives to colonize it. Caliban's famous speech marks the problems inherent in Prospero's colonization of the island:

> This island's mine by Sycorax my mother,
> Which thou tak'st from me. . . .
> I lov'd thee
> And show'd thee all the qualities o' th' isle,
> The fresh springs, brine-pits, barren place and fertile.
> Curs'd be I that did so! . . .
> For I am all the subjects that you have,
> Which first was mine own king. (1.2.331–41)

Here Caliban articulates the perspective of the colonized, representing all those who welcomed colonial Europeans, generously showing them "all the qualities" of their lands, only to have their lands overtaken by the same Europeans. The European colonizer, as Caliban notes, becomes "king," making the indigenous peoples his "subjects."

Prospero, of course, has a very different take on the situation. As far as he's concerned, there was nothing even resembling civilization on the island when he arrived; and, in fact, he feels that he has offered a fabulous gift to Caliban: European knowledge, skill, and culture. As Miranda, Prospero's daughter, says to Caliban, "I pitied thee/Took pains to make thee speak, taught thee each hour/One thing or other" (1.2.353–55). What she and Prospero get for their efforts, however, is summed up in Caliban's response: "You taught me language, and my profit on't/Is, I know how to curse" (1.2.363–64). Caliban doesn't *want* to be a European; he doesn't share their high estimation of their culture and language, and learns it only to "curse" those who have taken his home away from him.

Reading through this Calibanic perspective—through the eyes of the colonized "other"—is one way to mobilize and highlight the relevance of "postcolonialism." Indeed, this Calibanic perspective begins to answer the question of postcolonialism's relevance to literature, by pointing out the power of art in *responding* to colonization, in *forming* a new identity out of the old materials. The example of Caliban also teaches us that the very notion of culture or high culture is based on a distinction that we don't often acknowledge: In its modern manifestations, high culture is defined in relation to a primitive or low culture. Culture's opposite—barbarity or primitiveness—is carried along, however silently, in any definition of culture, just as any definition of a "man" presupposes certain things about its supposed other, "woman."

This, perhaps, is the most obvious set of links among the various "posts": All take the baseline of a cultural form (*Unforgiven* plays off the conventions of the Western; poststructuralism reworks the practices of structuralism), and each show the ways in which cultural discourses (modernism, structuralism, colonialism) are much more multiple, much more dangerous, and read or reworked in a certain way, much more liberating than they seem at first.

Indeed, much of the project of European colonization was carried on as a supposedly "civilizing" cultural mission. Consider, for example, German Enlightenment philosopher G. W. F. Hegel's thoughts on Africa in 1830:

The characteristic feature of negroes is that their consciousness has not yet reached an awareness of any substantial
objectivity—for example, of God or the law . . . . [The African]
is dominated by passion, and is nothing more than a savage. All
our observations of African man show him as living in a state
of savagery and barbarism. (*Lectures on World History*, 177)

Given this reading of Africans—Hegel goes on to argue that
they have no culture and no history—it's not surprising that some
argued *for* colonization as a civilizing mission. Such readings of
non-European cultures infantilizes them by interpreting whole populations as children in need of help and guidance, and reinforces,
as we've seen, the mythic superiority of Europe. Such cultural arguments were also widely deployed by less high-minded individuals,
who could care less about culture one way or the other. And many
saw the colonial system for what it was: a vast source of potential
wealth, regardless of the indigenous peoples and their cultures.

The discourse of postcolonialism highlights the fact that our
very definitions of culture, civility, and artistic achievement, as well
as notions such as political autonomy, economic development, and
modern progress, are firmly rooted in the history of colonialism and
its attendant images of savagery, backwardness, despotism, and
underdevelopment. The postcolonial moment, then, is one of constant redefinition of both "politics" and "culture" in a rapidly globalizing world. In this context, to be sure, culture comes from Bogota,
Nairobi, and Beijing just as surely as it comes from Paris, New York,
and London.

At the same time, we should note that the mechanisms for the
production and circulation of cultural images and texts worldwide
is hardly equal. Nor is access to those images, as many so-called
developing regions do not have electricity or clean drinking water,
and only 6 percent of the world's population is hardwired to the
Web. In fact, as of 1999, only about 20 percent of the world's population had regular access to a phone. As in the bad old days of

colonialism, this kind of symbolic inequality parallels and reinforces other kinds of inequality. The extreme unevenness of the
world's media and telecommunications operations finds its corollary in the growing inequality in the global distribution of wealth
and material resources, which seems to divide the world in ways
astoundingly similar to the era of colonialism. This state of affairs
raises many questions about the degree to which we are really living in a *post*colonial (as opposed to a *neo*colonial) world and the
degree to which the euphoric discourse of globalization is significantly different from, rather than an extension of, a centuries-old
colonial project.

Working Question

Figures 9.3 and 9.4 are stills taken from two Hollywood blockbusters: *Lawrence of Arabia* and *Raiders of the Lost Ark*. What do
these stills, spanning twenty years of representations of "Arabia,"
suggest about Arab identity as compared to its Western European
or American counterpart? How do representations of "the Arab"
change over time? How are men and women from the Middle East
currently represented in Hollywood film? Are there elements of this
constructed identity that stay the same? How are these representations both reflective of and legitimation for the political, cultural,
and economic contexts out of which they emerge?

For Further Reading

Postmodernism

Baudrillard, Jean. *America*. New York: Verson, 1989.
———. *Simulacra and Simulation*. Ann Arbor: University of Michigan
    Press, 1994.

Figure 9.3 Courtesy Photofest

Figure 9.4 Courtesy Photofest

Bauman, Zygmunt. *Postmodern Ethics.* Oxford: Blackwell, 1993.

Berman, Marshall. *All That's Solid Melts into Air: The Experience of Modernity.* New York: Penguin, 1988.

Foster, Hal, ed. *The Anti-Aesthetic: Essays on Postmodern Culture.* Port Townsend, WA: Bay Press, 1983.

Giddens, Anthony. *Modernity and Self-Identity: Self and Society in the Late Modern Age.* Cambridge, UK: Polity Press, 1991.

Harvey, David. *The Conditions of Postmodernity: An Enquiry into the Origins of Social Change.* Oxford: Blackwell, 1989.

Hassan, Ihab. *The Postmodern Turn.* Columbus: Ohio State University Press, 1987.

Jameson, Fredric. *Postmodernism, or the Cultural Logic of Late Capitalism.* Durham, NC: Duke University Press, 1991.

Jencks, Charles. *What Is Post-Modernism?* Rev. ed. 4th ed. London: Academy Editions, 1996.

Kellner, Douglas, and Steven Best. *The Postmodern Adventure: Science, Technology, and Cultural Studies at the Third Millennium.* New York: Guilford, 2001.

———. *Postmodern Theory: Critical Interrogations.* New York: Guilford, 1991.

———. *The Postmodern Turn.* New York: Guilford, 1997.

Lyotard, Jean-François. *The Postmodern Condition: A Report on Knowledge,* translated by Geoff Bennington and Brian Massumi. Minneapolis: University of Minnesota Press, 1984.

Nealon, Jeffrey T. *Alterity Politics: Ethics and Performative Subjectivity.* Durham, NC: Duke University Press, 1998.

———. *Double Reading: Postmodernism after Deconstruction.* Ithaca, NY: Cornell University Press, 1993.

Nicholson, Linda, ed. *Feminism and Postmodernism.* New York: Routledge, 1990.

Rorty, Richard. *Philosophy and the Mirror of Nature.* Princeton, NJ: Princeton University Press, 1981.

Rose, Tricia. *Black Noise.* Middletown, CT: Wesleyan University Press, 1994.

Poststructuralism

Critchley, Simon. *The Ethics of Deconstruction: Derrida and Levinas.* West Lafayette, IN: Purdue University Press, 1999.

Culler, Jonathan. *On Deconstruction: Theory and Criticism after Structuralism.* Ithaca, NY: Cornell University Press, 1982.

de Man, Paul. *The Resistance to Theory.* Minneapolis: University of Minnesota Press, 1986.

Deleuze, Gilles, and Felix Guattari. *Anti-Oedipus: Capitalism and Schizophrenia.* Minneapolis: University of Minnesota Press, 1983.

———. *A Thousand Plateaus: Capitalism and Schizophrenia.* Minneapolis: University of Minnesota Press, 1987.

Derrida, Jacques. *Margins of Philosophy,* translated by Alan Bass. Chicago: University of Chicago Press, 1982 (1972).

———. *Of Grammatology,* translated by Gayatri Chakravorty Spivak. Baltimore: Johns Hopkins University Press, 1976 (1967).

———. "Structure, Sign and Play." In *Writing and Difference,* translated by Alan Burns. Chicago: University of Chicago Press, 1978 (1967).

LaClau, Ernesto, and Chantal Mouffe. *Hegemony and Socialist Strategy: Toward a Radical Democratic Politics,* translated by Winston Moore and Paul Cammack. London: Verso, 1985.

Levi-Strauss, Claude. *The Raw and the Cooked,* translated by John and Doreen Weightman. Chicago: University of Chicago Press, 1983 (1969).

———. *Structuralist Anthropology,* translated by Monique Layton. Chicago: University of Chicago Press, 1983 (1976).

Payne, Michael. *Reading Theory: An Introduction to Lacan, Derrida, and Kristeva.* Oxford: Blackwell, 1993.

Saussure, Ferdinand de. *Course in General Linguistics,* translated by Wade Baskin. New York: McGraw-Hill, 1959.

Scholes, Robert. *Structuralism in Literature.* New Haven, CT: Yale University Press, 1974.

Sedgwick, Eve Kosofsy. *Epistemology of the Closet.* Berkeley: University of California Press, 1992.

Postcolonialism

Bhabha, Homi. *The Location of Culture.* New York: Routledge, 1994.

Cabral, Amilcar. *Unity and Struggle: Speeches and Writings,* translated by Michael Wolfers. New York: Monthly Review Press, 1981.

Cesaire, Aime. *Discourse on Colonialism.* New York: New York University Press, 2000.

Emerson, Ralph Waldo. *Selected Essays,* edited by Larzer Ziff. New York: Penguin, 1982.

Fanon, Frantz. *Black Skin/White Masks,* translated by Charles Lam Markmann. Grove Press, 1967.

———. *The Wretched of the Earth,* translated by Constance Farrington. Grove Press, 1965.

Hegel, Georg Wilhelm Friedrich. *Lectures on the Philosophy of World History,* translated by Hugh Barr Nisbet. Cambridge: Cambridge University Press, 1981.

James, C. L. R. *The Black Jacobins: Toussant L'Ouverture and the San Domingo Revolution.* 2d ed. rev. New York: Vintage, 1989 (1963).

Memmi, Albert. *The Colonizer and the Colonized.* Boston: Beacon, 1991.

Mohanty, Chandra Talpade. *Feminism without Borders: Decolonizing Theory, Practicing Solidarity.* Durham, NC: Duke University Press, 2003.

Mohanty, Chandra Talpade, ed. *Third World Women and the Politics of Feminism.* Bloomington: University of Indiana Press, 1993.

Poe, Edgar Allan. *Great Short Works of Edgar Allan Poe,* edited by G. R. Thompson. New York: Harper & Row, 1970.

Said, Edward. *Culture and Imperialism.* New York: Vintage, 1994.

———. *Orientalism.* New York: Random, 1979.

Spivak, Gayatri Chakravorty. *In Other Worlds: Essays in Cultural Politics.* New York: Methuen, 1987.

———. *The Post-Colonial Critic: Interviews, Strategies, Dialogues.* New York: Routledge, 1990.

Thiong'o, Ngũgĩ Wa. *Decolonising the Mind: The Politics of Language in African Literature.* London: Heinemann, 1990.

————. *Moving the Centre: The Struggle for Cultural Freedoms.* London: Heinemann, 1993.

Viswanathan, Guari. "Currying Favor: The Politics of British Educational and Cultural Policy in India, 1813–1854." *Social Text* 19/20 (Fall 1988): 85–104.

Notes

1. Structuralism does *not*, however, see that underlying consensus as ideological in the sense of being "false." On the whole, structuralists are more interested in exposing or *understanding* these underlying conditions than they are in doing an ideological *critique* of them. This critique, perhaps, is the work of *post*structuralism.

2. In this sense, it's not surprising that structuralism is most important in discourses like literary criticism and anthropology, both of which are interested in the meaning of a seemingly foreign and complex symbol system.

10

Differences

Perhaps it's best to begin this chapter with a series of questions. Does the race, gender, ethnicity, class, or sexual preference of a cultural producer like an author, a filmmaker, or an artist, or that of the reader as subject, make any *difference* in the interpretation of mass media, history, or literature? Do the categories of sexual, racial, economic, and ethnic difference make a difference in our reading and writing of the world? Among the many contexts that are important in producing meaning, are these contexts important or privileged ones? In sizing up the meaning of a context, are the differences between and among contexts just as important (or perhaps even *more* important) than the similarities? Is it important to attend to the respective "subject positions" of the cultural producers and readers as well as the actors or characters who animate social and cultural texts?

At first blush, we'd most naturally answer, "Well, sure, these things make a difference." As we've already discussed, history written from the viewpoint of the privileged reads differently than that written "from below." A film directed by a poor white lesbian will, it seems, read substantially differently than one written by a wealthy heterosexual Asian man. It only makes sense that it would. And our own reading and writing experiences clue us into the fact that we tend to identify with certain kinds of characters and certain kinds of situations depending on the investments we have as sexual, racial, economic, and gendered subjects.

For example, there are plenty of cultural phenomena that appeal quite directly to our investments in our own identity positions (or our curiosity about others' subjectivity); so there are "chick movies" and "guy movies," "queer" performances, "new black cinema" from directors like Spike Lee and the Hughes brothers (*Menace II Society*), working-class Scottish fiction like that by Irvine Welsh, unabashedly "poor white trash" American fiction like that by Dorothy Allison or Harry Crews, as well as ethnic restaurants, sports clubs (rugby, soccer, cricket), churches, and synagogues.

And, whether we realize it or not, we negotiate and account for these differences all the time. With or without a lot of high-minded rhetoric about "investments" in gender and sexual identity, you know that you shouldn't dial up a Lifetime movie on cable for entertainment when your dad's coming home from his Marine Corps drill sergeant assignment in Guam; and whether or not you think in terms of racial and economic "subject positions," you probably don't play gangsta rap or death metal when Mr. Bland, your classical harpsichord instructor, drops by for tea.

Clearly these racial, sexual, and economic differences make a difference in the ways we think, act, and interpret; as we noted long ago in chapter 2, it seems crucial to know that Marc Chagall was a Russian-born Frenchman, poor and Jewish, while Frida Kahlo was female, disabled, Mexican, and a socialist; Ludwig van Beethoven had a severe hearing disorder and became deaf in his thirties; Wolfgang

Amadeus Mozart was a child prodigy, mastering his first musical composition at age four in the space of half an hour; Toni Morrison, African-American and female, was an editor at Random House for twenty years prior to her literary successes; and Joseph Conrad was originally a seaman and emigré from Poland. But is it crucial to know, we might wonder, that Henry James was wealthy, while Melville died dirt poor? And that both James and Melville may have been what we now call "gay"? That Spike Lee comes from a black middle-class family, while the Hughes brothers come from black working-class backgrounds? That the Beatles and David Bowie come from England, whereas Van Morrison and U2 hail from Ireland?

Indeed, once we know these things, what *difference* do they (or *should* they) make in our interpretations? For example, do we go hunting for the biases of rich white men in James's fiction? And even if we find such biases, are we compelled to give him a break because he may have been a closeted gay man? Are we to read *all* of Melville's fiction through the lens of his subject position as "poor" and possibly "gay"? Does all of Chagall's work amount to a dense commentary on being Jewish? For that matter, does Spike Lee's work finally reduce to an extended commentary on "blackness" and/or "maleness"?

And what about the subject positions of the reader? If the reader is an important cog in the machine of meaning (one important context among several), does the reader's class, ethnicity, race, gender, and sexual preference need to be factored into his or her reading? Indeed, can a straight white male banker from London even read or understand the poems of a poor lesbian from Haiti? Is any identification possible from such disparate subject positions?

❖ Working Question

We think it's safe to assume that there are relatively few Rastafarians in our classes, but we're also willing to bet that there are a large number of you who have heard and enjoyed the music and poetry of Bob Marley and other reggae musicians from Jamaica.

How has reggae, a singular (and essentially *religious*) art form very specific to a small Caribbean island, become so popular and been so influential for other musical traditions: English punk (especially the Clash) and ska, American rap and jazz? Indeed, it seems that lots of people who know nothing about Jamaica or Coptic religious traditions somehow *identify* with reggae. How or why is that, do you think? And what, if anything, does such an identification suggest about reading and writing across ethnic, racial, gender, and class lines?

Clearly, while an attention to differences is crucial and necessary in determining meanings, in the end it seems that these differences are no more "essential" than the meaning that is produced in contextual interactions between readers and the cultural texts and practices they read. Just as there is no natural or simply authentic authorial or reading "self" who is finding meaning through reading or writing, there is likewise no natural or authentic "African-American" self, or "lesbian" self, or "working-class" self. These are *subject* positions in the sense that we outlined when talking about "subjectivity"; they are social categories of recognition that define us within a certain social *context.*

For example, preferring to perform certain acts with certain people (sexual preference) is no more *inherently* meaningful than having a certain skin color or having a great deal of money. Although they are incredibly important to our everyday lives, these states of sexual preference, ethnicity, and class are nevertheless *not* inherently or "naturally" meaningful; having brown skin does not inherently mean anything. But, as Frederick Douglass made clear, having brown skin in the American South in the 1840s certainly did carry very specific—and very deadly—significations. Likewise, the fact that certain adults prefer certain sexual acts or partnerships with other consenting adults is neither inherently "good" nor inherently "deviant." But, of course, in the context of contemporary

American political debate, homosexuality is consistently coded as "deviant" and remains technically outlawed—through "sodomy laws"—in many states. Although it seems impossible, in December 1998 two gay men were arrested in Texas for having sex in the bedroom of their own house. In fact, it wasn't until early 2003 that the Georgia legislature repealed its laws against consensual sex between unmarried adults, straight or gay. Recent passage of gay marriage laws may have changed some of this terrain, but the topic still remains hotly debated and contested in most of the United States.

As we stressed in talking about reading, we can't simply reduce the difference of the text to our opinions: Texts don't simply mean what we want them to mean. We must, rather, negotiate among contexts to produce meaning. The text and its context may be foreign to us (we may, for example, know close to nothing about Renaissance England and Shakespeare), but that doesn't mean the text is completely inexplicable. It does, however, mean that we have to engage it with some care and attention to its difference.

Like the contextual differences between readers and the texts, the differences among people (in terms of class, race, gender, ethnicity, sexual preference, able-bodiedness, age, weight, etc.) are not absolute either. As long as they share a common language, of course a rich black man can read and engage the texts of a poor white woman. Certainly they don't share the same field of experience, but, when you think about it, none of us does. There is after all a great deal of *difference* even among people who seem technically to fit within the same category or "subject position"; contrary to popular belief, not all people of African descent think the same way, nor do all straight white males.

At the same time, however, we need to pay attention to the differences within and among subject positions. Joseph Conrad, for example, was a white man writing in the late nineteenth and early twentieth centuries, but this doesn't *necessarily* mean he was or wasn't a racist, sexist, or homophobe. At the same time, however, a reading of his novella *Heart of Darkness* that pays attention to race and gender will come up with some troubling questions. Obviously, the text presents on one level a devastating critique of colonialism; Conrad had seen firsthand the stealing of land from people who are "different" and the naked greed that fuels the colonial enterprise, and he was determined to expose that colonial "darkness."

Keeping Conrad's intentions in mind, we'd nevertheless have to ask, how does *the text* play out or present the complexities of race (and, we might add, gender) within its critique of colonialism? Doesn't *Heart of Darkness*, despite Conrad's good intentions, present Africans as subhuman "nature-men," living in an evolutionary "blank space" of savage darkness? Is there a certain kind of racism present in the depiction of Africans as living in a state of nature? Likewise, in its (scant) presentation of women, we might note that *Heart of Darkness* presents a rather condescending picture. If Africans simply represent "nature," does Kurtz's fiancee—"the Intended"—similarly come to represent feminine "culture," which has to be condescendingly protected from the "darkness" of savagery?

Many people, of course, find such questions to be completely irrelevant to *Heart of Darkness*. Great art, they argue, should not simply be fodder for fashionable contemporary debates. And clearly it would be scandalously inadequate simply to dismiss Conrad out of hand as a racist or sexist. Just as certainly, however, the text brings up these questions of race and gender, and it seems that it would be condescending to Conrad not to follow the leads that the text gives us, not to ask *Heart of Darkness* the very same tough critical questions that it poses to the colonialist enterprise. The point, in other words, is not to *dismiss* Conrad or smugly celebrate our own enlightened understandings of gender and race but rather to add complexity to our understandings of the past and the present. While these concerns are certainly not the last word in interpretation, they shouldn't simply be ignored when they are present in a text.

In the end, attention to differences is what interpretation is all about. Interpreting texts in the broadest sense—whether we're talking about Pablo Picasso's *Guernica*, Francis Ford Coppola's

Apocalypse Now, Tupac Shakur's *T.H.U.G. L.I.F.E.,* CNN's coverage of the most recent events in the Middle East, a new ad campaign by Nike, the U.S. Supreme Court, or the president's latest economic stimulus plan—is not an attempt to *erase* difference (to come to a final meaning). Rather such attention is an attempt to highlight the complexities that the social world puts before us—as we work to understand and respond to events, practices, beliefs, institutions, and various cultural artifacts. Interpretation is perhaps best understood as a *response,* and certainly that response should be aware of the contexts—the race, gender, class positions—at play for the cultural producers and consumers within their respective social spaces. Such an awareness is not honed in the service of *judging* the text or dissing a group of dead white males ("This is sexist, so we don't have to read it!"); rather, attention to differences highlights the negotiation of contextual differences that is interpretation itself.

❖ Working Question

Do you feel inundated by "politically correct" rhetoric in your classes? Is political correctness all that attention to "differences" finally wants? Does anyone feel that this attention to "difference" has gone too far? Not far enough?

A critic recently wrote about such attention to differences in the context of literary study: "The fundamental, if only implied, message of [such] literary criticism is self-righteous, and it takes this form: 'T.S. Eliot is a homophobe and I am not. Therefore, I am a better person than Eliot. Imitate me, not Eliot'" (Frank Lentricchia, "Last Will and Testament of an Ex-Literary Critic," *Lingua Franca* [September/October 1996]: 60). Is this what attention to different "subject positions" necessarily boils down to: a smug celebration of the contemporary self, who has smoked out the racism, sexism, and homophobia of the past?

Gender

Gender theory has become a central mode of critical inquiry in a number of fields across the humanities and social sciences, raising critical questions about the social construction of masculinity and femininity, their ascribed social functions and forms of resistance, masculine domination, the politics of desire and the body, among other concerns in such disciplines as diverse as art, film, philosophy, geography, psychoanalysis, history, anthropology, and sociology. In literary theory, for example, gender criticism has its roots most specifically in debates over the literary canon. If you were awake at all in high school English class, you probably remember your teacher prattling on about the "universal" qualities of "great" literature. For example, Shakespeare's *Hamlet,* or so they say, embodies universal values and difficulties; the play dramatizes Hamlet's difficulties with decision ("to be or not to be"), valor (revenge for his father's death), family (his mother's remarriage to his father's rival), and the past (his father's ghost). According to the durable truism, these are universal themes that we can all relate to, even four hundred years later.

A gender theorist, however, might hesitate before the category of "universal" experience in the play. On further review, it seems that many of Hamlet's "universal" problems are rather suspiciously "male"; much of the play wouldn't make any sense, in its historical context anyway, if he were a woman. And certainly his rather abusive relationships with his girlfriend and his mother suggest a certain obvious hyper-masculinity—to say nothing of the play's central question (revenge) and its specifically male relation to the father in the play. Recall what are no doubt the most famous lines from *Hamlet:*

> To be or not to be: that is the question.
> Whether 'tis nobler in the mind to suffer

> The slings and arrows of outrageous fortune,
> Or take arms against a sea of troubles,
> And by opposing end them? To die: to sleep; . . .
> For who would bear the whips and scorns of time,
> The oppressor's wrong, the proud man's contumely,
> The pangs of dispriz'd love, the law's delay,
> The insolence of office, and the spurns
> That patient merit of the unworthy takes,
> When he himself might his quietus make
> With a bare bodkin? (3.1)

This speech, often pointed to as dealing with the "universal" theme of self-determination versus fate, seems on further examination to cast a pretty determinedly male eye on this question, and a fairly adolescent version of masculinity at that. The "question" posed here seems to go something like this: Is it "nobler" to "suffer" through the contingencies of life—the changes of time, the wrongs others do, the injuries to your pride, the difficulties of desire—or is it "nobler" to kill yourself "with a bare bodkin"? If I can't be completely in control of my circumstances, I'm outta here.[1] Let's just say that if this really were an accurate representation of a "universal" theme of "nobility," then the streets would be littered with corpses suffering from self-inflicted bodkin wounds.

From the perspective of gender theory, *Hamlet* begins to seem more like what Nina Baym calls a "melodrama of beset manhood" than a "universal" tragedy. And critic Judith Fetterley makes similar points about much "great" American literature. Classics from *Moby-Dick* through *The Adventures of Huckleberry Finn* up to *Catch-22* and *Gravity's Rainbow* all seem predicated on the conflation of universal experience with male experience: escaping to the frontier, going on the hunt, going off to war. And gender criticism might be said to get off the ground with the simple observation that the supposedly "universal" subject has a very specific gender: masculine.

✦ Working Question

Is it merely coincidence that when the recent "100 Best Novels of the Twentieth Century" were named by Random House's Modern Library series, only nine were written by women (who constitute 52 percent of the present world population, more at other times in the twentieth century)? The top book by a woman, Virginia Woolf's *To the Lighthouse*, came in at 15, aced out by such timeless classics as Samuel Butler's *The Way of All Flesh* (12) and Robert Graves's PBS-friendly *I, Claudius* (14).

Are the themes of "great" literature—the individual versus society, man versus nature, war, valor, etc.—somehow already "male" values? What difference does it make if they are or aren't?

In everyday circumstances, it seems that gender is a highly visible marker. One of the first distinctions you make when you meet someone, almost unconsciously, is whether he or she is a he or a she. But although gender is a pervasive difference in everyday life, there are surprising ways in which we *don't* notice it or don't pay proper attention to it. Certainly the questionable "universality" of *Hamlet* makes this point clear. To take a more pressing example of this same point, researchers into AIDS treatments have only recently realized a stunningly simple truth: that AIDS drugs, initially tested exclusively on men, do not work in the same ways and with the same effectiveness in women. It seems that it did not occur to researchers to factor in gender as one of the variables in testing new drugs—perhaps insofar as gender seems so *in*variable, so essential, everywhere and nowhere at the same time.

Indeed, there's a way in which this theoretical point is merely the logical upshot of a much more stunning and simple series of political points made by women's rights movements throughout the nineteenth and twentieth centuries. Women were denied the right to vote or own land on precisely this ground: The universal subject is the male subject. Of course, in the wake of the conclusion that there is no "universal" subject, one often finds substituted the equally durable cliché that "men and women are different." This seems clearly to be a fact, and one that demands a certain attention; it's important not to *forget* or *ignore* differences. But where you go from there remains a little unclear. Is there, we might ask, *a* difference between men and women, some sort of essential split, or are there *a series of* differences? Are these differences something to be mourned as an impossible bridge to cross ("they just don't get it"), or is gender difference in some senses a *good* thing? And where do these differences come from, anyway? Is the question of gender in the workplace somehow equivalent to the role of gender in the family, or the roles of gender in popular entertainment or in the military? Or is gender difference the same, no matter what the context?

Indeed, as theorists in the sense we've been developing here, wouldn't we have to be suspicious of the "fact" that there finally are only two genders? In almost any other context, you know you're talking to a fool when someone begins a discussion by saying, "there are two kinds of people in the world." But for some reason, we're perfectly willing to *believe* this when it comes to gender.

Perhaps this series of questions brings us back to the question of "essential" difference versus "culturally constructed" differences. The reason we're perfectly willing to accept that there are two and only two genders is because we tend to understand the difference between men and women as an *essential* difference. It seems, contra this book's suspicions, that if we're looking at sexual difference, we're looking at a "natural" difference: It's simply there, not constructed by a society.

And gender difference is a clearly *material* difference, not an airy ideological abstraction. Men have certain reproductive equipment, and women have different equipment (like the "male" and "female" hookups of a computer). And while gender or sexual difference has obvious cultural effects and manifestations, it seems difficult to argue that it's *not* a bedrock, "essential" difference. It's the biological roles set out in reproduction—the fact that the woman bears the child, and that the man cannot—that seems to make sexual difference an essential difference.

From this seemingly essential difference, many ideological implications follow. If this essential difference is biologically or naturally mandated, then it would seem to be common sense that women are naturally more fragile, more nurturing, weaker, passive, the stay-at-home type, whereas men would then seem naturally cut out to do the hunting and gathering and beer drinking and watching the Three Stooges on TV.

Of course, it is precisely because essentialism is translated into practice in this way—that biology is used as a warrant for the strict determination and limitation of social roles—that a gender critic would want to fight or question it. Biology has, from the get-go, had very specific cultural implications; "natural" roles in reproduction seem clearly to warrant certain similar roles in civic life. But, we might ask, how does "biology" become some kind of mystified bedrock? Isn't biology just as culturally constructed a discourse as psychology or sociology? Sure, there are differences among those beings we call men and women, but the differences themselves don't *contain* a specific meaning. Sure, men and women are different, but so are sofas and rocking chairs, and we don't tend to think of them as "essentially" different.

As theorist Judith Butler asks about the seeming naturalness of sexual difference,

> And what is "sex" anyway? Is it natural, anatomical, chromosomal, or hormonal, and how is a feminist critic to access the scientific discourses which purport to establish such "facts" for us? Does sex have a history? Does each sex have a different history or histories? Is there a history of how the duality of sex was established . . . [?] Are the ostensibly natural facts of sex discursively produced by various scientific discourses in the service of other political and social interests? (*Gender Trouble*, 6–7)

As Butler suggests, to say that gender difference is constructed in this way is similar to the claims made in this book about subjectivity or history: It's not that bodies don't exist, or that things don't happen; nor is it the case that history or subjectivity or sexuality can be arranged or rearranged any old way you want. Rather, "social construction" forces us to confront that the materiality of difference (x is different from y) doesn't determine what the difference means. Things don't already contain meanings; rather, such meanings are constructed in the very configuration of the seeming "fact" of difference.

The discourses that construct or mark difference also tend to tell us what those differences mean. For example, people are not born criminals, so the discourse of law obviously constructs the difference between criminals and law-abiding citizens (a criminal is nothing other than a person who has performed certain forbidden acts); the very construction of any difference (man/woman, criminal/citizen, normal/abnormal) also goes a long way toward telling us what that difference means. The difference between criminal and law-abiding citizen doesn't exist before the distinction is in fact made; there is no essential or natural difference of this kind. The difference only functions, only means something, in a particular context, one that's both configured and made meaningful by the discourses of criminality. It's only in the context of certain places or certain acts that one knows who the "criminal" is: Nelson Mandela was a criminal in South Africa for decades, then he became president. Same man, same acts, different context.

In other words, this point about gender construction is a subset of the point that this text has been making all along: Difference is all over the place; but precisely because of this fact, *what* something means (or even what it *is*) in a particular context is always going to be beholden to a *process* of disentanglement. In terms of gender differences, the simple fact of difference is too quickly translated back into an essentialism: Men are "like this," women are "like that." But it is in this way that gender difference is *constructed*. The fact that difference is there seems incontrovertible, but what that difference *means* is different in different contexts. If Army brass decides that women aren't fit for combat, for example, then they're not. Case closed. Recall again, however, that we don't get to choose what those contexts are, or what gender means in society at large. As Butler insists, it "is not a matter of choosing which gender one will be today" (*Gender Trouble*, 22), but of responding to already existing categories by disentangling them from determining notions of essence.

◈ Working Question

Study the following images by artist Barbara Kruger (figures 10.1, 10.2, and 10.3). What do they communicate about gendered identities? How are the seemingly objective discourses of science and history bound up with masculinity? Is Kruger challenging all males or certain norms that cluster around the sign of masculinity—what would be the difference?

Queer

So-called queer theory is very much related to the tactics and insights of gender theory: If gender theory demonstrates the disentanglement of "gender" from an essentialist notion of "sex" (and vice versa), queer theory demonstrates a similar disentanglement of sex acts from gender identity. If the primary insight of gender theory is, in Butler's words, that "gender does not follow from sex" (*Gender Trouble*, 17) (i.e., cultural categories do not simply follow along after supposedly natural laws), then the primary insight of queer theory might be the related argument that "sexuality is not an essentially personal attribute but an available cultural category"

Figure 10.1 Barbara Kruger. Courtesy Mary Boone Gallery, New York

Figure 10.2 Barbara Kruger. Courtesy Mary Boone Gallery, New York

Figure 10.3 Barbara Kruger. Courtesy Mary Boone Gallery, New York

(Jagose, *Queer Theory,* 79). In other words, queer theory will consistently show that there is no "natural" relation between anatomical equipment and what that equipment is supposed to mean or do in a given context—between a biological notion of sex and a particular sex act.

"Queer," of course, is at some level another word for "gay or lesbian," themselves substitutes for the nineteenth-century word "homosexual." And the terminology is important. As Annamarie Jagose recalls,

> The word "homosexuality"—coined in 1869 by a Swiss doctor, Karoly Maria Benkert—was not used widely in English until the 1890s, when it was adopted by the sexologist Havelock Ellis. It continues to have a certain currency, but, because of its unshakable association with the pathologizing discourses of medicine, it is seldom used nowadays as a term of self-identification. . . . In the 60s, liberationists made a strategic break with "homosexuality" by annexing the word

"gay," thus redeploying a nineteenth-century slang term which
had formerly described women of dubious morals. (*Queer
Theory*, 72)

The shift from "homosexual" to "gay" as a self-identifier is already
caught up in the denaturalization of sexuality. As Jagose continues,
"the popularity of the term 'gay' testifies to its potential as a non-
clinical descriptor unburdened by the pathologizing history of sex-
ology" (*Queer Theory*, 73).

Indeed, just as the man/woman essential split looks suspicious
to a gender theorist, the heterosexual/homosexual difference looks
equally so to a queer theorist. How do you get from the wide range
and variety of sex acts that people perform to the notion that there
are "two" sexualities? As Eve Kosofsky Sedgwick points out, there is
a dizzying array of things that people experience as "sexual"; the
same sexual act can mean very different things to different people.
For some people, sex is all about genital acts, while for others it's
more of a mind game, and may have little or nothing to do with
genitals; some people are very invested in sexuality as part of their
identity and spend a lot of time thinking about sex; others find it
inconsequential to their self-definition and spend little time thinking about it; some people can't have sex outside meaningful contexts of love, affection, marriage, etc.; others can't have sex inside
such contexts; for some, sex has to be spontaneous, while for others it has to be highly scripted, or has to be scripted in such a way
that it seems spontaneous.[2] In fact, we have former President Bill
Clinton and Monica Lewinsky to thank for making an obvious
point that's nevertheless very important to queer theory: Simply
put, people disagree quite widely on what constitutes "sex." It is, so
to speak, a slippery slope.

Obviously, this categorizing of what Gilles Deleuze calls "a
thousand tiny sexualities" could go on for a long time, but the point
of such a listing is to complicate what Sedgwick calls the
"axiomatic" understanding of sexuality, the reduction of myriad

kinds of sexualities and acts into two (maybe three) categories: homosexual or heterosexual (or bisexual). How, Sedgwick asks, does the gender (already a complicated notion, as we've seen) of your sexual object choice become the marker for the truth of your sexuality? Why is *that* the difference that makes all the difference? How does sex go from being about countless acts to being about two states of being?

Borrowing a term from linguistics, Sedgwick and Butler argue that gender and sexuality are "performative" discourses: They are all about acts and only secondarily about states of being. One is not born a man or woman or a homosexual; one becomes a man or woman or homosexual (becomes recognizable as such) only in the context of performing or not performing certain acts. Homosexual doesn't name a state of being; it names a being that performs certain acts, who's recognized and categorized by social categories rather than essential attributes. Or, to put it another way, the essential attributes of a person's identity are "backloaded," so to speak, from subjective actions; the "what" of sexuality or gender or race (what does it mean?) is always beholden to the "how" of sexuality, gender, or race (how does it work?). Subjective identity, as we've suggested all along, works from the outside in, rather than vice versa.

In the linguistic terms we reference above, any "constative" utterance (a speech act that desires merely to describe a fact or state a preexisting truism) is in fact already a "performative" utterance (one in which the statement "performs" the action it references). For example, "Hoboken is in New Jersey" is what one might call a "constative" speech act: It seems merely to restate a fact or describe a state of affairs that's already been proven to be true. In contrast, "I promise to pay you tomorrow" or the judge's "I now pronounce you man and wife" are distinctly "performative" speech acts, ones that require an *action* to be performed before they can be said to be "true" or "false." They actually bring about the state they claim to reference—marriage or the promise isn't something that exists already; the promise or the marriage is brought into being by the specific act of being married or promising. In a kind of shorthand, we might say that performative utterances are about *acts*, whereas constative utterances are about *facts*.

However, as we've seen time and again in this book, the status of facts is always and already beholden to certain acts, rather than vice versa. For example, the simple statement or simple fact that "Hoboken is in New Jersey" is already beholden to a number of prior "acts." The configuration known as "New Jersey," for example, is hardly a natural or essential entity; it's constituted by legislators, politicians, and mapmakers. A number of acts have had to happen to make any simple statement "true," and even a simple statement of truth is itself an act. Contrary to popular belief, saying something *is* doing something (hence the importance of "coming out" in the queer community). Truth, even the truth of one's sexuality, is beholden to acts, rather than vice versa. Who you are is an effect of what you do.

This is the primary insight of queer theory, and it has much in common with our previous chapters. In fact, this entire book has been suggesting that the categories of society and individuality are primarily *performative* ones, constructed in response to specific contexts.

Race

Race seems like yet another "natural" difference, but it becomes suspicious almost immediately upon reflection, for very good cultural, scientific, historical, and political reasons. A cursory look at its history reveals that the alleged "facts" of racial difference and racial hierarchy were grounded first in religious doctrine and then (as the hegemony of the Church waned in the increasingly secular world of the Enlightenment) in the discourse of science, where race was engaged initially through the study of language, then biology, and later genetics. At each turn, however, race remained an elusive and incoherent category. What religion could not fix or guarantee with

respect to racial difference, neither could biology, as it sought definitive answers in, for example, the measurement of skulls or intelli-
gence quotients. What, for example, constitutes a black man or
woman? This was an important legal question in the era of Jim
Crow, which each state addressed individually. Taken up as a function of "blood," some states argued that a person was black if he or
she had one-quarter black blood (i.e., a grandparent who was
black), others required one-eighth black blood, and still others
defined blackness according to the "one-drop rule." Of course, what
science now knows is that according to this last criterion, nearly all
residents of the United States would qualify as black. Nor did genetics make matters any less complicated when it was discovered that
there is often more genetic similarity between members of different racial or ethnic groups than among members of the same group.
In addition, race has been compared with or understood in terms
of "nation," "culture," "class," and "ethnicity" with a similar lack of
success. As a concept, "race" is both practically empty and too full.
Conceptually empty, race is able to chameleonically adapt itself to
a society's prevailing notions of truth, drawing legitimation from
them and changing as they change (Goldberg, *Racist Culture*, 61–89).

Rather than provide definite answers, however, the discourse of
race seems to open up myriad questions and contradictions, as it
shifts from a concept that explains all to one that requires explanation: Why can white women bear black children, but black women
cannot bear white children? How much blood do you have to have
to be of a particular race? What's the difference between race and
nationality—what does the marker "Irish" or "German" name, for
example? Are they races, or nationalities? Ethnicities? The Ku Klux
Klan hates Catholics, but is that because of their religion or because of
the national or ethnic groups that Catholicism often represents—
Poles, Slavs, Irish, Italians, Latinos? Exactly how does religion cut
across race and ethnicity? Jews, for example, are often thought of as
a "race," but Methodists seldom are. Race is clearly a structuring principle in American culture. In cities like Chicago, there is open talk

about "black" wards, "white" wards, and "Hispanic" wards; politicians seek the "black" or "Asian" vote; and school districts debate whether they should be "English Only," bilingual, or multilingual. Race is a ubiquitous feature of American social and political landscapes, and everyone seems to know what it means. Or do they?

Even pointing out the historicity of "race" flies in the face of our commonsense perception that race is a fixed, eternal, unchanging, and unchangeable fact of human nature. Making its first appearance in the English language about 1508, "race" is anything but natural and eternal. It is, on the contrary, quite profoundly social and political. What, for example, does it mean to be "Asian"? A brief look at how this term has been used in the United States reveals that it's a very slippery category indeed. As the *Chicago Tribune* reports:

> In 1978, the federal government redefined what it meant to be Asian. How? It simply drew a line on the globe. Beforehand, if one lived east of the line drawn between Bangladesh and Burma, one was Asian; if you lived west of that line, you were white, that is to say, Caucasian. Which meant that if you were from India, . . . even if your skin was black, you were white. And if you were northern Chinese, even if your skin was white, well, you weren't. Under the 1978 directive, the line is now drawn between Iran and Pakistan. So if you're Indian or Pakistani, well, you're now officially Asian. (November 29, 1998, 6)

So, if you're of Indian descent, your parents were likely "white" up until 1978, when they (and, subsequently, you) magically became "Asian." This is a very clear example of what we've been calling the "social construction" of race or gender or sexuality: The subject seemingly remains the same—same family, same descent, same skin tone, same sexual object—but what that subject position *means* is under constant re- and deconstruction. Which, again, does not mean you get to choose what race you want to be from: I'm feeling Caucasian today. What we're emphasizing is the *structural* point here: Race structures American society; it's not just added on after the fact by people who've decided it's a problem. Race is already there—it's already been there—through all the levels of American life. Like gender or sexual orientation or language itself, the fact that it's an arbitrary category doesn't mean that it's inconsequential or easily changed.

What the history of race reveals is that precisely because of its adaptive capacity—its power to constantly change as society changes—the concept of race remains a powerful and ongoing force in social life. Unfortunately, recognizing its constructedness neither explains nor challenges the persistence and depth of race thinking. Why does it remain such a powerful determinant in the distribution of social rewards and real life chances? Why is it such an overriding feature of identity, seemingly rendering all other dimensions of subjectivity irrelevant? Why is it that some racial categories are marked and others invisible; why, in other words, does the discourse of race signify "people of color" and not whiteness—as if white people aren't members of a racial or ethnic group? How has race affected the historic fate of nations?

People across the ideological spectrum continue to trade in fairly essentialized notions of race all the time. Some invoke it to underscore the correctness of a political position or the authenticity of a musical genre, while others make racialized claims about criminal predisposition or intellectual inferiority, even if the category itself remains a more or less vacuous and incoherent concept. Much more vivid, however, are the ways in which notions of race have been put in the service of the most sinister of historical outrages. Notions of sexuality or gender might seem innate and thereby benign—just the way things are—but the crimes that have been committed in the name or under the sign of race never seem so. From slavery to the Holocaust to ethnic cleansing, notions of race seem a bit easier to wrench from a "natural" context, or at least it becomes easier to see the deadly implications of a "natural" conception of race. American slavery was justified by employing such notions, as was the Nazi Final Solution; because Africans and Jews were said to be racially inferior, they could be treated accordingly by those who took themselves to be part of the master race. It's clear in these contexts that race is a highly ideological notion, a "fixed" or "naturalized" category constructed to foster nakedly political ends.

To make matters even more complicated, it seems that efforts to move "beyond race" are equally problematic and open to ideological manipulation. Recently, mainstream national rhetoric has championed "colorblindness" as a solution to the nation's history of uniquely tailored racial apartheid, fostering widespread debate about the meaning and significance of race. On the one hand, for example, politicians proclaim that the challenges of the civil rights movement in the United States have been successfully met, as the demand for racial equality and justice has been answered, at long last, by widespread adoption of "race neutral" or "race transcendent" public policy. On the other hand, as ACLU attorney Graham Boyd notes on the ACLU's website, the United States is

> incarcerating African-American men at a rate approximately four times the rate of incarceration of black men in South Africa under apartheid. Worse still, we have managed to replicate—at least on a statistical level—the shame of chattel slavery in this country: The number of black men in prison . . . has already equaled the number of men enslaved in 1820. . . . [And] if current trends continue, only 15 years remain before the United States incarcerates as many African-American men as were forced into chattel bondage at slavery's peak, in 1860. ("The Drug War Is the New Jim Crow," 2001: 1)

Such a stark contradiction underscores the ongoing political significance of race and the challenges posed by deeply antidemocratic policies that are clearly race-specific and yet are deployed under the banner of race-neutrality.

Class

The category of class, at first glance, seems very distinct from the "differences" we've identified so far, such as gender, sexuality, or race. First, it remains an open question what it is that class, as an index of social division, actually maps. Whereas we're pretty clear on what the concept of gender identifies, what class signifies remains rather murky. Is it simply a question of income? Occupation? Education? Or is it a condition more reflective of personal choice, a function of lifestyle, behavior, aesthetics, or taste, as when we describe certain individuals as having "real class" or "no class"? A college professor and a prison guard make about the same yearly income, for example, but the social distance between them is fairly staggering. How do we explain that? One analyst of the American class system, Paul Fussell, notes that how people define class reveals a great deal about their own class standing. "At the bottom, people tend to believe class is defined by the amount of money you have. In the middle, people grant that money has something to do with it, but think that education and the kind of work you do almost equally important. Nearer the top, people perceive that taste, values, ideas, style and behavior are indispensable criteria of class, regardless of money or occupation or education" (*Class*, 16).

Second, in spite of the definitional confusion, what seems to unite most Americans on the topic of class is a common belief in its fundamental irrelevance in what we tend to think of as a "classless" society. Mentioning class, in fact, often produces a lot of anxiety if not outright anger, especially in the realm of politics, where merely alluding to the concept is greeted with charges of "divisiveness," "class warfare," even "anti-Americanism." Whereas gender and ethnoracial distinctions are frequently foregrounded as crucial social (as opposed to biological) determinants, we seldom hear references to class differences, although they are just as readily accounted for and negotiated all the time. So why does class continue to lead such an underground existence? Part of the answer seems to be the fact of other, equally pervasive and strongly held ideologies: that U.S. society is fundamentally "egalitarian," "merito-cratic," and "fair." Under the presumption of "equal opportunity," for example, many people feel it is up to the individual to make it or break it in the "new economy." In the face of growing joblessness and downward mobility for many Americans, we often hear invo-cations of "personal responsibility" and "character" rather than calls for government intervention. At one level such rhetoric plays on the not unreasonable public fear and mistrust of government bureau-cracy and inefficiency, but it also hails, or interpellates, those who, like Ralph Waldo Emerson, champion "self-reliance" and rugged individualism as core values in American life. Even the most outra-geous examples of corporate malfeasance, such as we saw with Enron, WorldCom, and other multinationals in 2002, are often understood in terms of the personal greed and corruption of a few bad apples rather than structural components of a capitalist soci-ety that demand redress. It seems in the present era of deepening social inequality, individualism is a double-edged sword: Success bespeaks individual initiative, hard work, and perseverance, and fail-ure just as often translates into laziness, stupidity, ineptness, and moral turpitude. And this brings us to our third point.

Although we are born into a particular socioeconomic class just as surely as we're born with a gender and race, class seems a far more malleable condition than either gender or race. Unlike the concept of caste, which ascribes to subjects a fixed social position at birth, class recognizes that society is stratified, or divided into unequal groups, but people are free to start "movin' on up." Although there is a strong correlation between class origin and class destination, being born into a poor family doesn't necessarily guar-antee a life lived in poverty. Or so we tend to assume. The belief in class mobility is woven deeply into the fabric of American life. The American dream is founded on the presumption that "success" is just around the corner for those willing to put their noses to the grindstone—coupled, perhaps, with a little bit of luck.

A definitive characteristic of national identity, class denial shapes public consciousness and public memory. According to the chroniclers of conventional history, colonists came to the "New World" in search of a better life, one free of the feudal traditions and rigid class hierarchies associated with England and other European societies, as well as the repression and poverty of their rapidly industrializing urban centers. For the early settlers who forged a new nation, America represented a land of unlimited opportunity, with vast frontiers, ample natural resources, and a constitutional commitment to the rights of all people, regardless of birth or station, to life, liberty, and the pursuit of happiness. Although the Southern economy was based on chattel slavery, the impoverished conditions of many Northern cities rivaled those of Europe, and unpropertied young men were denied the right to vote until the Jacksonian era, the dominant perception of American heritage suggests that we are and have always been a stalwartly hard-working, middle-class people.

But just how much mobility actually is there? Contrary to popular belief, it's pretty difficult to ascend the social ladder, just as it's equally unlikely to fall from the top rungs. In a February 18, 2000, *New York Times* editorial, "America's Rags-to-Riches Myth," Michael Weinstein cited a University of Michigan study looking at the plight of poor children in recent decades. Separating children into five groups by family income, about six in ten children in the lowest group—the poorest 20 percent—in the early 1970s were still in the bottom income group in the early 1980s. Almost nine in ten children in the bottom group remained in the bottom two income groups ten years later. Further, the study indicates that neither of these figures had changed by the early 1990s, providing solid evidence that mobility in that twenty-year period was largely a myth. While mobility hasn't changed, what has sharply increased in the same twenty-year period is inequality: The rich have gotten much richer and the poor have gotten poorer—and the vaunted middle-class society seems to be disappearing altogether. Former counsel to the U. S. Senate Committee on Finance Jeff Gates notes that

- The financial wealth of the top 1 percent of households now exceeds the combined wealth of the bottom 95 percent.
- In the fifteen-year period between 1983 and 1997, only the top 5 percent of households saw an increase in their net worth, while wealth declined for everyone else.
- The wealth of the Forbes 400 richest Americans grew an average of $1.44 billion each from 1997 to 2000, an average daily increase in wealth of $1,920,000 per person ($240,000 per hour or 46,602 times the U.S. minimum wage).
- Executive pay at the nation's 365 largest companies rose an average of 481 percent from 1990 to 1998, while corporate profits rose 108 percent.
- The pay gap between top executives and production workers grew from 42:1 in 1980 to 419:1 in 1998 (excluding the value of stock options). ("Modern Fashion or Global Fascism," *Tikkun* [January/February 2002]: 30)

Inequality seems to widen by the day as a result of the restructuring of the nation's tax system in favor of the rich, the removal of restrictions on CEO pay, and the massive loss of blue-collar work with the advent of deindustrialization. Yet many Americans are still more likely to blame weaknesses in individual character than structural conditions to explain poverty and joblessness. Committed, as we've suggested, to equality of opportunity if not equality of outcome, many cite the role of schools as the "great levelers" of the economic playing field. But a cursory glance at the nation's public school system makes a mockery of this presumption. Mostly funded by local property taxes, as opposed to a national system of taxation as in every other industrialized country, America' schools are fundamentally unequal. Jonathan Kozol explains that

A typical wealthy suburb in which homes are often worth more than $400,000 draws upon a larger tax base in proportion to its student population than a city occupied by thousands of poor people. Typically, in the United States, very poor communities place high priority on education, and they often tax themselves at higher rates than do the very affluent communities. But even if they tax themselves at several times the rate of an extremely wealthy district, they are likely to end up with far less money for each child in their schools. (*Savage Inequalities*, 55)

In fact, poor districts wind up with as much as $5,000 less per child than their suburban counterparts. The upshot is that poor school districts do not have enough money for quality teachers, up-to-date textbooks, computers, or even a safe and healthy school infrastructure. According to the General Accounting Office, it would take $112 billion to bring the nations' public schools up to building code. Many schools in poor districts have been condemned by the local boards of health but remain open on emergency waivers because students simply have no place else to go. Not only does Kozol document vast inequalities in financial support, but public schools in the 1990s were more segregated than they were in the 1890s. And we see the same tiering at the postsecondary level, where a credential from an Ivy League school will open doors for its graduates in the Fortune 400 in the same way that a credential from Podunk U will likely qualify one to join the ranks of underpaid laborers in the service sector.

The persistence of class inequality in American life not only bespeaks differences in socioeconomic status, which define both people's access to goods and services, as well as their capacity to buy political influence. Class is also lived culturally. It significantly influences, if not determines, the kinds of social relationships we form and the social worlds we navigate. This is evident in the workplace, where one rarely finds industrial workers or mall clerks enjoying a "power lunch" at the Ritz-Carlton with corporate executives, lawyers, or doctors. Members of different socioeconomic groups live in different neighborhoods, attend different churches and increasingly different schools, and spend their leisure time in vastly different ways. The high cost of tickets to the opera, the symphony, or even the Mets puts such amusements out of reach for most folk, who can perhaps afford movie rentals from Blockbuster and an occasional visit to the pool hall or the bowling alley. Dietary habits are also likely to vary sharply, as are favored nightclubs or pubs, reading materials, places to shop, and participation in sports.

Considering these differences, it seems that what one might have taken as evidence of personal choice in the realm of taste, discrimination, values, and behavior looks more and more like a function of the material wealth and privilege that only certain groups enjoy. Not only do wealthier classes enjoy all the benefits of excess economic capital, but they also reap the rewards of what the renowned French sociologist Pierre Bourdieu called "cultural capital." Cultural capital—access to certain ways of speaking, certain cultural codes of behavior, taste, and discrimination—pays just as surely as economic capital. The corollary lack of cultural capital among poorer classes further reinforces inequality. A working-class student hoping to attend college, for example, faces a double disadvantage: Not only is she found wanting in terms of economic capital, but also of cultural capital. Unlike the middle-class student who likely hails from the same background as her teacher and thus shares a mutual understanding and set of expectations, a lower income student will not be able to "read" as well what the teacher wants or expects. Cultural capital determines who has "class" and who doesn't. This is not merely a question of taste, but one of social authority. It is no coincidence that one of the linguistic derivatives of class, "classic," confers authority on whatever it modifies.

Given the growing inequalities between the rich and the poor within the new global economy, it seems likely that an analysis of class differences will become more emphatic, as we take measure of the social costs of this ever-widening divide—what Bourdieu eloquently called "the weight of the world" we now live in.

❖ Working Questions

1. Pick up a copy of a men's or women's fashion magazine and look at the advertisements for "high end" merchandise like Gucci, Armani, Versace, or Prada. Compare these with ads for folks with a little less pocket change, like Old Navy, the Gap, or J. C. Penney. Clearly the two sets of ads hail different market niches. How do the ads differ aesthetically: how do they use space, color, imagery, text, etc.? How do they variously construct their audiences? What lifestyles, values, interests, and social roles do they assign them? How do gender roles differ across classes? Are classes configured racially? How?

2. What goals do you have in your life, and what means do you have to attain them? Where do these aspirations come from? Is there anything you consider "out of reach"? Why?

Concluding Differences

We can see a possible response shaping up to this rather esoteric discourse on "differences" (and of course the list of categories could go on and on: able-bodiedness, age, national origin, religion, etc.). Okay, we can hear the skeptical student say, this is interesting enough, but why does all this discussion of theory matter to everyday people living their lives? With some help, I can see how "ideology" or "subjectivity" relates to the study of various cultural texts: Music, poetry, and art are produced in a social context rife with ideologies, and the production of "subjects" seems to be a central theme of virtually all artistic production, both reading and writing. We learn a lot about who we are and who we want to be from cultural products. But if you're not queer or nonwhite, sexual orientation and race seem like somewhat marginal categories—not, the skeptical student might say, that there's anything *wrong* with inhabiting these subject positions, but race or disability or queerness hardly seem to be *central* questions in most people's lives. Nor it is clear that these categories are all that *central* to the study of those seemingly less social and more esoteric fields of the humanities.

Well, like most things that seem obvious, it's not entirely clear that this is really the case. Again, let's think about what the study of cultural texts entails. *Huckleberry Finn* may not be about race, gender, or sexuality, but if it's not, then what the hell is it about? Huck's companion is a slave, with whom he has a very close relationship; he does cross-dress in the book as well, and ends by lamming out of a feminized "sivilization" for the butch individuality of the frontier. So, while it's not essentially "about" these categories, *Huck Finn* is not essentially "about" metaphor or irony or friendship or anything else for that matter. Remember the primary lesson of our reading on "Reading": Meaning is beholden to context, and "differences" give us a wider array of contexts in which to explore culture in its myriad manifestations.

Indeed, these categories of subjectivity are important for studying culture precisely because of their slippery quality and their relations to personal investments, which shape not only our perception of texts but also personal relationships, social norms, public policy, and the rule of law. Art teaches you about these "inner" states; it teaches us how to feel about who we are, and how we're supposed to feel about who others are. Precisely because they're so slippery, ideological determinations tend to stick to these categories of "difference," making the disentangling and denaturalizing work of theory even more important at these sites.

In the end, the point of these analyses of "differences" is not to *prove* a conclusion—everything is socially constructed—because that's finally too simple. That things are "socially constructed" tends to suggest that we simply get to *choose* how something is constructed or that it's easy to reconstruct it in any way we want it to be; but the theoretical importance of differences—or topics like race, gender, and sexuality—is that they represent sites where we *don't* get to choose. At the same time, however, we are not wholly determined by these categories. You don't get to choose your race—

in ways that are importantly different from the ways you don't get to choose your sexuality—but the attributes of your race or sexuality are not finally decided, do not make you lockstep into this or that subject.

For Further Reading

Gender

Bordo, Susan. *The Male Body: A New Look at Men in Public and Private.* New York: Farrar, Straus & Giroux, 1999.

———. *Unbearable Weight: Feminism, Western Culture, and the Body.* Berkeley: University of California Press, 1995.

Butler, Judith. *Gender Trouble.* 10th ed. New York: Routledge, 1999 (1989).

Cixous, Hélène, and Catherine Clement. *The Newly Born Woman,* translated by Betsy Wing. Minneapolis: University of Minnesota Press, 1986.

De Beauvoir, Simone. *The Second Sex,* translated by H. M. Parshley. New York: Vintage, 1989.

De Lauretis, Teresa. *Technologies of Gender: Essays on Theory, Film and Fiction.* Bloomington: Indiana University Press, 1987.

Fraser, Nancy. *Justice Interruptus: Critical Reflections on the "Post-socialist" Condition.* New York: Routledge, 1997.

Grosz, Elizabeth. *Volatile Bodies: Toward a Corporeal Feminism.* St. Leonards, Australia: Allen and Unwin, 1994.

Irigaray, Luce. *An Ethics of Sexual Difference,* translated by Carolyn Burke and Gillian C. Gill. Ithaca, NY: Cornell University Press, 1993.

———. *This Sex Which Is Not One,* translated by Catherine Porter with Carolyn Burke. Ithaca, NY: Cornell University Press, 1985.

———. *Speculum of the Other Woman,* translated by Gillian C. Gill. Ithaca, NY: Cornell University Press, 1985.

Kristeva, Julia. *The Portable Kristeva.* Updated ed. Edited by Kelly Oliver. New York: Columbia University Press, 2002.

Moi, Toril. *Sexual/Textual Politics: Feminist Literary Theory.* New York: Routledge, 1988.

Pateman, Carole. *The Sexual Contract.* Cambridge: Polity Press, 1988.

Queer

Butler, Judith. *Bodies That Matter*. New York: Routledge, 1993.

———. *Gender Trouble*. 10th ed. New York: Routledge, 1999 (1989).

Crimp, Douglas. *Melancholia and Moralism: Essays on AIDS and Queer Politics*. Boston: MIT Press, 2002.

Dyer, Richard. *The Culture of Queers*. London: Routledge, 2002.

Freud, Sigmund. *Three Essays on the Theory of Sexuality*. Rev. ed. New York: Basic, 2000.

Jagose, Annamarie. *Queer Theory: An Introduction*. New York: New York University Press, 1997.

Sedgwick, Eve Kosofsky. *Epistemology of the Closet*. Berkeley: University of California Press, 1992.

Warner, Michael. *Publics and Counterpublics*. New York: Zone, 2002.

———. *The Trouble with Normal: Sex, Politics, and the Ethics of Our Life*. New York: Free Press, 1999.

Warner, Michael, ed. *Fear of a Queer Planet: Queer Politics and Social Theory*. Minneapolis: University of Minnesota Press, 1993.

Wittig, Monique. *The Straight Mind and Other Essays*. Boston: Beacon Press, 1992.

Race

Baker, Houston, ed. *Black British Cultural Studies: A Reader*. Chicago: University of Chicago Press, 1996.

Collins, Patricia Hill. *Black Feminist Thought: Knowledge, Consciousness, and the Philosophy of Empowerment*. 2d ed. New York: Routledge, 2000.

Crenshaw, Kimberlé, ed. *Critical Race Theory: Key Writings That Formed the Movement*. New York: New Press, 1996.

Dyson, Michael Eric. *Open Mike: Reflections on Racial Identities, Popular Culture, and Freedom Struggles*. New York: Basic Civitas Books, 2002.

———. *Race Rules: Negotiating the Color Line*. New York: Vintage, 1993.

Gilroy, Paul. *Against Race*. Cambridge, MA: Harvard University Press, 2000.

———. *The Black Atlantic*. Cambridge, MA: Harvard University Press, 1993.

————. *There Ain't No Black in the Union Jack.* Rev. ed. Chicago: University of Chicago Press, 1991.

Goldberg, David Theo. *The Racial State.* London: Blackwell, 2001.

————. *Racist Culture: Philosophy and the Politics of Meaning.* London: Blackwell, 1993.

Gordon, Lewis R. *Bad Faith and Anti-Black Racism.* Atlantic Highlands, NY: Humanities Press, 1995.

Hall, Stuart, Paul Gilroy, Lawrence Grossberg, and Angela McRobbie. *Without Guarantees: In Honour of Stuart Hall.* New York: Verso, 2000.

Hall, Stuart, David Morley, and Kuan-Hsing Chen. *Stuart Hall: Critical Dialogues in Cultural Studies.* New York: Routledge, 1996.

hooks, bell. *Black Looks.* Boston: South End Press, 1993.

————. *Talking Back.* Boston: South End Press, 1989.

Mercer, Kobena. *Welcome to the Jungle.* New York: Routledge, 1994.

West, Cornel. *Race Matters.* New York: Vintage, 1994.

Williams, Patricia. *The Alchemy of Race and Rights.* Cambridge, MA: Harvard University Press, 1992.

Winant, Howard. *The World Is a Ghetto: Race and Democracy since World War II.* New York: Basic, 2002.

Winant, Howard, and Michael Omi. *Racial Formation in the United States from the 1960s to the 1990s.* New York: Routledge, 1994.

Class

Aronowitz, Stanley. *Class: The Anthology.* Oxford: Blackwell, 2003.

————. *The Crisis in Historical Materialism: Class, Politics, and Culture in Marxist Theory.* Minneapolis: University of Minnesota Press, 1990.

————. *False Promises: The Shaping of American Working Class Consciousness.* New York: McGraw-Hill, 1974.

Bourdieu, Pierre. *Distinction: A Social Critique of the Judgement of Taste,* translated by Richard Nice. Cambridge, MA: Harvard University Press, 1984.

————. *The Weight of the World: Social Suffering in Contemporary Society,* translated by Pricilla Parkhurst Ferguson. Stanford, CA: Stanford University Press, 1999.

Bourdieu, Pierre, and Jean-Claude Passeron. *Reproduction in Education, Society and Culture,* translated by Richard Nice. London: Sage, 1977.

Fussell, Paul. *Class: A Guide through the American Status System.* New York: Ballantine, 1983.

Giddens, Anthony. *The Class Structure of Advanced Societies.* New York: Harper & Row, 1975.

———. *Classes, Power, and Conflict: Classical and Contemporary Debates.* Berkeley: University of California Press, 1982.

Giroux, Henry A. *Theory and Resistance in Education: A Pedagogy for the Opposition.* South Hadley, MA: Bergin and Garvey, 1983.

Kozol, Jonathan. *Savage Inequalities: Children in America's Schools.* New York: Harper Perennial, 1992.

Lukacs, Georg. *History and Class Consciousness: A Study in Marxist Dialectics,* translated by Rodney Livingstone. Cambridge, MA: MIT Press, 1971.

Poulantzas, Nicos. *Political Power and Social Classes.* London: New Left Books, 1973.

Sennett, Richard, and Jonathan Cobb. *The Hidden Injuries of Class.* Cambridge: Cambridge University Press, 1977.

Thompson, E. P. *The Making of the English Working Class.* New York: Pantheon, 1964.

Willis, Paul. *Learning to Labour: How Working Class Kids Get Working Class Jobs.* New York: Columbia University Press, 1981 (1977).

Notes

1. In the context of the play, it's plausible that Hamlet is well aware of the absurdity of this position, that this speech is part of his *acting* mad. In either case, it's a wonderful example of exaggerated adolescent male angst, and hardly a universal conundrum.

2. See Sedgwick's "Axiomatic," the introduction to her *Epistemology of the Closet* (1992).

11

Life

"Then, what is life? I cried."

—Percy Bysshe Shelley, from his unfinished poem,
"The Triumph of Life" (1822)

We concluded our discussion of differences with a set of remarks that gesture toward understanding how theory matters to "everyday people living their lives." Lest this be read as a backdoor return to some version of transcendence, truth, or grand metacontext that we all share despite our multiplying differences—that is, this thing we call life—we'll endeavor now to take a closer look at that category. Though there's probably no concept more seemingly obvious than "life" (always been around, always been more or less the same at its core), as we'll soon see, there is also no category as relentlessly invoked nor as shot through with power. As we hear in constantly used phrases ranging from "life itself" to "everyday life," from the "life of the mind" to "lifestyle," "pro-life," the "meaning of life," "extraterrestrial life," or "making life better," the concept of "life" really has quite a life of its own. Life, in short, seems like an always-and-everywhere essential concept, something we've all shared since the beginning, this hard-to-define thing that we all have in common with other humans, as well as other living species, and maybe even with the ecosystems of the earth itself.

In other words, while the historical contexts and technological ways of living this thing called life have changed significantly over the centuries (for example, humans have gone from expressing how life works on cave walls and stone tablets to writing blog posts about it using word processors, mobile phones, or voice-recognition software), it's tempting to think on the other hand that the bedrock of the whole larger operation, "life itself," really hasn't changed much over the past few thousand years. Nor, it would seem, has our fascination with the topic. As Italian philosopher Giorgio Agamben argues, for example, much of Western thought grows out of a seemingly simple opposition in Aristotle between two contrasting forms of life: zoe and bios. For Aristotle, zoe corresponds to animal life: the raw, personal, unfettered quality of our biological existence— our basic desires for food, water, companionship, avoiding pain. On the other hand, Aristotelian bios corresponds to what we might call political life, which is to say a form of life that is not wholly "free" but circumscribed in various ways by larger social categories (gender, class, race, ethnicity, sexuality, nationality, disability, and so on) that should be familiar to us from our discussion of subjectivity. So in Agamben's reading of Aristotle, we see a distinction between something we might be tempted to call "life itself" (zoe), the substrate of each individual's existence; then there's a series of particular *kinds* or *forms* of life (bios)—the constrained "biopolitics" of our social existence (the roles we fulfill in the family, school, workplace, and so on).

However satisfying this initial distinction between "raw life" and "political life" (zoe and bios) may seem, as we've seen relentlessly throughout this text, it's always a suspicious ideological move to say that there's a version of something "in itself" (a natural, basic, always-existing "way things really are"), to which the difficulties of social structures or politics are merely added, after the fact as it were. And Agamben himself argues as much when he shows that "bare life," the mere existence of zoe, has itself become a highly charged, biopolitical category within modernity—one that has authorized, among other things, all kinds of genocidal political policies. "The enemy," in short, is another convenient modern name for he or she who "merely exists" like a wild animal or invasive plant does; as such, the enemy has no tradition of cultural or biopolitical life that needs to be recognized as legitimate and thereby can be slaughtered with no more guilt than one experiences in killing a mouse or pulling a weed.

Or, to put the biopolitical point somewhat differently, given the work we've done up until this point, it should be clear that the (social, political, linguistic) way that you describe or understand something like "life itself" inexorably changes what that life "is." For example, in any kind of us/them political situation, "their" life will not look like "our" life, just as Tibetan Buddhist life doesn't necessarily look much like North American college life or Darwinian life; likewise, the Christian medieval conception of what life "is" and what's important within it differs radically from the Native American conception of life or the version of life you'd get from a contemporary molecular biologist.

In point of fact, the organized body of knowledge dedicated to studying "life itself"—the discipline of biology, queen of the life sciences—is nowhere to be found before the word *biology* is coined by Jean-Baptiste Lamarck in 1802, which is at least initially to suggest our modern, biological ideas about studying life would have been quite foreign in most of human history. Indeed, philosopher Michel Foucault provocatively insists that until the nineteenth century, "life itself did not exist. All that existed was living beings, which were viewed through a grid of knowledge constituted by natural history" (*The Order of Things*, 128). In other words, Foucault suggests that, prior to Lamarck's coining of the word and concept "biology" in the early nineteenth century, life was not necessarily understood (at least in western science) as we think of it today—a kind of substrate that connects all "living" things. Rather, from ancient times through the eighteenth century, it was generally understood there were different kinds of live things (plants, animals, people) and the job of science (understood as natural history) was to categorize them properly. Life, in other words, was not a general animating principle, hidden inside things, secretly connecting them. Rather, there were simply many different kinds of things that were alive, offered to the gaze of the scientist for classification. Prior to the 1800s, Foucault argues, natural life wasn't the kind of thing that developed or changed, nor was it kept secret within the heart of things; it was just "there," awaiting classification. Following Aristotle, human beings in the West were for more than two thousand years classified as a species of animal life (zoe) that had an additional capacity for political life (bios), largely made possible by our capacity for reason and language (logos).

Of course, to argue that "life" as a concept was born in the early nineteenth century is not to suggest that anyone from that period would or could share "our" understanding of life. The dominant way of understanding or studying biological life today, at the molecular or subgenetic level, would in fact seem bizarre (and simply unavailable) not only to Aristotle but also to the likes of Lamarck. For many vitalist philosophers of the nineteenth century, "life" was understood, contra Aristotle, not as a naturally existing thing to be classified, but as an overflowing force of transformation and/or adaptation (think of Nietzsche's "overman" here, or Darwinian evolution). However, by the time we were halfway through the twentieth century, with the discovery of DNA in 1953, the entire understanding of life had shifted again: there was broad consensus that life was to be conceptualized not as a developing vital "force," but rather life was to be understood primarily as a kind of "information" contained in genetic patterns.

In other words, far from remaining the same from Aristotle to today (roughly 2,400 years), the basic scientific and cultural understanding of what constitutes "life" has in fact changed drastically several times in the past sixty years alone. With the discovery of the double helix of DNA, "life" was transformed from an excessive vital force into the kind of thing that was "written" in a genetic "code," and the life sciences thereby morphed into a discipline or branch of knowledge that doesn't so much track or categorize the transformative forces of living things, but rather "interprets" what's called only half-ironically the "book of life." Genetic patterns, on this explanation, contain "meaning," and thereby the life sciences come to be understood specifically as interpretive sciences. However, as the discoveries of biology since the mid-1950s have become ever more miniaturized and technical (as we not only "discover" or "interpret" genetic information, but are also able to alter the very structure of genes), the contemporary discourse of the life sciences has undergone yet another shift of dominant paradigms. Life is no longer primarily understood on the genomic analogy of the book (containing a hidden secret, requiring the scientist's interpretation), but on model of the microscopic or molecular, the smallest particles that can be manipulated by scientists.

So, with an ironic nod to Marx, one might say that contemporary biology is not merely interested in *interpreting* genes, but *changing* them. Which is to say, biological life is studied today not so much through its end products (life as a vital force that's developing or degrading, or life as an interpretive puzzle that you have to solve in its entirety before you can get a sense of its meaning); rather, life is today understood as a kind of super-origin. Scientifically speaking, life most purely "is what it is" not in its social manifestations or effects, but in its minutest, most original and hidden molecular incarnations. As sociologist of science Nikolas Rose writes, contemporary biology has largely become molecular biology, and has come to visualize life taking place primarily at the submicroscopic region. But of course, such contemporary understandings of life owe their efficacy to a series of breakthroughs in other social and scientific arenas, outside biology itself: most obviously, ever more powerful microscopes and other subatomic visualization technologies quite literally make this molecular understanding of life possible.

Working Question

The way you look at something changes what it "is." This statement comprises a kind of theoretical truism in the humanities and arts—an idea that we see very clearly on display, for example, in Wallace Stevens's poem "Thirteen Ways of Looking at a Blackbird" or in the impressionist paintings of Claude Monet or the cubism of Picasso. We're used to this as a grounding insight for literature, art, or even history (where different angles of examination change our understanding of, say, Abraham Lincoln's legacy); but is this true for science as well? Is this the case for the very study and understanding of life itself?

For example, how have advances in visualization techniques, increased computational speed for data crunching, government and private funding decisions (funding this kind of research and not that kind), or even Facebook for that matter inexorably changed the way people end up understanding this thing called life? Or, most simply put, does looking at something under a high-powered microscope, rather than a magnifying glass or the naked eye, change how you understand that thing? Does life "magnified" on Facebook look different from life in the mirror? How, exactly?

Biopower

One way to sum up this discourse concerning life is to think about the question in terms that German philosopher Theodor Adorno uses. Quoting Ferdinand Kürnberger, Adorno begins his *Minima Moralia: Reflections on a Damaged Life* with the paradoxical sentiment that "life is not alive"—which is, among other things, to suggest that the animating principle we so often associate with life (pure vitality, energy, striving) is not in any way contained within the concept of life, any more than freedom is free or the word "bird" can actually fly. Life is not lively, not living—it has to be animated, configured, or deployed within a context, given a particular sense, for it to live. So, for example, even if within a particular sociopolitical context, life on earth isn't thought to be as important as life in the next world (as some religious doctrines hold), that understanding of the ultimate irrelevance of social life nevertheless comes out of a particular social situation.

In other words, "life is not alive" suggests that all life at this historical juncture is biopolitical life, organized and played out under a series of sociopolitical constraints. Life—whatever that may be, mean, or do in a particular context—is always inexorably subject to external practices of power (which is true for human political struggles, as well as plants' fights for sunlight in the forest or salmon making their way upstream to spawn). Another way to put this may be that life has to be embodied because you can never point to "life itself," only to living things. The specific term that Foucault coined for that series of material relations where life gets determined is "biopower," which he and many other social theorists see as our dominant form of power today. Indeed, what else are the hot political fights in the United States over health care, abortion, assisted suicide, gay marriage, or the death penalty if they're not fights about life and the proper or improper ways of understanding or protecting it?

Of course, understanding life in terms of biopower does allow life (the "bio" in "biopower") to remain a kind of odd "always and everywhere" concept, and we learned in our earlier reading that any such misty, elastic abstraction tends to fall under the rubric of "ideology." But if life has become a kind of dominant ideology, the discourse surrounding it is not ideological in that it's merely false because life in fact has become a political issue, probably *the* political issue of our time. In short, life has become a kind of ideological commonsense notion in the contemporary world: Nearly everywhere you look these days (advertising, politics, art, education), there is an appeal to this thing called "life"—making life better, enjoying life more, living the life of the mind, or even la vida loca. Which is to say the notion of biopower shows us that social modes of power at this historical juncture don't so much work *on* life as they do *through* life: Social modes of power (everything from government programs to advertising campaigns) make constant appeals to this amorphous thing called "life." In order to do its social job, contemporary power mobilizes a certain form or understanding of life—hence, it's biopower. Indeed, as Agamben argues in his work on the Holocaust, even the death-dealing Nazi genocide, a death-power that seems exactly the opposite of bio- or life-power, was made possible by a strange appeal to life. In a nutshell, the twisted logic of the Holocaust was that Germanic Aryan life needed protection from being infected by a whole series of supposedly inferior forms of life (most tragically, Jews—but also Gypsies, homosexuals, communists, and others), so these other forms of life had to be eradicated. In short, Nazi power was biopower, a political program of laws and discriminatory practices that makes a bedrock appeal to an authentic form of life. The Holocaust justified its horrible work *through* notions of life, not *outside* or *in spite of* them.

Or, on a more everyday level, one could also take the example of modern crime and punishment. In his cornerstone study of criminology *Discipline and Punish*, Foucault argues that life and law have come together over the past hundred years most obviously under the rubric of biopower. In prior historical regimes, dominant social networks and institutions (the state, the school, the police, the company, the family) were primarily interested in gaining power over what people did—listen, obey, do the things you're supposed to do. Foucault calls this earlier mode of power "discipline," and its main modality is training people at various institutional sites—you learn from the family how to be a proper man or woman, you learn from school how to be a pupil and citizen, you learn from the police not to break the law, you learn from the store how to shop. So-called disciplinary power is then primarily concerned with what you do, or what you shouldn't do, and its norms (its tests of right and wrong) fall primarily on your actions. For example, there's a series of right ways to fulfill your familial role as son or daughter (get good grades, work hard, do what you're told, date the right people), and a series of wrong ways.

And the punishments for transgression under a disciplinary regime tend also to be aimed at redirecting or limiting your actions—you get a timeout, you're grounded, you lose your license, you get expelled, or you go to prison. These disciplinary practices try to affect or curtail your actions: disciplinary practices, on Foucault's reading, evidence very little interest in "who you really are." As practices of power, they simply entice you to act in certain "normal" ways and not act in other ways, which are by definition "abnormal."

As Foucault writes, in the modern mutation from disciplinary power to biopower (roughly, from the nineteenth to the twentieth century), the central figure of power's drama remains the so-called abnormal subject, but the basis on which that abnormality is diagnosed or discovered changes radically. In short, social discourse of norms and the "normal" comes to pivot less on an individual's actions and more on the person and his or her life as an explanation for what he or she does. In short, the central focus for biopower is the abnormal *subject* rather than the (disciplinary) criminal *act*—abnormality is to be found in who you are rather than what you do. As Foucault writes, the "[biopolitical] delinquent is to be distinguished from the [disciplinary] offender by the fact that it is not so much his act as his life that is relevant in characterizing him. . . . The legal punishment bears upon an act; the punitive technique on a life" (*Discipline and Punish*, 251–52). How's that? Well, the criminal act remains within a fairly well-defined disciplinary realm, with a more or less binary system of "guilt": in the end, you *are* or you *aren't* guilty of a crime (you either got convicted or you didn't). Biopower, however, further multiplies the concepts and practices of potential guilt by its invention of a species or life-form lurking behind the acts of criminality: the delinquent, the monster, the sociopath, the pervert. These are subjects who may or may not have *done* anything illegal or transgressive, but their lives are nonetheless outside the slippery slope of biopolitcal normativity. As Foucault insists, biopolitical "delinquency must be specified in terms not so much of the law as of the norm" (*Discipline and Punish*, 253).

In short, the disciplinary criminal is known through her transgressive *act*, while biopower's delinquent is known through his abnormal *personality*. And, on Foucault's account, this emergence of subject-centered biopower becomes the gateway to the present, to the proliferation of "abnormal" subjectivities that characterizes today's even more highly intensified biopolitical society: "At this point one enters the 'criminological' labyrinth from which we have certainly not yet emerged" (*Discipline and Punish*, 252). As a concrete example of such biopolitical production of subjectivities, and biopower's mutation from the strictly speaking disciplinary investment in acts, one could note here that the homosexual is the paradigmatic example of the "delinquent" in Foucault, the subject whose supposedly "abnormal" conduct is most obviously saturated and explained by his or her life: "The nineteenth-century homosexual became a personage, a past, a case history, and a childhood, in addition to being a type of life, a life form, and a morphology" (*History of Sexuality*, 43). In the transition from discipline to biopower (from power targeting the act to targeting the life), the emergence of modern homosexuality is paradigmatic for Foucault insofar as homosexuality becomes understood "less as a habitual sin than a singular nature" (43). In short, homosexuality was "transposed from the *practice* of sodomy onto a kind of *interior androgyny*, a hermaphrodism of the soul" (43, our emphasis), from an occasional and discontinuous set of actions into the continuous manifestation of a supposed personality defect. In short, Foucault argues that the homosexual used to be understood as a person who occasionally *did* certain things; we now understand the homosexual as a certain *kind of person.* And that's biopower in a nutshell—power is now interested first and foremost in who you (really) are; and once we figure that out, we'll be able to explain what you do and why you do it. And all of this is of course based on the substrate of life, as that secret buried somewhere *within* the subject and his or her actions, the enigmatic (often genetic) explanation lurking behind the actions of the "abnormal" or "deviant."

And with our changing notions of what causes abnormal behavior like crime also come changes in our notions of treatment or punishment. Prison, for example, used to be a place for rehabilitation, a place to get an education and/or learn a trade, so you can become a productive member of society when you get out. The primary understanding of punishment was disciplinary in Foucault's sense: change the bad acts to good acts. These days, by contrast, prison has largely become just a holding pen for what the criminal justice system thinks of as incorrigible sociopaths, dangerous individuals, people who are genetically just "that way," so there's no point in teaching them a trade or anything else in prison. If we understand crime as caused by a personality defect (as bearing on an entire life rather than a single bad decision), then that inexorably changes the way we "treat" crime (or don't) as well.

Working Question

Following along, perhaps unhappily, from the example of historical changes in crime and punishment, we wonder: How has the experience of being a student changed, do you think, in the mutation from discipline to biopower? When we were in primary school in the dark ages of the 1960s and '70s, if you weren't paying attention or were caught goofing off, you sat in the corner facing the wall, stayed after school, and/or went to the principal's office. (A decade or two before that, you might have been hit on the knuckles or the butt with a ruler.) With problem students today, however, it seems as if it's all counselors and medical diagnoses (Attention Deficit Hyperactivity Disorder, for example), followed up not by stints wearing the dunce cap or going to detention, but by a life spent taking expensive prescriptions (Adderall, Ritalin).

Is this an example of biopower at work, taking over from a notion of discipline—from treating the act to treating the abnormal personality supposedly "behind" the act? Is one way of treating problem student behavior (prescriptions or punishments) necessarily better than the other? Better for what, do you think?

Resistance

When thinking about power and how it works, we most often end up talking about some version of resistance as well. In other words, because power (like life) is so ubiquitous that it's nearly impossible to localize, it's easiest to locate social power (what's considered normal and what's abnormal) at those points where power clamps down on various forms of resistance. In other words, we can see forms of power most clearly when they are brought to light against "resistant" acts or practices that power wants to eradicate. For example, it's the widespread use of certain illicit substances that brought drug laws into existence—marijuana was legal in the United States until 1937, LSD until 1966, and as any Internet search shows, there are thousands of compounds out there awaiting the inevitability of either a Phish show or government regulation.

But, as the (more or less) arbitrarily chosen example of drug regulation shows, we also tend to think about power and resistance in terms of the State (the government, maybe even the "man") and its (almost always repressive) relation to the individual. Our dominant understandings of power lead us to think about it as top-down, repressive, anti-individualistic, nay-saying, and pleasure-denying: power versus resistance. As films often portray it, we tend to think of power in black and white, as something that denies us color, fun, and life itself. We think here especially of the 1998 film *Pleasantville*, which portrays a grim, repressive, disciplinary 1950s invaded by gnarly, time-travelling 1990s California teens portrayed by Tobey Maguire and Reese Witherspoon. When the hip future invades the film's complacent world of the 1950s, objects on the screen magically change from black and white to color. With the arrival of individualism, fun, and rebellion (in short, resistance) comes the color and thickness of life itself.

We should perhaps be suspicious of a Hollywood film that promises to save us from a repressive world that now we only know through Hollywood films and sitcoms (how film and TV escape being part and parcel of the "repressive '50s" is never made clear in such filmed representations of it), but *Pleasantville* offers us a very familiar story about repression and resistance: Normative, repressive power wants to take the color of life away. While in contrast, we resist by being ourselves, having fun, being perky like Reese Witherspoon. And it's precisely that resistance to the norm that puts the color right back into our lives. The "man" represses by taking away fun and pleasure, wanting us all to be the same, and we rebel by living it up, doing our own thing, fighting for the right to party.

But, if we reexamine the drama of power and resistance in terms of the Foucaultian story outlined earlier concerning the shift from discipline to biopower, one begins to wonder what that story means for our still-dominant notions of repression and resistance. In the face of repressive "discipline" (trying to train people to be the same or similar), resistance seems relatively easy to locate or enact: you simply have to be yourself, refuse to be like everyone else. But how do you resist the biopower that precisely works through expanding forms of life and lifestyle? How does one resist the fact that soda pop commercials now ask you to "trust your gut," car companies urge you to "choose your own road," or governments want to provide you with health care (asking you not, as under disciplinary regimes of war, to die *en masse* for your country but paradoxically to live longer for it)?

As Thomas Frank writes in his essay "Why Johnny Can't Dissent," we may have a pretty good handle on how contemporary biopower works, but our notions of resistance to that form of power have become, perhaps, hopelessly outdated. As Frank notes, "life" has changed exponentially over the past few decades, but

> our notion about what's wrong with . . . life and how the figures responsible are to be confronted haven't changed much in thirty years. Call it, for convenience, the "countercultural idea." It holds that the paramount ailment of our society is conformity. As existential rebellion has become a more or less official style of Information Age capitalism, so has the countercultural notion of a static, repressive Establishment grown hopelessly obsolete. However the basic impulses of the countercultural idea may have disturbed a nation lost in Cold War darkness, they are today in fundamental agreement with the basic tenets of Information Age business theory.

Prevailing modes and practices of power have changed, rapidly and all around us, from a dominant disciplinary mode to a dominant mode of biopower; but it may be that our sense of what might resist power has become antiquated as well.

Working Question

Black Sabbath's "Iron Man" (1970) has become one of the most recognizable songs in the classic rock canon, and the song is now a standard pop cultural reference, showing up everywhere from commercials for Nissan to Christmas song parodies ("I Am Santa Claus")—not to mention the fact that it's become a staple on band playlists at high school football games and served as a theme song for the summer 2008 Hollywood blockbuster of the same name.

But there's something really weird about this—primarily because if you would have told us in the 1970s that any song from Black Sabbath's drug-addled *Paranoid* album could be used to sell cars, or would soon become a favorite of high school administrators everywhere, we'd have said you were high (and, it being the '70s, you very well might have been). In the business world of the 1970s, it would simply have been *unthinkable* that the music of loud, greasy-haired British rockers could help you to move Japanese pickup trucks. And anyone who was in high school at any point in the '70s can, I think, attest to the fact that suggesting Black Sabbath songs be added to the school band playlist would bring on a locker search rather than a nod of approval.

So how does "Iron Man" go from being a confused underground stoner anthem about a mixed-media B-list superhero who goes on a killing rampage to being a nifty way to sell products and/or boost school spirit? The song's the same, so obviously the context surrounding it has changed somehow. Is there something different about our understanding of consumer products themselves and what they offer us today? Can products offer resistance to mainstream culture? Or is some notion of resistance (the "cool" of counterculture) part of what sucks us into mainstream culture these days?

The Economics of Culture; or, The Biopower Business

We know, we know—you didn't become a humanities or arts major because you enjoyed reading the business section of the newspaper. And economics is an area of inquiry that, even its proponents tend to agree, is fully deserving of its nickname: the Dismal Science. But the news these days is full of economics, obscure business numbers:

something called "the Dow" went up or down today, on the heels of what happened with the "Nikkei" (Japanese), "Hang Seng" (Chinese), or "FTSE" (British) markets overnight. Huh? And all this means precisely what for college students, at least ones who are studying something other than business? What's it all got to do with life or biopower?

Well, it's pretty clear that economics is important to contemporary life: as the global near-depression of 2008 showed, bursting bubbles, recessions, and credit problems end up affecting all of our lives sooner or later. Depending on the larger state of the global economy, it's harder or easier to make your payments, get a new job, a student loan, or a hold of dad's credit card for a trip to the store. It's pretty well known that, sooner or later, there are widespread and serious consequences for individuals' lives that follow along from this more nebulous general story about economic ups and downs— the so-called trickle-down theory of economics. But Foucault's notion of biopower tends to suggest that these larger changes in the functioning of power have more direct consequences on our everyday life, restructuring not just the realm of the economic but the very mechanisms of how we understand our everyday world, and increasingly ourselves. Maybe these days life doesn't so much change in the wake of economic fluctuations (no study abroad next fall if you can't get a job this summer), but it may be that economics today is directly implicated in our lives, our understandings of ourselves.

Me and economics, you say? You gotta be kidding—I am something that happens outside my job. A college career spent studying the arts, humanities, and most of the social sciences is precisely designed to dedicate yourself to something other than, maybe even in opposition to, the workaday world of business. And this drama of "work versus life" certainly was the case in the past—as a passing example, take a look again at the Van Gogh painting *A Pair of Boots* that we reproduce in chapter 9. This painting, from the high modern period of the late nineteenth century, certainly contains, among many other things, an allegory about work and its relation to life: While art is of course a kind of work (those shoes don't paint themselves), the artist's work is portrayed here as something that inevitably takes place after the hard work of manual labor. As the shoes rest, so does their peasant wearer, and such moments of enjoying life, away from back-breaking toil of field work, are the only moments available for either the production or consumption of higher things like art.

Likewise, Van Gogh here subtly presents the job of art as the what we might call the "redemption" of peasant work by the artist's work: Everyday hard work is transformed, simply by being included as the topic of high artwork, into something sublime, artistically important, metaphysically meaningful (just think of what James Joyce's *Ulysses* does for a single drab day in Dublin). Likewise, Van Gogh's painting subtly portrays itself as a "way out" of dead-end, everyday manual labor: The world of backbreaking toil that the painting so effectively summons can itself be escaped or trans-formed through the work or the life of art. Van Gogh's painting shows us how life, or the life of the artist, can transform the mere objects of workaday living.

But one of the major effects of biopower over the past decades has been the increasing collapse of such a rigid distinction between life and work for many people. Under the factory regimes of disci-pline, you went to work at 9, clocked in, and left the job behind when you clocked out at 5. (In the old days, students were one of the few groups of people who were on the job 24/7.) Increasingly, though, we don't leave our jobs at the office anymore. And even when we do leave work, as something like Warhol's painting *Diamond Dust Shoes* suggests, we increasingly pass not into a work-less space of life-as-leisure, but into other "jobs"—as consumer, gen-dered subject, someone always competing for scarce social goods (recognition, love, fame, a great pair of shoes) even when we're away from our jobs: Everybody's a dreamer, and everybody's a star. Unlike the world portrayed in Van Gogh's painting (where one can leave the economics of work behind, if only for a time), today even our leisure time is saturated by the economic imperatives of our era—money and competition. Warhol confronts us with this new reality when he literally covers the surface of his painting with diamond dust: art, he insists, is no escape from the world of commodities. Art is a commodity, too.

Life-as-leisure, even the work of the artist, is no longer so separated from the economic work of the world. In fact, today, leisure presents its own kind of economic imperatives (as you know if you've ever been on "vacation" at places like Disney World: leisure has become a job). In other words, outside of our money-making jobs, each of us has the additional biopolitical task of building ourselves and our lifestyles through the consumption of products, what we might call the branding of our individuality—the shoes we wear, the music we listen to, the books we read (or don't read), the car we drive, the movies we like. These things that surround us are, as far as the world's concerned, who we are. Which is to say that our lives these days are under constant re- and deconstruction by the undulations of biopower—a form of power that, oddly, we often wield on ourselves. In contrast to the older, disciplinary forms of power (which have hardly disappeared altogether and continue to work on us at institutional sites—school, work, army, shopping mall), the emergent form of biopower bears directly on "life itself" (our everyday lives, our lifestyles). And it works on us all the time—in our living rooms, dining rooms, and bedrooms. We are all these days what theorists like to call "prosumers," people who produce themselves and their lives through consumption.

But, to return to our question about resistance, the "everywhere" quality of biopower hardly means that we are all necessarily dupes for power. Because power as biopower works on and through a kind of resistance (through an emphasis on life, on ourselves), then the whole drama of power and resistance needs to be rethought in our era. Resistance is no longer the purview of a handful of avant-gardists, those brave or wealthy enough to *really* be themselves, but is rather the common fabric of society. Oddly, resistance may be the thing, like life, that we all have in common these days. Think of the health care debates of the last two decades in the United States: one side resists a government takeover of health care, while the other side resists the skyrocketing costs of private insurance. The two sides of this debate have little in common, other than that both of them are invested first and foremost in a notion of resistance—both see themselves speaking in the name of life (the good, or at least better, life), against a system that would have terrible, detrimental effects on that life.

So, biopower is at work not only in the public or social sphere, but we learn from Foucault that it's also at work in your sex life, your relation to your friends, your family, your health, even in your relation to yourself. And this is as true for the president of the United States as it is for your mom, Angelina Jolie, your classmates, or your next-door neighbor. So at that level of generality—there is no outside of biopower—what good are Foucault's insights concerning power? Well, as a conclusion ("yep, power's at work everywhere in the contemporary world, even in our relations to ourselves"), the value is not much. But this diagnosis of biopower's spread is a starting point for the contemporary analysis of power rather than an endpoint. In other words, this increasing scope of biopower is cause neither for celebration nor despair. In Foucault's work, it's first and foremost a descriptive claim: as power becomes increasingly more invested in the minute details of our lives, so, too, have our modes of resistance become increasingly subtle and intense. Foucault reminds us, "There are no machines of freedom, by definition" ("Space," 136). Just as our dominant understandings of power are becoming anachronistic, Foucault shows us that many of our categories of resistance remain as holdovers from prior understandings of power. Resistance, like power, is known in its *effects*, not in its *intentions*, so critical analysis would likewise have to focus on the discontinuous, social effects of power and resistance rather than the supposed authenticity of the original intentions of the persons involved.

▓ Working Questions

1. On the occasion of the fiftieth anniversary of the publication of William Burroughs's *Naked Lunch* in 2009, we read the following on the NPR website:

> Regina Weinreich, who teaches Beat Generation literature at New York's School of Visual Arts, believes the novel represents an alternative way of life, one that focuses on the individual as opposed to the masses. "It cuts through the norms of society— the way that we all have to be polite, the way we all have to follow our institutions, our governments, our addictions," Weinreich explains. "The alternative is to be [an] individual, and to go to those places on our own."

Does our analysis of biopower pose any relevant questions to *Naked Lunch* as presenting an alternative way of life—against the masses, the government, and for the individual? Are *Naked Lunch's* celebrations of the individual self, more than fifty years later, still modes of guaranteed resistance to our dominant culture? Why or why not?

2. Two songs by classic rockers The Kinks may help us to make some sense of the shift from discipline to biopower. Their 1971 song "20th Century Man" takes us into the heart of the disciplinary society: "I was born in a welfare state/ Ruled by bureaucracy / Controlled by civil servants / And people dressed in gray / Got no privacy / Got no liberty / Cause the 20th century people / Took it all away from me." The song later implores us, "We gotta get out of here / We gotta find a solution."

A year later, in 1972, though, The Kinks recorded "Celluloid Heroes," which conjures a very different kind of world, where "Everybody's a dreamer / And everybody's a star / And everybody's in movies / It doesn't matter who you are / There are stars in every city / In every house and on every street." Which seems pretty cheery, but the song later warns, "Those who are successful / Be always on your guard / Success walks hand in hand with failure / Along Hollywood Boulevard."

There are two very different worlds represented here (in our terms, the disciplinary world of obedience to authority, contrasted with the biopolitical world where everyone is invited to sculpt his or her own "star" identity). But is the world of "Celluloid Heroes" the "solution" that "20th Century Man" longs for, a return of the "liberty" taken away by the disciplinary society? Or are there simply new challenges and difficulties introduced by a new kind of system where you're no longer so much molded into a rigid norm like everyone else but invited (told?) to be your true self, be all you can be, a star at whatever you do—the star fry cook at your local McDonalds?

For Further Reading

Agamben, Giorgio. *Homo Sacer: Sovereign Power and Bare Life,* translated by Daniel Heller-Roazen. Stanford, CA: Stanford University Press, 1998.

Canguilhem, Georges. *Ideology and Rationality in the History of the Life Sciences,* translated by Arthur Goldhammer. Cambridge, MA: MIT Press, 1988.

———. *Knowledge of Life,* edited by Paola Marrati and Todd Meyers, translated by Stefanos Geroulanos and Daniela Ginsburg. New York: Fordham University Press, 2008.

Cooper, Melinda. *Life as Surplus: Biotechnology and Capitalism in the Neoliberal Era.* Seattle: University of Washington Press, 2008.

Doyle, Richard M. *Darwin's Pharmacy: Sex, Plants, and the Evolution of the Noösphere.* Seattle: University of Washington Press, 2011.

———. *On Beyond Living: Rhetorical Transformations of the Life Sciences.* Stanford, CA: Stanford University Press, 1997.

Esposito, Roberto. *Bios: Biopolitics and Philosophy,* translated by Timothy Campbell. Minneapolis: University of Minnesota Press, 2008.

Foucault, Michel. *The Birth of Biopolitics.* New York: Picador, 2010.

———. *Discipline and Punish: The Birth of the Prison.* 2d Vintage Books ed. Translated by Alan Sheridan. New York: Vintage Books, 1995.

———. *History of Sexuality, Volume 1,* translated by Robert Hurley. New York: Vintage, 1980.

———. *The Order of Things: An Archaeology of the Human Sciences.* New York: Vintage, 1970.

———. "Space, Power and Knowledge." In *The Cultural Studies Reader,* 134–41. Edited by Simon During. New York: Routledge, 1999.

Frank, Thomas. "Why Johnny Can't Dissent." In *Commodify Your Dissent,* by Thomas Frank and Matt Weiland. New York: Norton, 1997. Available at http://www.nytimes.com/books/first/f/frank -dissent.html. Accessed March 19, 2011.

Krell, David Farrell. *Daimon Life: Heidegger and Life-Philosophy.* Bloomington: Indiana University Press, 1992.

Margulis, Lynn, and Dorion Sagan. *What Is Life?* Berkeley: University of California Press, 2000.

Mitchell, Robert. *Bioart and the Vitality of Media.* Seattle: University of Washington Press, 2010.

Rose, Nikolas. *The Politics of Life Itself: Biomedicine, Power, and Subjectivity in the Twenty-First Century.* Princeton, NJ: Princeton University Press, 2006.

Schrödinger, Erwin. *What Is Life? The Physical Aspect of the Living Cell.* Cambridge: Cambridge University Press, 1944.

Sunder Rajan, Kaushik. *Biocapital: The Constitution of Postgenomic Life.* Durham, NC: Duke University Press, 2006.

Wolfe, Cary. *What Is Posthumanism?* Minneapolis: University of Minnesota Press, 2010.

12

Nature

Of course, critical attention to the proliferating points of contact between life and power shouldn't stop with human life. Indeed one of philosophy's consistent preoccupations since antiquity has been locating, maintaining, and policing a meaningful line between human and nonhuman life, between culture and nature—from Aristotle to Agamben as we've seen. We should note at this belated moment in our investigations that we have referred to the concept "nature," and the related descriptor "natural," throughout this text without pausing to consider what we mean by such terms. Though like life, it presents itself shrouded in the same blanket of obviousness, there are variable, even opposite, ways in which nature is invoked in theoretical argumentation and everyday conversation. Recalling the Gang of Four tune "Why Theory?" with which our journey began, the tagline "Every day seems like a natural fact" is repeated seven times in twenty-four lines, much like the ways that unreflective insistence about the inevitability and inviolability of "the way things are" often dog efforts to open up spaces for thinking otherwise, for imagining or theorizing alternative possibilities. Certainly it is in the interests of challenging the unconscious, taken-for-granted assumptions that too often inform daily life—the ones that seem so spontaneous, transparent, and, yes, natural—that our earlier analysis of ideology as a form of cultural common sense unfolds. Yet, we understand nature not only as a kind of intrinsic value or essence but also in opposition to the very tricky concept of culture, as when we insist that "ideology is the making natural of cultural phenomena." In the first sense, declaring a quality, condition, or event natural renders it timeless and immutable; in the second instance, the natural summons the material world, the environment, and forms of nonhuman life that make up the "natural order," which we define as wild or uncultivated—all that stands apart from, and indeed is often perceived to threaten, civilization or humanity. Consider the so-called debate over global warming—a natural occurrence or unfolding human-made catastrophe? Some politicians and business interests invested (literally) in "business as usual" subscribe to the former interpretation, fending off the need for costly changes in things like the regulation of emissions and other pollutants with the assurance that climate variation and fluctuations in the earth's temperature are both natural and cyclical.

To complicate matters further, in contrast to the paired oppositions between nature/the nonhuman and culture/humanity, sometimes humans are located within the "state of nature," as when we examine in chapter 4 the assertion of a transcendent "human nature" as against the concept of socially constructed subjectivity. Sigmund Freud famously theorized the relation between nature, located in the external world, and an internal, or human, nature by claiming that both needed to be controlled or tamed in the interests of civilization and social progress. According to Freud, "Our civilization is, generally speaking, founded on the suppression of instincts" (cited in Barry, *Environment and Social Theory*, 85). In short, cultural advancement only happens when we successfully repress other "less lofty" time- and energy-consuming activities; principally for Freud, this means quelling the urge to satisfy rapacious sexual desire and other instinctually driven pleasures through the purifying activity of work (and we can assume a lot of cold showers). Such comparisons between animal and human behavior are hardly the special preserve of psychoanalysts. Debates among religious fundamentalists aside, consider the utterly conventional scientific assertion that *homo sapiens*, Latin for us humans, are a particular species within the animal kingdom, similar to other higher primates in the ability to manipulate systems of communication and form complexly structured social relations, among other behaviors, and whose closest ancestral relation is the chimpanzee. It is in recognition of our genetic commonality with nonhuman life that, for example, clinical researchers study the onset of pathology in, or run drug trials on, various species to make observations and determinations about the trajectory of certain diseases or the appropriate course of medical treatment for humans. So in the end, the concept of nature can work to remove or separate humanity from the nonhuman or natural order, or it can bring them together in a kind of organic unity (Barry, *Environment and Social Theory*).

It is for all the preceding reasons that "nature," according to Raymond Williams, is "perhaps the most complex word in the [English] language" (*Keywords*, 219). Yet in spite of the linguistic challenges that the concept of nature poses, we manage pretty well the task of negotiating different registers of meaning, even when they are sometimes used all at once. Consider the following passage from Shakespeare's *King Lear*:

Allow not nature more than nature needs,
Man's life's as cheap as a beast's . . .

. . . one daughter

Who redeems nature from the general curse
Which twain have brought her to.

That nature, which condemns its origin,
Cannot be border'd certain in itself . . .

. . . All shaking thunder
Cracked nature's moulds, all germens spill at once,
That make ungrateful man . . .

. . . Hear, nature hear; dear goddess, hear.

In *Lear*, Williams observes a broad range of often conflicting meanings: "from nature as the primitive condition before human society; through the sense of an original innocence from which there has been a fall and a curse, requiring redemption" (*Keywords*, 222). It signifies the "special sense of a quality of birth," to be found in the Latin root *natura*, which literally means "birth" and links "nature" to related terms like "native" and "nation." Further still, he notes, a paradoxical juxtaposition between the "destructive natural force of thunder" and "that simple and persistent form of the goddess, Nature herself" (*Keywords*, 222). Such usages betray not only an uncertainty but also a tension; "nature," Williams concludes, "was at once pure innocent, unprovided, sure, unsure, fruitful, destructive, a pure force and tainted and cursed" (*Keywords*, 222). An abiding question for our consideration thus concerns the *ethical and ecological consequences* of the conflicts, contradiction, opacities, and aporias that structure human understandings of nature and non-human life. In other words, how have such widely varying perceptions of the natural world shaped human action and behavior toward it?

To be sure, thinking about and theorizing the natural world and our relation to it is one of the most enduring aspects of human thought and has occupied a central place in philosophy from the beginning, but this is most particularly—and ambivalently—so in the modern era, as the *Lear* passage serves to illustrate. Hence, why, how, and what nature and related terms come to mean for literary and social theory are not only very interesting questions, given the layers of complexity involved, but absolutely crucial, as we observe over and over the various ideological uses to which the invocation of nature is put to legitimate or justify an existing, and quite often unequal, status quo. As we argue in chapter 6, labeling something "natural" implies that it is impervious to change, inevitable, a given—and appropriately so; we cannot and should not do anything to alter it. Thus categorizing certain behaviors "natural" or "unnatural" serves a very powerful normative function indeed.

Working Question

Moral panics about what constitutes appropriate and inappropriate reading material for children have a long history in American life, sending the nation's youth scurrying off to read such "trash" as *Huckleberry Finn, Romeo and Juliet,* and *Catcher in the Rye* under the bed covers with a flashlight since well before we were kids. Currently the number-one banned book in the United States is Justin Richardson and Peter Parnell's *And Tango Makes Three,* a picture book for the four-to-eight-year-old set. In fact, it has held steady at the top spot since its publication in 2006. *Tango* tells the true story of Roy and Silo, two male penguins currently living in the Central Park Zoo, who share a nest and raise together an orphaned baby penguin. Seems harmless enough, yet it has spawned an avalanche of national media attention and so much controversy along the way that it also came in number-one on the American Library Association's annual list of "works attracting the most complaints from parents and school officials," surpassing even the allegedly anti-Christian, pro-witchcraft Harry Potter series (Associated Press, "Book on Male Penguins"). Cathy Collett, a literary theorist whose research focuses on romantic conceptions of childhood and education, raises a compelling question: "Why this book? Why not *Mom And Mum Are Getting Married?*—a picture book for the same age group, published the same year, that tells the story of a couple of same-sex *humans* raising two children?" (2–3).

What do you think? Why all the hubbub about heretofore adorable penguins? How does *And Tango Makes Three* complicate the desire to categorize what is natural or biological versus what is cultural or social—and by extension what we assume to be "normal" versus "aberrant" identities or behaviors? Which laws—those of nature or culture—would appear more iron-clad or resistant to rebellion?

But there is another obvious and pressing reason to engage questions of nature in relation to society, which has everything to do with the magnitude of the environmental problems that involve not just some regions or some populations of the globe—spawning competition and cooperation, anxiety and aggression among them—but the very viability of the planet. Global warming and attendant forms of climate change, deforestation, desertification, acid rain, air pollution, water contamination, endangered species and the loss of biodiversity, genetically modified or "frankenfood," famine, floods, food and water scarcity, depletion of natural resources, factory farming—all grab big headlines these days. So, too, related controversies over the benefits and costs, the legality and morality, of biotechnical innovations in reproductive technologies, genetic engineering, and cloning, to say nothing of the ecological consequences of new biological, chemical, and nuclear weaponry that constitute central preoccupations in contemporary society. As a result of rapid and astounding breakthroughs in science and technology that mark the modern (and postmodern) era, humans have the capacity to radically transform—and utterly endanger—the earth's ecosystems large and small. Over the course of the last century, in fact, such "advances" have led to the capacity to level densely populated cities, if not destroy the entire planet, in pretty much the time it takes to boil an egg. Yet the stockpiling of weapons of mass destruction (WMD) by a minority of the world's nations remains a generalized threat, in spite of Strategic Arms Limitation Talks and other treaty agreements, as "rogue" nations and populations remain committed to the relentless research and testing in pursuit of their own WMDs. And the Hollywood blockbuster machine turns out one terrifying visual narrative of apocalypse after another.

As we have already discussed at some length the ideological power of references to nature in chapter 6, we focus here on the latter set of concerns. As we shall see, how nature is *theorized* over time and in different cultural contexts has everything to do with how the natural world is *acted upon* by humanity. Our primary interest is in the distinctively *modern* way of thinking about the natural world, particularly the differences between nature and culture, which have tended for the most part to set nature and society sharply apart from each other. The political philosopher Thomas Hobbes, for example, defined life in the "state of nature" as "solitary, poore, nasty, brutish and short" (*Leviathan*, 96), hence he designed and defended the necessity of a strong, centralized sovereign power in the form of the modern nation-state to provide stability and security as the very precondition for human sociality. His conception of nature, in fact, marks an important rupture in the history of political thought. Political theorist Thomas Lemke notes that for Hobbes (and liberal modernity more generally) the recourse to the natural world "makes it possible to leave nature behind, or more precisely to leave behind a certain concept of nature that conceives of it as eternal, holy or unchangeable" (*Biopolitics*, 46). If in the Middle Ages good government was thought to be "part of the natural order created by God's will," thus foreclosing the necessity for political action and intervention in deference to divine law, in modernity, nature becomes the main point of reference for state imposition of order out of chaos. Thus Hobbes proposed the Leviathan, an artifice through which "brutish" nature was to be controlled and curtailed. In contrast, Jean-Jacques Rousseau provides a dissenting view from the vision of the natural world pitched in a war of "all against all" offered by Hobbes and many of his contemporaries. Rousseau insists that man was by nature cooperative rather than relentlessly competitive and self-interested. For Rousseau the *costs* of civilization—alienation from nature chief among them—were far greater than the alleged benefits. And indeed, Rousseau's doubts about the Enlightenment faith in science and technology as the primary motor for civilizational progress have been echoed by subsequent thinkers up to the present era. We should note quickly in passing that neither of these contrasting visions of the "state of nature" result from putatively objective or value-free observation and research; rather, Hobbes and Rousseau, like all thinkers henceforth, read into the natural world characteristics amenable to his own perception of human tendency and political possibility. In other words, nature serves as a kind of mirror reflecting—and so revealing—much more about the observer than about what is objectively out there.

So what does it mean to make nature the object of state action, as opposed to taking the hands-off approach to "God's creation," as the medievals had done? Well, as an extension of this new way of thinking about nature, modernity ushered in a number of revolutionary changes in social, economic, and political thought, but basic to all these intellectual shifts is an abiding obsession with *order*. According to sociologist Zygmunt Bauman, the commitment to order is expressed in myriad ways: through the will to dominate nature through the force of state reason, as we saw in the earlier Hobbesian example; through the rendering of nature transparent by discovery of the "laws of nature," a metaphor that invites comparison to the (equally inviolable) laws established by sovereign power. Further, order is created through the act of naming, ranking, and classifying the natural world according to systems of scientific thought like those of Linnaeus. And order enables the mastery of nature, understood here in both nonhuman and human manifestations, by way of "*design, manipulation, management, engineering*" (italics in original; *Modernity*, 7). So we see the drive to order in the scientific categorization and arrangement of all forms of life. In terms of governance, the principle of order is made visible in new bureaucratic modes of organizing and managing populations and in legal codification; in economics, it is manifest through the laws of the market and reason's "hidden hand." As a result of the imposition of order, nature's opacity and obscurity are supposed to give way to rational transparency and regularity; indeterminacy and ambivalence are to dissolve into predictability and certainty; irrationality and chaos give way to reason and rational self- and social determination. In short, Bauman and Tim May observe that in modernity

> nature and society were "discovered" simultaneously. What was in fact discovered was neither nature nor society, but the distinction between them and especially the distinction between the practices that each one enabled or gave rise to. As human conditions appeared more and more to be products of the legislation, management and intervention in general, "nature" assumed the role of a huge depository for everything which human powers could not yet or had no ambition to mould; everything, that is, which was seen as being ruled by its own logic and left by humans to its own devices. (*Thinking Sociologically*, 125)

Success in the establishment of order (culture) over chaos (nature) requires the transformation of what was once improbable into the necessary and inevitable. As Hobbes understood, nature must be restrained or "moulded" in the interests of security and stability; order thus became a matter of power—a matter of willful imposition and force as much as rationalization and calculation. Yet we also see that in the incessant drive to order and control the natural world, what comes to constitute culture as opposed to nature necessarily shifts with every technoscientific advancement that renders nature a little more knowable and a little more manipulable. The ironic upshot of the obsession with security and protection offered by the vision of a perfectly ordered world is that, ecologically speaking, the world is more insecure and vulnerable than ever—and it is now nature that needs protection from human contact, given ongoing decimation of the planet's resources. In the end, we may find ourselves more free from the vicissitudes of nature, but will we be more free in general? Bauman and May raise the chilling question as to whether the regulating, ordering, and ecologically devastating force of culture "may appear to the individual in much the same way as the laws of nature: it is a fate against which one cannot rebel, or against which rebellion is, ultimately, a futile gesture" (*Thinking Sociologically*, 127).

Central to modernity's ordering logic is the desire to classify and distinguish, to set things and people apart through acts of segregation and discrimination—to master and subjugate. As we saw with Freudian psychoanalytics, the perceived need to dominate, control, and thus tame external nature through the use of reason is also manifest in the imperative to repress man's natural instincts. But not all humans were perceived to be equal to the task. The modern man of reason excluded categorically all women and nonwhite populations, who were understood to be biologically inferior, where not animal or subhuman, from public life. (Recall, for example, the preamended U.S. Constitution defined a black man as three-fifths of a man.) And it is in view of the violence that results from the double imperative to order and control both nature and humanity that later theorists take up and build upon Rousseau's doubts about modernity's civilizing mission. Surely one result of the Enlightenment faith in rationality is the reduction of the natural environment to mere instrumentality. The natural world thus became disenchanted. Stripped of any intrinsic worth, nature is seen to possess value only insofar as its vast resources prove useful, profitable, or otherwise amenable to human needs and desires. But the critique of instrumentalism has not only aimed at the astonishing and radically unequal diminishment of the earth's recourses by a small minority of its population. In their influential work *Dialectic of Enlightenment*, the Frankfurt school theorists Max Horkheimer and Theodor Adorno examine the perils of an ever "advancing" scientific, technological, industrial society governed through the logic of control and domination. Like Rousseau before them, they question whether modernity's grand vision of a world literally designed to order actually led to an improvement in the human condition—or to its imminent self-destruction: "What men want to learn from nature is how to use it in order wholly to dominate it and other men" (4). From their perspective, the imperial aspirations of emerging nation-states, new capitalist markets, new technologies, new modes of instrumentalist thinking and acting—all of these structured and perpetuated the gross exploitation of the natural world and would eventually and inevitably come to define and degrade human social relations. Thus the domination and exploitation of nature leads to domination and exploitation of humans. Horkheimer and Adorno conclude, "Men have become so utterly estranged from one another and from nature that all they know is what they need each other for and the harm they do to each other" (*Dialectic of Enlightenment*, 253). But it is Frederick Douglass, reflecting on his situation as a slave charged with the task of taming two wild oxen in his second autobiography, *My Bondage and My Freedom*, who most succinctly, eloquently, and eerily captures the unfolding logic of modernity's underside: "I now saw, in my situation, several points of similarity with the oxen. They were property, so was I; they were to be broken, so was I. Covey was to break me, I was to break them; break and be broken—such is life" (132).

For all the allegedly civilizing work of the last several centuries, humanity would appear to remain more often than not mired in the Hobbesian war of "all against all." Zygmunt Bauman explains:

> Modernity legitimizes itself as a "civilizing process"—as an ongoing process of making the coarse gentle, the cruel benign,

the uncouth refined. Like most legitimations, however, this one is more an advertising copy than an account of reality. At any rate, it hides as much as it reveals. And what it hides is that only through the coercion they perpetuate can the agencies of modernity keep out of bounds the coercion they swore to annihilate; that one person's civilizing process is another person's forceful incapacitation. The civilizing process is not about the uprooting, but about the *redistribution* of violence. (*Life in Fragments*, 141)

In confrontation with "savage" populations—Hegel's benighted subjects frozen in the state of nature, denied development and so history—the rules of civility do not apply, as histories of colonization and enslavement painfully attest. To be sure, coercion and force can find justification even within modernity's well-ordered and civil spaces, Bauman elaborates, provided they are *rationally deployed*, that they become a "known necessity." In this instance, "civilized violence" is "violence rendered civil" through the standardization and routinization of forced restrictions or impositions on targeted populations. Violence here is the effect of instrumental rationality and the reifications it inevitably produces rather than a naturalistic or transcendent principle. It is against this image of an increasingly more volatile and constrained world that another member of the Frankfurt school, Herbert Marcuse, called for the "liberation of nature," which did not mean turning back to or recreating a pretechnological, idyllic age by packing it in, buying a farm, or living on a commune—if such a thing were even possible or desirable. Rather, he proposed freeing both humanity and nature by harnessing to those ends the vast achievements of science and technology all too often unleashed in the service of gross exploitation and exclusion.

Of course there have been more conservative conceptions of and justifications for forms of violence and suffering inflicted on various populations, which are also grounded in a particular understanding of human interaction with the natural world and the growing realization of ecological limitation. As far back as 1798, Thomas Malthus challenged prevailing Enlightenment wisdom and criticized its leading philosophers and social theorists for thinking that the future of humanity was destined to be one of ongoing progressive improvement in social, political, and economic conditions.

In the first of six editions of his *An Essay on the Principles of Population as It Affects the Future Improvement of Society*, published that year, Malthus takes to task those intellectuals who imprudently and unscientifically speculate that the Age of Reason—which gave birth to the French Revolution, or in his view a murderous campaign to destroy government by blood-thirsty masses—would eventually realize the dream of a society "devoid of war, crime, government, disease, anguish, melancholy, and resentment, where every man unflinchingly sought in the good of all" (cited in Barry, *Environment and Social Theory*, 61). Against such confident predictions, he declares utopian visions of social improvement impossible precisely on natural grounds. Malthus argues that population growth results from times and regions of plenty and contracts when the population exceeds the ecological resources necessary to sustain it. Not only does he assert that throughout human history and in every society a certain segment of the population is inevitably relegated to poverty by virtue of this calculus, but also that aid to the poor would only artificially increase their numbers (lacking as the "lower classes" did, or so he believed, any moral restraint around sexual activity) and add to their eventual and inevitable misery. "In all societies," he writes, "even those that are most vicious, the tendency to a virtuous attachment is so strong that there is a constant effort towards an increase of population. This constant effort as constantly tends to subject the lower classes of the society to distress and to prevent any great permanent amelioration of their condition" (18). If enlightened social and political thought answered the challenges posed by the excess of population with, paradoxically, more population (i.e., more workers and more soldiers equaled more production, more acquisition, more growth, more happiness, and in turn more power), Malthus theorizes "surplus population" as a variety of human waste to be disposed of, lest its presence gum up a smoothly running economy and bring about the decline and fall of the entire society.

Unsurprisingly then, Malthus staunchly opposes state aid to the poor, suggesting instead that the withdrawal of governmental forms of support would only serve to "motivate" them to shake off sloth and seek gainful employment. A man of religious faith and a member of the clergy, he believes that the constant threat of poverty and hunger are part of God's design and teaches the preeminent virtues of hard work and virtuous behavior. Catastrophic events like famines, epidemics, and wars serve as natural checks on population growth when it stretches beyond a region's inviolable ecological limits and are *productive* occurrences that call for neither prevention nor intervention, for without the test of such struggles, human society he feels would never have evolved beyond of its initial state of savagery: "Evil exists in the world not to create despair, but activity" (*An Essay on the Principles of Population*, 138). Thus Malthus not only insists on the inevitability but also the desirability of poverty and inequality within society (Barry, *Environment and Social Theory*, 61).

Working Question

Does Malthusian logic sound familiar? It should. Malthus was satirized in the character of Ebenezer Scrooge, whose disgust for the poor in Charles Dickens's *A Christmas Carol* was matched only by his praise for prisons and workhouses. Recall those heartwarming lines that follow Scrooge's refusal to help alleviate the suffering of the poor and destitute. Two gentleman request a small donation:

> "What shall I put you down for?"
> "Nothing!"

"You wish to be anonymous?"

"I wish to be left alone. Since you ask me what I wish, gen-tlemen, that is my answer. I don't make merry myself at Christmas, and I can't afford to make idle people merry. I help to support the prisons and the workhouses,—they cost enough,—and those who are badly off must go there."

"Many can't go there; and many would rather die."

"If they would rather die, they had better do it, and decrease the surplus population."

More recently, around Christmas 2010, condemnation of state aid for the poor was voiced once again, not as satire, but as straight-forward public policy. While championing the rich and claiming that they don't get justice, a Fox news pundit "debunked" the "lie" that the poor are suffering. He said,

When you get things for free you don't appreciate them. We don't appreciate the things we have, and I mean even me, we don't appreciate our country because it was handed to us. Instead, we just long for things other people have. We never have enough. We shouldn't begrudge millionaires or billion-aires. Our grandparents would have taught us that we could be the next millionaire or billionaire. Hell, it's America. (LiveLeaks.com)

Where do you stand on this hot-button issue of the day? What responsibility does government have to help its citizens or residents who fall on hard times, get sick, or get old—what kind of safety nets should people be provided in exchange for the taxes they pay? Should the state provide services to the poor, or does aid only serve to promote dependency and sloth? Are the poor people poor by choice or natural inclination—or is there any truth to the claim that poverty is an effect of systemic economic exploitation?

Although Malthus had many critics—William Godwin, Shelley, Marx, and Engels most famously among them—his controversial doctrines were deeply influential for thinkers as diverse as John Stuart Mill and Charles Darwin. Darwin in fact exalted Malthus as a "great philosopher," readily acknowledging his authority, though he clearly departed from orthodox religious beliefs about creationism in support of his own theory of human evolution. In his autobiography, he describes the influence Malthus's essay on population had on his theory of natural selection: "In October 1838 . . . I happened to read for amusement Malthus on *Population*. . . . It at once struck me that under these circumstances favourable variations would tend to be preserved, and unfavourable ones to be destroyed. The result of this would be the formation of new species" (*The Autobiography of Charles Darwin*, 128). Applying this logic to human affairs, social Darwinists, as they came to be called, were fond of echoing Malthusian claims that helping the poor merely enabled the unfit to artificially survive and thus held back the course of social evolution, which was premised on the survival of the fittest. Just as the study of natural selection and species interaction rendered "nature, red in tooth and claw," the study of social evolution and the interaction between individuals and groups in society, especially within the economic sphere, were imagined to be governed by the same ironclad laws of nature. For social Darwinists of the late nineteenth century, as for today's economic Darwinists, the basest forms of competition, self-interestedness, and ruthlessness in economic life could be and were justified on the grounds that such behavior is rooted in the science of social evolution and its particular conception of human nature, a disposition generally devoid of the capacity for cooperation, compassion, and solidarity.

Animals

If Freud blurs the line of demarcation between human beings and animals by theorizing the comparable role of instinct in guiding human social behaviors as well as the need to harness an untamed human nature, Darwin, as we've already discussed, obliterates the human–animal distinction by insisting unequivocally that humans *are* animals, more specifically a subspecies of primates. Since Darwin, evolutionary biology and related empirical sciences have continued to attack hard and fast dichotomies between human and nonhuman life, preferring instead a kind of continuum that describes differences among living organisms only by degree. Similarly, scholars in the social sciences and humanities have also experienced difficulty in maintaining what Heidegger once called the "vast abyss of essence" that separates animals from humans, though the challenge to think critically and capaciously about non-human life has been only belatedly and ambivalently engaged. As Peter Atterton and Matthew Calarco observe, the same philosophical traditions that have largely rejected what figures like Descartes and Kant have claimed on behalf of man as a rational, independent, and free self (a critique we examine in chapter 4) and proclaimed in turn the "end of humanism," the "death of God," the "death of Man" and the "death of the author," have been strangely silent on the flip side of the constitutive human/animal distinction (*Animal Philosophy*, xv). While the romance with man appears to have come to an end, philosophy can't quite quit him. In fact those occasional efforts to theorize animality, even to question the priority of human life and human need over and against that of animals, consistently betray shored-up, hidden, and not-so-hidden humanist presumptions of animal lack and anthropological plentitude (Clark, "Towards a Prehistory of the Postanimal," 4).

With rare and always problematic exception, animals are defined, as the critical theorist David L. Clark explains, in terms of their perceived intellectual impoverishment, incompetence, and imbecility; they are "without consciousness, without self-consciousness, without language, without representation, without judgment, as they are without secrets, history, love, without the capacity to respond to inquiry or to address another, without the ability to laugh or mourn or make contracts, and finally, in Heidegger, without a form of death-oriented life" ("Towards a Prehistory of the Postanimal," 4). These explicit or implicit anthropocentric assumptions mark the limits of philosophical investment in engaging the "question of the animal" in moral and ethical terms. Denying animals even death, to say nothing of the sanctity of animal life, has been deeply consequential for theorizing notions of rights, justice, and responsibility to nonhuman life—as well as to those humans similarly denied rationality. Historically, we've seen not an extension of rights and protections but their violent and pervasive suspension. The distinguished philosopher Thomas Taylor, for example, reacted to Mary Wollstonecraft's stirring *Vindication of the Rights of Woman* (1792) with the bitterly satirical *Vindication of the Rights of Brutes* that same year, equating in their apparent absurdity the rights of women and the rights of animals. One exception to the generalized indifference to animals is the philosopher Jeremy Bentham, who advocates for women's rights, gay rights, and prison reform. Comparing and condemning the moral repugnance of slavery with animal sadism, Bentham asserts, "The question is not, Can they reason? Nor, Can they talk? but, Can they suffer?" (*An Introduction to the Principles of Morals and Legislation*, chapter 17, footnote 122). After all, he surmises, a mature horse or dog surely has more rational capacity and more ability to communicate than a human infant a day or a month old, yet we do not value the dog over the child. Neither the faculty of reason nor the faculty of discourse can provide an adequate justification for countenancing the priority of human over animal life. That said, it is important to note the rationale underpinning Bentham's sense of animal obligation, which is not a repudiation of killing animals for consumption or some other utilitarian ends, but of inflicting suffering. Rather, he holds that by engaging in cruel and tyrannical acts, we diminish *ourselves*; we violate not just animals but (more importantly, the implication seems to be) our humanity, particularly under those circumstances, like slavery, where such ascription to fellow humans is actively denied.

There remains in Bentham's philosophy and in philosophical thought more generally an abiding anthropomorphism that constrains political and legal conceptualizations of injustice in so far as injustice is inevitably understood as inhumanity. The subject of injustice, in other words, is always imagined to be, and necessarily is, a human subject. A similar limitation emerges in various forms of animal advocacy that appeal to rights discourse as it pertains to animal protection. In *The Philosophy of Animal Rights*, for example, Tom Regan seeks to demonstrate that animals are in many significant ways identical to humans, that they are "being subjects-of-a-life" or "subjects with personal preferences, desires, and a stake in how they are treated" (cited in Calarco, *Zoographies*, 8). Matthew Calarco counters that Regan's efforts still fall prey to anthropomorphic tendencies; he does not build a compelling case for animal rights but rather the rights for *subjects*. In other words, it is only "in as much as animals manifest morally relevant human, or subject-like traits, they are brought under the scope of moral consideration" (*Zoographies*, 8). One of the principle challenges for animal theorists like Calarco involves recognizing the limits of philosophical, legal, and moral discourses that presume an implicit anthropocentric, subject-centered model. This is no small task. As we explore in chapter 4, the notion of who is constituted by the law, hailed by the institutions of modern life, and seeks recognition from family, friends, and fellow workers through forms of communicative exchange that remain beholden to rational and linguistic competence is one of many discourses of capacity that has been used to deny animals even basic moral standing for centuries and in turn disavow obligation toward them. Jacques Derrida writes,

> It is *not just* a matter of asking whether one has the right to refuse the animal such and such a power (speech, reason, experience of death, mourning, culture, institutions, clothing, lying, pretense of pretense, covering of tracks, gift, laughter, crying, respect, etc.—the list is necessarily without limit, and the most

powerful philosophical tradition in which we live has refused
the "animal" *all of that*). It also means asking whether what
calls itself human has the right rigorously to attribute to man,
which means therefore attributing to himself, what he refuses
the animal, and whether he can ever possess the pure, rigorous,
indivisible concept, as such, of that attribution. (*The Animal
That Therefore I Am*, 135)

Indeed there are multiple conditions humans confront—infants and
very young children, those with have suffered brain injuries or the
end stage of terminal illness, soldiers and others traumatized by war,
the mentally challenged, the elderly afflicted with dementia, to name
just a few in extremis—that will invariably translate into their fail-
ure to meet the benchmark capacities that divide human from nonhuman, as Jeremy Bentham muses. We—whoever "we" are—do not
deny them humanity, but can we be said inevitably to have afforded
each life dignity or justice?

Another related and significant issue in the emerging field of
inquiry called "animal studies" concerns the very concept of animality itself, or the degree to which one can assume a shared essence
that binds all animals together in any kind of coherent or meaningful way. Functioning much like the critique of essentialism that we
explore in chapter 10, animal theorists reject the ways in which the
concept of animality functions both to mark off and separate out
humanity from the realm of animals and to impose a reductive
sameness across what appears to be radically different forms of life
(Calarco, *Zoographies*, 2–3). What might it be that could possibly
subtend and unite the staggering differences among one-celled creatures like amoebae and primates, fish and mammals, birds and
insects of infinite variety? If theorizing the differences between
humans and animals have proven difficult if not impossible for philosophy, so, too, have efforts to grasp the multiplying and myriad
distinctions among animals. One of the most incisive and compre-
hensive philosophical treatments of this question to date is to be

found in Derrida's *The Animal That Therefore I Am*. There he argues against the discursive tendency to refer to animals in what he calls the general singular, "The Animal," and invents the term "l'animot" to use in its place, which is meant to invoke the immense play of differences, the very plurality of animals. More significantly, Derrida challenges the very drive to homogenize the multiplicity of nonhuman life as both a "sin against rigorous thinking" and a "crime," a charge that is particularly consequential given, as Derrida readily acknowledges, the alarming upswing in the levels of violence visited on animals in the last two centuries, from the abuses that take place in animal testing laboratories to ever-expanding factory farms. He writes:

> among nonhumans and separate from nonhumans there is an immense multiplicity of other living things that cannot in any way be homogenized, except by means of violence and willful ignorance, within the category of what is called the animal or animality in general. From the outset there are animals and, let's say, l'animot. The confusion of all nonhuman living creatures within the general and common category of the animal is not simply a sin against rigorous thinking, vigilance, lucidity, or empirical authority; it is also a crime. Not a crime against animality precisely, but a crime of the first order against the animals, against animals. Do we agree to presume that every murder, every transgression of the commandment "Thou shalt not kill" concerns only man (a question to come) and that in sum there are only crimes "against humanity"? (48)

As philosophers and theorists past and present remind us, the field of animal studies opens up a staggering number of questions, from the most basic—What is an animal? Does such a being exist?—to the most intellectually and ethically challenging: How are we to engage the question of human understandings of and obligations toward nonhuman life, especially that infinite variety of life that is reduced too quickly to the singular conception of the animal? Do nonhuman animals oblige "us," whoever "we" are? Are responsibilities toward animals best expressed by the concept of rights—can they be the subjects of inviolable if not quite human rights? Or do we require a new language that is less subject-centered? Can animals speak—or be heard? Do they die or do they just stop living? Do they experience pleasure or joy? Loss or mourning? Do they suffer? If the concept of the animal represents an urgent challenge to ethics and to politics, to say nothing of the very anthropocentric foundation of modern and postmodern thought itself, how might a more rigorous and critical engagement with the discourse of the natural—to return once again to our favorite punk tune—change what we *do and how we act*? It is to this question of agency that we now turn.

Working Questions

1. In the November 2008 general election, ballots in the state of California listed a number of propositions upon which citizens were invited to vote. A vote "yes" for Proposition 2 on Standards for Confining Farm Animals addresses issues with veal calves, egg-laying hens and pregnant pigs—mandating they "be confined only in ways that allow these animals to lie down, stand up, fully extend their limbs and turn around freely." Exceptions are made for "transportation, rodeos, fairs, 4-H programs, lawful slaughter, research and veterinary purposes" (LA Law Library). A vote "yes" for Proposition 8, Eliminates Right of Same-Sex Couples to Marry, changes the California constitution to eliminate the right of same-sex couples to marry in California and provides that only marriage between a man and a woman is valid or recognized in California (LA Law Library).

How are traditional constructions of nature challenged or reinforced in each case? In the first instance, how is the line between animality and humanity—at least in terms of rights discourse—effectively blurred, challenging how we understand and

Figure 12.1 Egg Hen House.
© iStockphoto.com/rrodrickbeiler

construct our responsibilities to the natural world? In the second instance, what kind of ideological work does the question of nature perform in relation to gay rights? On what grounds are rights in this instance not extended but curtailed? Is it an advancement to support the rights of certain animals over a certain population of humans?

2. Martin Heidegger argues that animals do not die; being instances of what he calls "mere life" or "just-plain-life," animals thrive and then stop living. More recently Isaac Bashevis Singer asserts the counterpossibility that animals not only die, but are also subject to systemic and hideous murder, comparing the conditions that factory-farmed animals endured en route to their slaughter to that suffered by the Jews in the Nazi death camps. Life for animals, he argues, "is an eternal Treblinka" (cited in Clark, "Towards a Prehistory of the Postanimal," 31). To say the very least, Singer's allusion to the Holocaust is both consequential and controversial, although he was not the first to make the comparison. To satisfy the world's appetite for meat, for clothing, for décor, are animals not only slaughtered but also murdered? Does the Final Solution (the systematic killing of the European Jews, the infirm, gays, and other supposed enemies of the Nazi state) share a history with the industrialization of farming—the agrobusiness—of pigs, chickens, and cows for human consumption and use? Or is there inevitably a kind of violence to this thing called life?

Even if we refuse to accept this admittedly shocking analogy, animals theorist David L. Clark encourages us to ponder "how the denial of 'death' to the animal and, for that matter, the attribution of a certain privileged mortal 'life' to human Dasein can form a dreadful alibi for all sorts of murderous violence, for what Derrida calls the 'non-criminal putting to death . . . not of animals but other humans as well by marking them *as* animal'" ("Towards a Prehistory of the Postanimal," 2).

For Further Reading

Associated Press. "Book on Male Penguins Tops Complaint List." August 30, 2008. Available online at http://today.msnbc.msn.com/id/20480366. Accessed April 3, 2011.

Atterton, Peter, and Matthew Calarco, eds. *Animal Philosophy*. New York: Continuum, 2004.

Barry, John. *Environment and Social Theory*. 2d ed. New York: Routledge, 2007 (1999).

Bauman, Zygmunt. *Life in Fragments: Essays in Postmodern Morality*. Oxford: Blackwell, 1995.

———. *Modernity and Ambivalence*. Oxford: Polity Press, 1993.

———. *Wasted Lives: Modernity and Its Outcasts*. Cambridge: Polity, 2003.

Bauman, Zygmunt, and Tim May. *Thinking Sociologically*. 2d ed. Oxford: Blackwell, 2001 (1990).

Bentham, Jeremy. *An Introduction to the Principles of Morals and*

Legislation. Oxford: Clarendon Press, 1907. Library of Economics and Liberty. Available online at http://www.econlib.org/library/Bentham/bnthPML18.html. Accessed March 21, 2011.

Bookchin, Murray. *Ecology of Freedom: The Emergence and Dissolution of Hierarchy*. Oakland, CA: AK Press, 2005 (1991; 1982).

Calarco, Matthew. *Zoographies: The Question of the Animal from Heidegger to Derrida*. New York: Columbia University Press, 2008.

Clark, David L. "Towards a Prehistory of the Postanimal: Kant, Levinas, and the Regard of Brutes." Unpublished Manuscript. Available at http://www.humanities.mcmaster.ca/~dclark/documents/courses/767/PrehistoryofthePostanimal%20Oberlin.pdf. Accessed March 23, 2011.

Collett, Cathy. "And 'Tango' Makes It to the Top of the Banned Book List: Censoring the Queer in Children's Picture Books." Unpublished Manuscript.

Darwin, Charles. *The Autobiography of Charles Darwin 1809–1882*, edited by Nora Barlow. London: Collins, 1958.

———. *On the Origin of Species by Means of Natural Selection, Or, The Preservation of Favoured Races in the Struggle for Life*. London: Hurst, 1911 (1861).

Derrida, Jacques. *The Animal That Therefore I Am*, edited by Marie-Louis Mallet, translated by David Wills. New York: Fordham University Press, 2008.

Dickens, Charles. *A Christmas Carol*. New York: Dover, 1991.

Douglass, Fredrick. *My Bondage and My Freedom*, edited by William L. Andrews. Urbana: University of Illinois Press, 1987 (1855).

Freud, Sigmund. *Civilization and Its Discontents*, translated by David McLintock. New York: Penguin, 2002 (1930).

"Glenn Beck Calls the Suffering of the Poor a Lie, Just in Time for Christmas." LiveLeaks.com. Available at http://www.liveleak.com/view?c=1&i=be1_1291338231. Accessed January 22, 2011.

Heiddegger, Martin. *Being and Time*, translated by John Macquarrie and Edward Robinson. New York: Harper & Row, 1962.

Hobbes, Thomas. *The Leviathan*, edited by A. P. Martinich. Peterborough, ON: Broadview Press, 2002 (1651).

Horkheimer, Max, and Theodor W. Adorno. *Dialectic of Enlightenment*, translated by John Cumming. London: Allen Lane, 1973.

LA Law Library. "California Ballot Propositions 2000–2009." Available online at http://www.lalawlibrary.org/research/ballots/2000/2008 .aspx. Accessed April 3, 2011.

Lemke, Thomas. *Biopolitics: An Advanced Introduction*. New York: New York University Press, 2011.

Malthus, Thomas Robert. *An Essay on the Principles of Population as It Affects the Future Improvement of Society*. 2d ed. Edited by Philip Appleman. New York: Norton, 2004 (1798).

Marcuse, Herbert. *Counterrevolution and Revolt*. London: Allen Lane, 1972.

———. "Ecology and the Critique of Modern Society," *Capitalism, Nature, Socialism* 3, no. 3 (1992): 29–38.

Nussbaum, Martha. *Frontiers of Justice: Disability, Nationality, Species Membership*. Cambridge, MA: Belknap/Harvard University Press, 2006.

Rousseau, Jean-Jacques. "Discourse on the Origin and Foundations of Inequality among Men or Second Discourse." In *Rousseau: The Discourses and Other Early Political Writings*, edited by Victor Gourevitch, 111–13. Cambridge: Cambridge University Press, 1997 (1754).

Singer, Peter, ed. *In Defense of Animals: The Second Wave*. Malden, MA: Blackwell, 2006.

Williams, Raymond. *Keywords: A Vocabulary of Culture and Society*. Rev. ed. New York: Oxford University Press, 1985 (1976).

13

Agency

This book has been loosely organized around what you can *do* with critical concepts: how you can deploy them in writing and thinking about culture and society. So, to that extent, we have been posing questions about *power and agency*. Given a particular set of constraints on our subjectivities, what actions, operations, and powers can be brought to bear in an interpretation or analysis?

Agency, in its simplest definition, is the power to *do* something. In the *American Heritage Dictionary*, the entry for "agency" illustrates this meaning by offering a helpful quotation: "We cannot ignore human agency in history." We cannot, in other words, ignore the fact that people create history by doing things; history is *made* rather than *found*. Subjects have agency—the ability to *respond* to their historical contexts and, with any luck at all, *change* them in the process. But the quotation also raises an interesting question: Why the need for such a warning? Why might we be likely to ignore or forget that people are agents? Although humans certainly do make history, everyday people tend not to see their actions as having much if any impact on the grand historical stage. Rather, history is often thought of as a kind of impersonal force that acts on them, "behind their backs" in Marx's famous formulation. Recall from chapter 7 that dominant narratives tend to exclude popular culture and everyday people from their plots, ascribing historic action to the very wealthy and/or powerful. In light of such representations, the reminder that people are agents who make history is all the more necessary, given the inclination to view the present as inevitable, the future as nothing more than a repetition of the past.

But how do we square this capacity for individual action with our earlier discussions about subjectivity? Doesn't such action presuppose the return of a free and independent self? Not so fast. One of the things we've been consistently trying to confront throughout our investigation of theory is the fact that people are *subject to* their historical contexts rather than *master of* them. None of us is in control of the social spaces that we inhabit; nor are we completely in control of the subject positions that we occupy. Take, for example, Woody Allen. He is a male, filmmaker, writer, white guy, jazz performer. These are all tags that may or may not apply to him. Yet his subjective agency—the things that he *does*—will finally have a lot to say about whether or not people apply these labels to him; one obviously has to exercise agency to become a writer or to become a musician.

But at the end of the day, these choices are not simply or unproblematically "our own." The contexts in which any particular agent acts and makes decisions have a good deal of influence on those decisions; for example, it's not merely a coincidence that there are a lot of Canadians and Russians in the National Hockey League or that polo hasn't caught on as a participant sport in the inner city. There are, it seems clear, contextual factors that make certain people more likely to engage in certain acts.

In any case, the point is this: Our choices always are made in contexts that we do not control. We are not born with an innate longing to play soccer, hockey, or basketball; we learn to want the things we desire in the context in which we find ourselves. Even what we think of as our deepest secret dreams—to be a writer or an astronaut or a rock star—are, on further reflection, effects of our surroundings. Our agency—what we want, what we strive for—has contextual sources rather than some source deep inside us.

And, we might add in passing, there are some even more obvious limits to one's agency: None of us has chosen the racial identity we inhabit, for example, nor can we simply renounce that subject position. Agency is obviously crucial in determining who you are, but it just as obviously has its limits. Our agency is both *constrained* and *enabled* by the contexts in which we find ourselves.

Working Questions

1. What could that last sentence possibly mean? How can agency or action be *enabled* by something that *constrains* or *limits* it? Isn't agency an escape from the limits imposed on us? Following that metaphor, how can such an "escape" be enabled by the "imprisonment" that it presupposes? Say, for example, you're stuck in a bad relationship—your agency is constrained by it, so you decide to get out. How is it that such a situation (stuck in a go-nowhere relationship) actually enables agency rather than simply limiting it?

2. Consider the following spoof ads put out by Adbusters (figures 11.1, 11.2, and 11.3). How do they work? What's their point? As a form of response to the corporate takeover of public spaces, or a challenge to the dubious claims of advertisers, how do the ads reflect subjective agency?

Figure 11.1 Image courtesy of www.adbusters.org

Figure 11.2 Image courtesy of www.adbusters.org

Another way of stating this point about constraint and possibility would be to discuss the workings of power. To have agency, you'd seem to need to wield a certain amount of power. But you also need to have a sense of how power in its various manifestations is at work on you.

But how does power work? For starters, it's important to recognize what power isn't. It isn't a singular force, a kind of stable monolithic structure with a center. Nor is it a commodity that some have access to and others don't. It is a much more diffuse, multiple, decentered, social field that is continually shifting and always negotiated. The critical terms we've covered in this book are all imbricated in the workings of power. Authority, for example, is frequently used as a synonym for power, as when we warn potential intruders that we'll call the authorities if they come into our homes. Further, forms of authority vary; there is the abstract authority of the Law

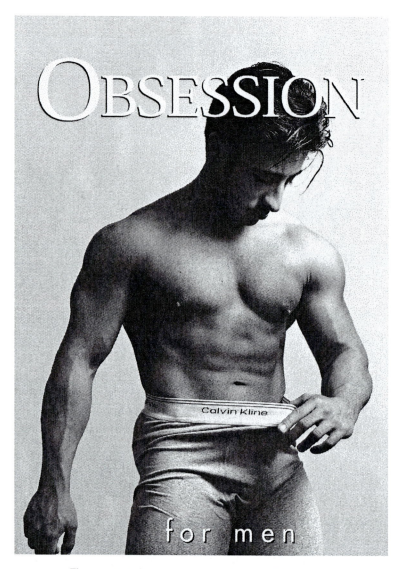

Figure 11.3 Image courtesy of www.adbusters.org

and its embodied enforcers, the police and the military; religious authority, parental authority, and the authority claimed by myriad "professionals" from medical doctors to housing inspectors to electrical engineers. And the nature of our responses to all of these also varies. The capacity of institutions or individual "experts" to define the rules of reading, that is, delimiting what is considered "appropriate" inquiry across disciplines and fields, to determine what constitutes an "acceptable" interpretation of texts—whether we're talking about an artist's body of work, a historic event like 9/11, or the U.S. Constitution—or to frame the terms of particular public or scholarly debates wields considerable power in constructing "legitimate" forms of knowledge.

The capacity of some ideologies to gain the force of common sense—a given that requires no thought and certainly no questioning—bespeaks another form of power. And as we've read, subjects are conceived in and through ideology. By virtue of social norms operative in any given society, certain subject positions exercise more power and experience greater freedoms than others. Being wealthy, for example, often translates into greater capacity to make choices, to take control over one's time, to enhance one's mobility—all of which create the conditions for improved security, health, and happiness, but not across all contexts. We can imagine an alternative scenario in which being rich makes us targets for various scams, even violence. Complicating matters further, recognition—how others see us—plays a central role in the construction of our identities. The subject positions we occupy are never simply a function of what we choose for ourselves. Granting or withholding recognition, then, is another manifestation of how we use power and how power is used on us.

Selecting, shaping, and circulating particular images and stories through media or history books privileges certain understandings of the world and censors others. Such activity also requires no small amount of power. We've discussed those discourses characterized by the prefix "post"—postmodernism, poststructuralism, and postcolonialism—that are in different ways challenges to traditional forms of authority, dominant beliefs, legitimate knowledge, and "universal truths." And such challenges require agency, our capacity to make choices and act, another form of power.

Power is generally conceived as force that dominates, but as this laundry list of examples indicates, it's never simply that. Its operations are far too multiple and complex. Think about it: When you're ordered to do something by a parent, teacher, cop, or other authority figure, do you always comply? Why not? Shouldn't a "superior" power or authority always dominate an "inferior" one? Shouldn't power simply repress your individual desires and force you to obey or conform? Shouldn't the power of "constraint" add up to power as "control"? Doesn't power seek and cause repression and obedience? Don't authorities keep citizens in line by making sure that they refrain from doing certain forbidden things? In the end, doesn't power simply say, "No, you can't do that"?

Of course, power certainly does repress. And it represses in different ways. The power that your father wields is different from that of a government official, a cleric such as a priest or rabbi, or the masked figure who holds a gun to your head as he robs you blind. And transgression carries different kinds of consequences. For example, your father can take away your car or starve you financially, a police officer can toss you in jail, and a priest can threaten you with eternal damnation. Different forms of power demand different responses—some require our participation; others require total passivity. In other words, we give consent to some forms of authority, while others are achieved through coercion. We tend to listen to our parents to the degree that we love them and they deserve respect. Other forms of power allow no negotiation and do not require our participation in any way, as in the case of being car-jacked.

But power, as we've insisted, isn't simply about repression; it also produces. Sometimes when your father said no, it made you all the more determined to go ahead and do it anyway, against his wishes. Although one of the functions of power is to repress or control, power also produces lots of other things: resistance, anger, conflict, knowledge, and even pleasure. As philosopher Michel Foucault writes:

> In defining the effects of power by repression, . . . one identifies power with a law that says no. . . . Now, I believe that this is a wholly negative, narrow, and skeletal conception of power. . . . If power was never anything but repressive, if it never did anything but say no, do you really believe that we should manage to obey it? What gives power its hold, what makes it accepted, is quite simply the fact that it does not simply weigh like a force which says no, but that it runs through, and it produces things, it induces pleasure, it forms knowledge, it produces discourse; it must be considered a productive network which runs through the entire social body much more than as a negative instance whose function is repression. (*Power/Knowledge*, 119)

How, we might wonder, does power "produce" things as well as repress things? Aren't these contradictory modes? How can the power of repression—the stifling of agency—be the same as the power of liberation? How can the power that constrains be the same power that enables? Wouldn't there have to be a distinction between the "good" power that enables and the "bad" power that controls? And what if repressive power happens to produce good things? Consider Freud's thesis in *Civilization and Its Discontents*: Repression advances cultural achievement!

Certainly one can make such distinctions after the fact; any particular deployment of power can be judged by its "good" or "bad" effects. But power or agency "is" never anything but its effects. The potential to do something is neither here nor there, neither good nor bad. As with performativity, agency is agency only in action. Acts, like words, don't mean something outside a particular context; what's repression in one context is liberation in another.

❖ Working Question

Simple question: George Washington was of course commander of the U.S. Revolutionary Army and first president. So, was he a hero or a traitor, a force of righteous liberation or a force of unlawful insurrection? Or does it depend on whom you ask? He was certainly a terrorist to the English, while he remains a hero to Americans. But in 1776, one way or the other, he was a dangerous revolutionary, no?

Subjects and their actions aren't meaningful or describable outside a historical and social context—recall our insistence that meaning is not *inherent*—but at the same time, subjects are not *merely* or *simply* determined by their contexts. But if subjects are determined and made meaningful by their contexts, how can they ever break out of or remake those contexts?

How, in short, can you have "agency" if all subjects are social constructions? Logically speaking, aren't the subjects who are *created* by a system simply going to *follow* that system slavishly? Wouldn't any resistance to social contexts—any real agency—have to come from elsewhere, perhaps from the shadowy unconstrained "self" rather than the socially constructed "subject"? Indeed, is there any agency at all in such a socially constructed system, where a subject's decisions are not so much *actions* as they are programmed *effects* of the system?

To put the question straightforwardly, if we are all subject to social contexts (if our subjectivity is *created* in social contexts), why and how does anyone ever *resist* or *remake* dominant norms? Why does anyone ever *do* anything not endorsed by the social context of norms? If societies produce subjects like assembly lines produce cars, how does a Taurus factory of a society ever produce a Camaro or a Jaguar? Most pointedly put, the question might be this: How is it that the norms of a society produce resistance, when logically they should produce only obedience?

First of all, it may be important to point out that to say that something is *constructed* doesn't mean that it's determined in some lockstep way. One need look no further than literature to see this: Shakespeare's plays or Joyce's novels are very intricately constructed, but that doesn't mean that their meaning is somehow determined in their creation; likewise, Einstein's work on atomic physics did not somehow determine the deployment of nuclear weapons and the Cold War. The social construction of something is a far cry from determining what it does or what it means; this is true both of human subjects and more seemingly inert social constructions like books or scientific knowledge.

Rather, what something does or what it means depends on how it is used. As we've insisted all along, race or meaning or subjectivity are not inherently meaningful categories; what they mean depends on the contexts in which we find them. And, in turn, those contexts are not essential; they are, in both theory and practice, always changing and changeable. Recall the idea from philosopher Jacques Derrida: "There is no meaning outside of context, but no context permits saturation" ("Living On—Border Lives," 81). Because there is no "saturated" or final context, one can always recontextualize something from another angle. Because all meaning is contextual, all meaning presupposes an agency, an act, an analysis, a critical reading, to bring it about.

It is important to point out once again that this does not boil down to the formula "it means what I think it means." The subject itself is produced in a context, and its agency, as we noted above, is inexorably constrained and enabled by the contexts it finds itself in. Your knowledge of English allows you to read Shakespeare or the King James Bible or mediaeval chronicles, but at the same time your reading of these texts is constrained by your lack of knowledge in other areas: the specific vocabulary, the texts' historical contexts, the interpretative history, etc.

Shakespeare or a medieval history text is already "there," so to speak, when you come to it; it already exists in a number of contexts.

Likewise, everything you come upon in the world is not simply something that's in your control; this language that we're writing and the people that we know are not simply or even primarily "ours." A word is a bridge erected between oneself and the other.

While we do all sorts of things, we don't so much act as react to situations in which we find ourselves. Everyday we find ourselves constantly in contexts that are not of our own creation; it is in the way that we respond to situations and others that our agency is born. Contexts constrain us, but they likewise give us the means to respond specifically to situations and other people. Even when someone says "Hi" to you in the hall, that is a kind of constraint, something that you could not have predicted or brought about, something that's done "to" you. When you say "howsagoin?" in response, you've practiced a certain "agency" by responding correctly. Although this may seem a trivial example, the ability to respond—that response-ability—is the birth of all agency. And you don't get to choose, really; even not responding is a kind of response, one that has effects and consequences.

There is no response, no agency, no power, outside a context; the options for responding and for doing something meaningful or effective are given by the situation at hand. Agency, then, is always a response to already given contexts, and, as we've seen throughout the semester, in this sense the ways we respond to the everyday world are bundled up with the ways we respond to cultural texts. The creativity of the response—the way it works and reworks preexisting codes—is finally the measure of a subjective action. Similarly, the care and contextual creativity that we bring to the critical reading of a text decide the extent to which we've performed a successful or compelling critical reading or contextual response.

In the end, perhaps the key terminology to take away from this text is Saussure's reading of the linguistic signifier, which suggests that meaning is not inherent in words or things but comes about in social and contextual negotiations of differences. Saussure's insight here might be called the paradigm for all theoretical discourse, what's often called "the linguistic turn in the human sciences." If there are no "given" essences (Saussure: "there are no positive terms"), then all meaning must be worked out in a social process of signification. Saussure teaches us that things don't mean in themselves; they mean according to contexts.

So, for example, we've seen this insight worked out in terms of the subject: Who you are is not a "given" (or "positive term") but is rather beholden to ideology, history, race, gender, culture, and so on. There's a way in which, as we stated at the very beginning of this Toolbox, the first step of any "theory" is away from a naturalist or organicist understanding of the art object or the social space, toward the specific complexities of context: the work's context, the author's context, the reader's context, the subject's context. We've been trying to move away from a supposed "universalism" (which sees differences as insignificant or to be overcome) toward the specificities of response, toward an examination of the specific material processes or practices that make meaning: reading, authority, subjects, ideologies, histories.

To redeploy Saussure's linguistic insight, we might say that we've learned nothing but these powerful assertions: Wherever you think you see a noun, you're in fact already looking at a verb; wherever you think you see a conclusion, there's been a process or practice at work; and if you want to know what something means, you'd better take into account the process of meaning's production. What something means is inseparable from how it means (or historically how it's come to render things meaningful), on both the textual level of individual reading and the social level of social debate. Even in the places where things seem static, there's actually a lot going on.

And that's why we need a toolbox, to work on the present, to affect it, to build a present to live in.

For Further Reading

Butler, Judith. *The Psychic Life of Power: Theories in Subjection.* Stanford, CA: Stanford University Press, 1997.

Canetti, Elias. *Crowds and Power*, translated by Carol Stewart. New York: Farrar, Straus & Giroux, 1984 (1962).

Chomsky, Noam. *Understanding Power: The Indispensable Chomsky*. New York: New Press, 2002.

DeCerteau, Michel. *The Practice of Everyday Life*, translated by Steven Rendall. Berkeley: University of California Press, 1984.

Derrida, Jacques. "Living On—Border Lives." In *Deconstruction and Criticism*, edited by Harold Bloom et al., translated by James Hulbert. New York: Seabury Press, 1979.

Foucault, Michel. *Discipline and Punish*, translated by Alan Sheridan. New York: Vintage, 1979.

———. *Power/Knowledge: Selected Interviews and Other Writings 1972–1977*, translated by Colin Gordon. New York: Pantheon, 1980.

Hartsock, Nancy. *Money, Sex and Power: Toward a Feminist Historical Materialism*. New York: Longman, 1983

Hegel, G. W. F. *Phenomenology of Spirit*. Oxford: Oxford University Press, 1977 (1806).

Lukes, Stephen. *Power, A Radical View*. London: Macmillan, 1974.

Lukes, Stephen, ed. *Power*. Oxford: B. Blackwell, 1986.

Mills, C. Wright. *New Men of Power: America's Labor Leaders*. New York: A. M. Kelley, 1971 (1948).

———. *The Power Elite*. New York: Oxford University Press, 1956.

Parenti, Michael. *Power and Powerlessness*. New York: St. Martin's Press, 1979.

Russell, Bertrand. *Power: A New Social Analysis*. New York: Norton, 1969 (1938).

Credits

"Why Theory" written by Andy Gill, Jon King, David Allen, and Huge Burnham © Bug Music Ltd. (PRS)/Administered by Bug Music and Carbert Music Inc. (BMI)/Administered by Carlin America Inc. All Rights Reserved. Used by Permission. Reprinted by permission of Hal Leonard Corporation.

"Metaphors of a Magnifico" by Wallace Stevens. From *The Collected Poems of Wallace Stevens* by Wallace Stevens, © 1954 by Wallace Stevens and renewed 1982 by Holly Stevens. Used by permission of Alfred A. Knopf, a division of Random House, Inc.

"Before the Law" by Frank Kafka, translated by Ian Johnston. www.kafka.org/index.php?id=162,165,0,0,1,0. November 2003. Used by permission.

"Community" from *Franz Kafka: The Complete Stories* by Franz

Index

Italicized page numbers locate illustrations

About the Authors

JEFFREY NEALON teaches in the English Department at Penn State University. He is author of several "theory" books: *Double Reading: Postmodernism after Deconstruction* (1993), *Alterity Politics: Ethics and Performative Subjectivity* (1998), and the coedited collection *Rethinking the Frankfurt School: Alternative Legacies of Cultural Critique* (2002).

SUSAN SEARLS GIROUX is associate professor of English and cultural studies at McMaster University in Hamilton, Ontario. She is the author of *Between Race and Reason: Violence, Intellectual Responsibility, and the University to Come* (2010) and the coauthor, with Henry A. Giroux, of *Take Back Higher Education: Race, Youth and the Crisis of Democracy in the Post–Civil Rights Era* (2004). She has been managing editor of the interdisciplinary *Review of Education, Pedagogy, and Cultural Studies* for over a decade.